THE
CHEESE
BIBLE

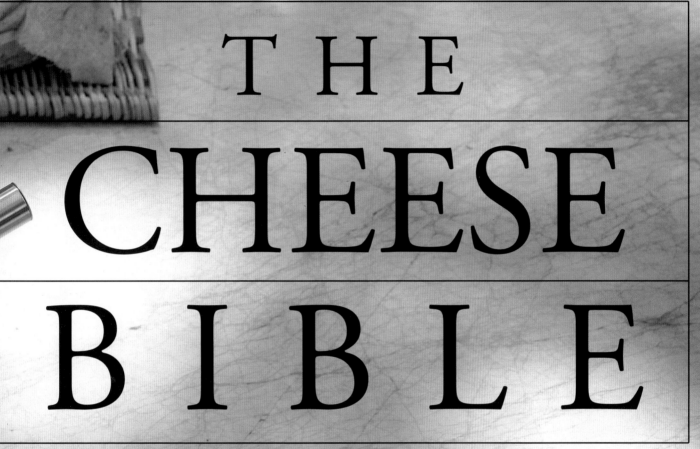

THE
CHEESE
BIBLE

Idea and concept: Christian Teubner
Cheese encyclopedia: Dr. Heinrich Mair-Waldburg
Recipes: Friedrich-Wilhelm Ehlert

PENGUIN
STUDIO

PENGUIN STUDIO
Published by the Penguin Group
Penguin Putnam Inc., 375 Hudson Street,
New York, New York, 10014, U.S.A.

Penguin Books Ltd, 27 Wrights Lane,
London W8 5TZ, England

Penguin Books Australia Ltd,
Ringwood, Victoria, Australia

Penguin Books Canada Ltd,
10 Alcorn Avenue, Toronto, Ontario
Canada M4V 3B2

Penguin Books (N.Z.) Ltd,
182-190 Wairau Road, Auckland 10, New Zealand

Penguin India,
210 Chiranjiv Tower, 43 Nehru Place, New Delhi,
11009 India

Penguin Books Ltd, Registered Offices:
Harmondsworth, Middlesex, England

First published in the United States of America
by Penguin Studio, a member of Penguin Putnam Inc., 1998.

10 9 8 7 6 5 4 3 2 1

Original edition published under the title *Das grosse Buch vom Käse*, 1990
Copyright © Teubner Edition, Germany, 1990

English language text
Copyright © Transedition Ltd, England, 1998
All rights reserved

Photographs other than those listed in the Picture Credits:
Christian Teubner, Dorothee Gödert, Kerstin Mosny (photojournalism)

Layout: Birgit Braun
Origination: PHG-Lithos GmbH, Planegg
Editorial management: Barbara Horn
Design and production: Richard Johnson

Library of Congress Catalog Card Number: 98–66955

Without limiting the rights under copyright reserved
above, no part of this publication may be reproduced,
stored in or introduced into a retrieval system, or transmit-
ted in any form, or by any means (electronic, mechanical,
photocopying, recording, or otherwise), without the
prior written permission of both the copyright owner
and the publisher of this book.

ISBN: 0–670–88129–5
Printed and bound in Italy by Mondadori

Contents

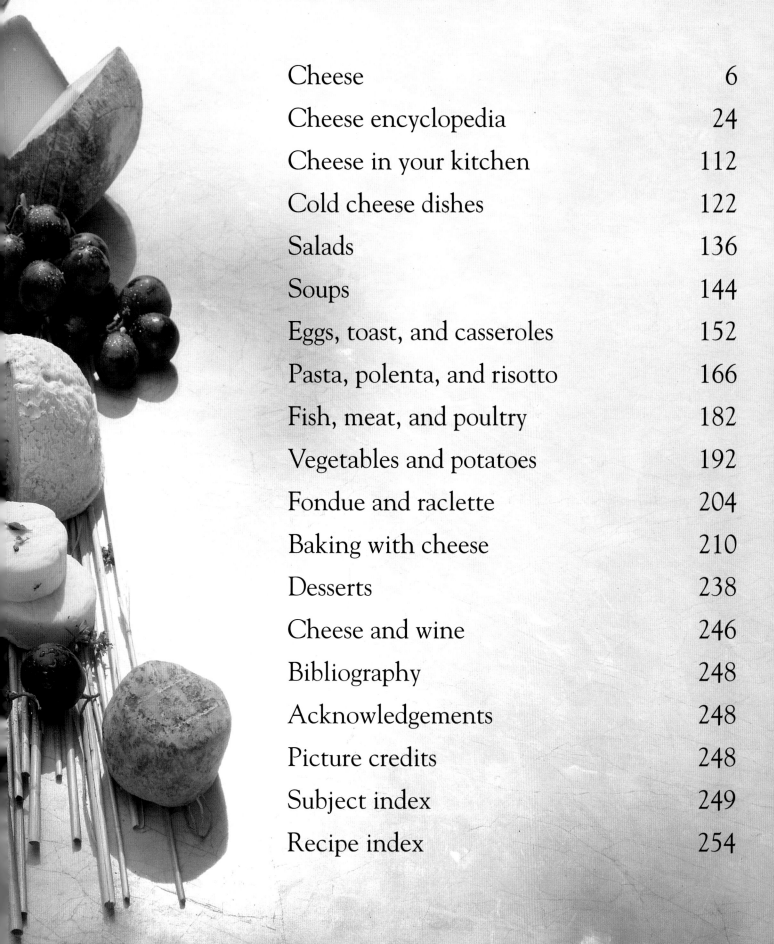

Cheese

In the beginning …

No matter how far back archeological finds go, we can only guess at when and how the first cheese came into being. We *do* know that more than seven thousand years ago humans progressed from simply hunting animals to domesticating certain species — goat, sheep, cow, and ox — and have incorporated the milk of such animals in their diet since then. Although we do not know exactly when people began to understand the properties and behavior of milk, from which cheese is made, there is evidence that cheese was eaten even in prehistoric times. Perhaps it began when people put out milk as an offering to their gods, and then observed that the milk became thick after a while — the effect, then as now, of bacteria that convert lactose to lactic acid. People living in areas where the climate changed seasonally would also have noticed the effect of temperature on this process: in the warm cave, by the fire, and in warmer weather the milk would curdle faster than in the cold. This can be considered the first technological cheesemaking discovery. The next was that when the curdled milk was allowed to stand, liquid drained off and the curdled mass became firmer. Later, this process was encouraged by pouring the curdled milk into woven baskets or other containers with holes and allowing the whey to drain off. This produced a firm, white substance: the first fresh curd cheese, which is still made according to the same principle.

The third discovery in cheesemaking was rennet, an extract derived from rennin. This digestive enzyme in the stomach of young animals causes casein, a milk protein, to precipitate, forming curds. Perhaps hunters found curdled milk in the stomach of a young animal that had been suckling from its mother. Or perhaps they discovered the curdling effect when they used the stomachs of young animals as containers for milk, as nomads did even in neolithic times. However the curdling effect of the stomach contents was discovered, at some time thereafter people put this chance observation to use, deliberately adding rennet to milk to curdle it and thus make cheese. Thousands of years later rennet remains the optimal coagulant for making cheese, derived not only from animal but also plant sources.

Although the very early history of cheesemaking rests on conjecture, the first pictorial testimony dates back to the third millennium B.C. The oldest known illustration of how milk was obtained and processed into cheese is the frieze of El Obeid at the Temple of the Great Goddess of Life, Ninhursag, in

Mesopotamia. The first literary testimony is in the Greek and Roman eras. Homer's *The Iliad* refers to "fig rennet coagulating the milk quickly" (from which we can see that the coagulant effect of many plants, such as the sap of the fig tree, bedstraw, and some types of cardoon, were known at an early date). In his satirical play *Cyclops*, Euripides has fig juice thicken the milk. In *The Odyssey*, Polyphemus, the one-eyed giant, poured the "curdled milk into woven baskets" in his cave. Elsewhere, "the noble Aphrodite fed Odysseus and his companions cheese and sweet honey." The Greek satirist Aristophanes, writing in Athens in 400 B.C., has a son say irascibly to his father: "...nothing thereof is thine, but the curd cheese of the court pay apportioned to thee." In about 350 B.C. Aristotle reported that goat's milk was mixed into ewe's milk "in Sicily, or wherever else it is still very creamy." Martial spoke for the refined taste of Ancient Roman gourmets, asserting that smoked cheese tasted good only when "smoked in the smoke of the Velabrum," the delicatessen quarter on the Aventine. The special status accorded to cheese in ancient Rome can also be inferred from the comedies of the playwright Plautus: for him, the word cheese formed part of such flattering pet-names as *dulciculus caseus* (sweet little cheese) and *meus molliculus caseus* (my tender little cheese).

The cheese trade flourished in ancient Rome. Cheese was brought to the capital from every province, from the Italic region, and from such faraway areas as present-day Nîmes and Savoy, as well as from Dalmatia. From Raethien, the area of modern Switzerland and the Allgau, *caseus alpinus* (alpine cheese) was exported to Rome.

Starting with these early references, the long

Market scene from the Middle Ages. This woodcut from *Hortus Sanitatis*, which appeared in Mainz in the fifteenth century, shows a cheese seller at a German marketplace.

This 1548 woodcut from the *Swiss Chronicles* of the historian Johannes Stumpf documents how cheese was made in the sixteenth century.

the infant can make it through this sensitive stage in life until weaning. The compositions of the different types of milk arose during the course of evolution and were determined by the adaptation to the task of fulfilling nutritional and growth requirements. In addition to these important species-specific functions, other natural characteristics (for example, breed, stage of lactation, age and state of health of the mother animal), rearing, and feeding , and environmental factors (such as season and climatic conditions) contribute to the great variety in types of milk and to the fluctuations in quality, which are of crucial importance in cheese production.

Even different types of milk have certain characteristics in common. They all contain components that can be classified in the same

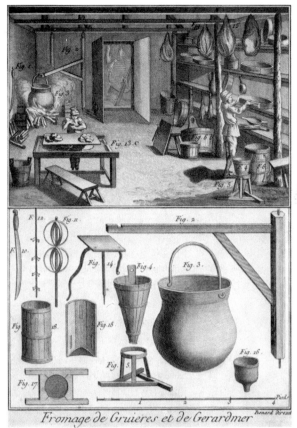

A cheese dairy with equipment from the second half of the eighteenth century; Gruyère and Gérardmer were made here. The illustration is from the *Encyclopedia of Diderot and D'Alembert* (c. 1770).

history of cheese and cheesemaking can be traced through the centuries, from ancient times to the modern era. Although interesting, that would exceed the scope of this book. Our purpose here is to explain how cheese, in all its wonderful variety, is made, stored, and used.

Milk

In general, milk is the fluid produced by the mammary glands of mammals, such as cows, sheep, goats, and buffalo, as well as camels, llamas, yaks, and reindeer. It is approximately 85 percent water, with the remaining 15 percent composed of lactose (milk sugar), fat, protein, minerals (such as calcium and phosphorus), trace elements, vitamins, and enzymes.

Milk has quite specific tasks. It must ensure efficient transmission of the most important nutritional and growth-promoting components to the newborn creature, as well as support the young animal's limited immunity in its new environment. There is a direct relationship between the protein content of the mother's milk and the time required for doubling birth weight; that is, the speed with which

categories. In some cases it is mainly the percentages of these components that vary; in others, the composition of the individual components (such as fat, protein or salts) differs. The table on page 8 illustrates the average composition of some types of milk that are used in the human diet. Human milk has a comparatively low total protein content (0.9 percent), and half as much casein as whey protein (0.3 and 0.6 percent, respectively).

The milk of cows, sheep, goats, and buffalo is of economic importance in cheesemaking. The biologically determined lactation cycle of different animals limits the availability of each type of milk. In general, this means a period of 300 days a year for cows, 240 days for goats, and 150 days for sheep. In addition, there are regional seasonal differences, especially in the case of sheep- and goat-milk production. Yield is also influenced, of course, by the size of the animal. A fully grown cow is expected to yield at least ten times her own weight in milk each year. Depending on the breed, annual yields per cow are between 5.5 and 7.75 tons of milk, or about 1,375 to 2,062 gallons. For goats, milk yield usually fluctuates between 140 and 230 gallons, and for sheep, between 115 and 140 gallons.

The individual components of milk are of differing importance for cheesemaking. Lactose is the only sugar that occurs in milk in relatively large quantities, and contributes to its slightly sweet taste. The structure of lactose is the same in the milk of all mammals, but the percentage of lactose in dry matter, or milk solids, varies: it is 37 percent in cow's milk, 25 percent in sheep's milk, and 40 percent in goat's milk. Its

contribution to cheese yield — the amount of cheese that can be produced from a given quantity of milk — is very limited, since most of it is drawn off with the whey during manufacture. Lactose does, however, serve as an important metabolic energy source for dairy cultures. For many cheese products, its value resides in bringing about the necessary acidification, which improves the natural preservative qualities of the raw

material, the so-called cheese milk and, at the end of a long chain of biochemical transformations, produces the most important by-product, lactic acid.

Milk protein consists of two main groups, casein and whey proteins, which differ markedly from each other in structure and characteristics. Casein is the basic cheese matter, the colloidal protein that, under the influence of rennet or acids, can be made to curdle. It is the framework within which all the other components of milk are contained. Bound to the casein are important organic and inorganic minerals, such as calcium and phosphorus. Casein constitutes the largest percentage of the total lactoprotein, on average 80 percent for cow's milk, 84 percent for sheep's milk and 79 percent for goat's milk. This, in turn, is an indication of the cheese yield.

The whey proteins are not precipitated by acidification or by the effect of the rennet. In the normal cheesemaking process, they remain in solution and are retained only in small amounts in the cheese. Their great sensitivity to heat, which makes precipitation possible, sets limits on the temperatures used in the heat treatment. The white appearance of the many small protein particles gives milk its typical color.

Milk fat is essential for the nourishment of the newborn mammal. Its composition and yield are influenced by the animal's feeding conditions, and so may be subject to great fluctuations. In fresh milk, the fat occurs in the form of little globules, consisting of a nucleus of fat surrounded by a protective shell. The majority of the milk fat consists of triglycerides, the basic building blocks of which are three fatty acids. In comparison with other animal and vegetable fats, the milk fat of ruminants contains a high proportion of short- and average-length fatty acids with fewer than twenty carbon atoms in their chains. In cow's milk, every tenth fatty acid is a butyric acid. Sheep and goat's milk contain a higher proportion than cow's milk of these fatty acids, which contribute to the typical aroma and flavor of the cheese. Their structure also enables a slight degrading by fat-ripening enzymes.

Milk from these animals can also be important in

The milking process has been the same for centuries. In exactly the same way as this twelfth-century dairy worker milks a goat, the present-day Sicilian farmer in the photo (above right) obtains milk from his sheep. The sheep's milk is then made into the famous Pecorino.

Mammal	Water content	Dry matter	Fat content	Total protein	Casein	Whey protein	Casein: Whey protein	Lactose	Ash
	%	%	%	%	%	%	%	%	%
Cow	87.3	12.7	3.7	3.4	2.8	0.6	4.7	4.7	0.7
Sheep	80.7	19.3	7.4	5.5	4.6	0.9	5.1	4.8	1.5
Goat	88.7	11.3	3.5	3.4	2.7	0.7	3.8	4.5	0.8
Buffalo	82.5	17.5	7.6	4.2	3.6	0.6	6.0	4.8	0.9
Camel	86.2	13.8	4.5	3.6	2.7	0.9	3.0	5.0	0.7
Llama	83.5	16.5	2.4	7.3	6.2	1.1	5.6	6.0	0.8
Yak	82.1	17.9	6.5	5.8	–	–	–	4.6	1.0
Reindeer	66.9	33.1	16.9	11.5	–	–	–	2.8	-

the human diet. Milk fat contains a small quantity of the fat-soluble vitamins essential for human health — A, D, E, and K — as well as carotene. Carotene is a natural colorant of plant origin, and a source of vitamin A. Just how much carotene is contained in milk depends on the breed of cow and the amount of carotene in the animal's diet. This is why, for example, cow's milk is somewhat more yellow in color in the summer than in the winter. The milk of sheep and goats do not contain carotene, and is pure white, as are the cheeses produced from it.

Milk also contains a number of water-soluble vitamins, including B1, B2, B6, B12, and a very small amount of vitamin C, and a complex mixture of minerals. Thus milk can provide the human body with calcium, phosphorus, and magnesium, as well as with trace elements such as zinc, iron, and copper, which are involved in the secretion of enzymes and hormones. The fact that the calcium and phosphorous content of the different types of milk is equal to their casein content promotes rapid growth. The majority of the calcium in fresh milk is bound to the casein particles — only about one-third is found in dissolved form — and it therefore plays an important role in cheesemaking. It is involved in the linking of the casein particles, which leads to coagulation. As acidification progresses, calcium is released from the casein into the whey. Sour-curd cheeses (see below) have a very low calcium content, while the calcium remains bound to the casein in rennet cheeses, which therefore have a high calcium content. The presence of citrate in the milk enables the development of several important flavors by specific lactic acid bacteria.

These specific characteristics of milk must be taken into account in the cheesemaking process. Occasionally, for economic or technological reasons, reconstituted powdered milk, cream, buttermilk or whey is used in addition to fresh milk in the manufacture of cheese.

How cheese is made

Cheese is a fresh or ripened product made from coagulated milk. The basic principles of cheesemaking were initially learned by humans from observing nature, and are still based on the gradual separation of the solid constituents of milk from the water in which they are dissolved or very finely distributed. The solid part still contains some water, and the liquid part — the whey — still contains some solid components. The basic principle of cheesemaking can be summarized in the following simplified sequence of events:

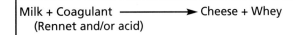

Milk + Coagulant ⟶ Cheese + Whey
(Rennet and/or acid)

Preparing milk for cheese production improves its preservative qualities and even its suitability for cheesemaking. Milk is made into cheese with or without prior maturing, according to cheese type or regional tradition. For some cheeses, the milk is processed shortly after milking, while still warm; however, it can also be allowed to stand for a while and to mature, or ripen, at ambient temperature until it is processed. Sometimes the milk obtained from the evening milking is left to stand overnight and is mixed, frequently after being skimmed of butterfat, with the fresh morning milk.

When milk is left to stand, the cream rises to the top; if the cream is not stirred back in, but skimmed off, the fat content of the milk decreases. The risen fat is not skimmed off uniformly in every case, which results in varying fat content. We distinguish between whole milk, partially skim or cream-enriched milk, and skim milk, which contains only a slight residue of fat. The fat content of milk is standardized for cheesemaking, and the fat content of the cheese is stated on the label of the finished product.

In modern cheese factories, the raw milk is subjected to mechanical purification using separators. If the cheese is not to be made from raw milk, the milk is then "thermized" or pasteurized. Pasteurizing, or heating the raw milk to 162°F for a short time, destroys any harmful bacteria. Thermization, heating the milk to 135 to 155°F, is less severe than pasteurization; holding the milk at the higher temperature range can affect not only the ultimate flavor but also the texture.

Ripening

After being heated, the milk is cooled to about 43–54°F. A small quantity of a specific bacteria is then added to it, which changes some of the lactose in the milk to lactic acid. This, in turn, begins to precipitate the curd from the whey. Additional starter cultures can be used to accelerate or intensify this acidification process. Two major types of bacteria are used: mesophilic bacteria, which grow best at temperatures of between 68 and 86°F, and thermophilic bacteria, which prefer temperatures of about 95–113°F and primarily form lactic acid and lactic-acid salts when the lactose is broken down. The type and quantity of bacteria used are determined by the degree of acidification required and their metabolic activities during ripening. Here, we will refer to them in general as "lactic acid bacteria." The time the milk is left to coagulate is relative to how ripe it is, and generally ranges from ten minutes to two hours or longer.

Rennet

Both acid and rennet have a strong coagulant effect on lactoproteins. As in the stomach of a suckling baby mammal, the coagulation of milk in the cheesemaking process is usually caused by the ratio of acid to rennet. The more acidic the milk, the greater the effect of the rennet, so the less rennet needed. The protein can be precipitated through acidifying the milk with lactic

acid bacteria alone. The milk sours and clots, a process that can be observed when milk is left to stand. Many fresh cheeses are made in this way. Clotting can also occur through the combined effects of acid and heat, as in the case of Ricotta. Many goat's-milk and soft cheeses are produced with very little rennet by letting milk sour and thicken. With some other cheeses, for example Burgos, coagulation is achieved exclusively with rennet.

Rennet pastes, which have strong protein- and fat-ripening properties, are prepared mainly from rennet obtained from lambs and kids. Rennet from calves' stomachs, available in liquid or powdered form, is added to the milk. The active substance in it is the enzyme chymosin. During coagulation it affects the casein, and later is involved in the ripening of the cheese, where it also has the effect of breaking down protein. Commercial calves' rennet consists not only of chymosin, but also pepsin. The latter can come from cattle, pigs or other animals, and has a stronger protein-ripening effect than chymosin. Other rennets, so-called rennet substitutes, are increasingly being used in a number of cheeses. Among these are microbiol rennet, whose coagulant and protein-degrading enzymes are produced by different strains of mold and bacteria, and rennet substitutes of plant origin (such as fig-tree sap, bedstraw, and cardoon), both of which are being used to a limited extent, particularly in producing cheese for the vegetarian and kosher markets.

In addition, other ripening cultures (such as blue mold, red bacteria, or yeasts, depending on the type of cheese), can be added to the milk along with the rennet solution. In order to promote the coagulation of the milk and the metabolic activity of the ripening cultures, the milk will be held at a temperature of between 78 and 104°F, again depending on the type of cheese. For most cheeses, the temperature range lies between 86 and 95°F, but a number of cheeses, especially goat cheeses, are coagulated at 68–77°F, and some Pecorino and Italico cheeses at 95–104°F.

If we now take into account the method of coagulation of the cheese milk, we can identify three main cheese groupings: sour-curd cheeses, sour-rennet curd cheeses, and rennet cheeses.

If the milk is kept absolutely still during the coagulation process, it turns into a smooth, gelatinous mass referred to as the "coagulum." If, however, the milk is stirred or subjected to any movement during coagulation, a type of coagulum is formed from protein and fat flakes that contains only a portion of the whey. This initiates the separation of solid and liquid components (whey separation); further processing will gradually concentrate the important milk components, casein protein and fat.

Fresh milk is not synonymous with milk for cheesemaking, which, according to the type of cheese being made, may be preripened, skimmed, or enriched with cream.

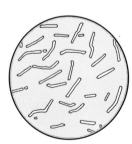

Lactic acid bacteria cause the milk to ripen. They convert lactose into lactic acid and sometimes produce a slight souring, which is a desirable preparation for curdling.

Scooping and cutting

Scooping the curd is a simple step in making a cheese. A large ladle or scoop is used to transfer the coagulum to molds. Doing this separates the whey, just as inserting a spoon into yogurt can cause the solid and liquid to separate. This scooping is still the norm with traditional cheeses, such as Brie de Meaux and Camembert, and with goat's milk cheeses, such as Selles-sur-Cher.

The coagulum is also worked simply by stirring by hand or with an implement, even with twigs. Mostly, however, the curd is cut lengthwise and crosswise with a knife, a saber, or a Swiss harp (see illustration above right) into fragments or cubes of the desired size.

The smaller the curd, the firmer the cheese

For soft cheeses, a large curd, about the size of a walnut, is prepared; for firmer cheeses, a medium-sized curd, about the size of a hazelnut or a kernel of corn, is cut; for hard cheeses, the curd is cut small, to about the size of a grain of rice. The reason for this is that larger cheese curds contain more water than small ones. The dry-matter and water content of the cheese can be controlled by the size and firmness of the cheese curd. Knowing just when to scoop out or cut up the coagulum and prepare the curd also affects its consistency, whether it is soft or firm, elastic or "short," and is considered an art.

For many cheeses, a medium-sized curd is prepared first. It then gives off more whey when it is stirred and warmed. The curd becomes smaller as a result of both manual or mechanical cutting and the shrinkage produced by the progressive acidification, known technically as syneresis. Carefully raising the temperature of the mixture of separated curds and whey or adding hot water to it after partially removing the whey leads to increased syneresis, and hence to obvious shrinkage of the curd. The temperature may be raised

Rotating Swiss harps cut up the curdled milk (the coagulum) into grains, which, depending on cheese type, are relatively large or small; the cut-up mixture is called the curd.

slightly, to a few degrees above the renneting temperature; to 50–59°F above the renneting temperature; or considerably, as much as 68–77°F above the renneting temperature, which is referred to in the industry as "scalding" or "cooking." The temperature is seldom raised above 132°F. Generally, the higher the

Emmental curd is heated to 125°F. This heating, known technically as "cooking," causes the individual cheese grains to shrink and become firmer.

temperature to which it is heated, the smaller the curd will be, and the firmer the cheese. However, there are also hard cheeses that are produced without cooking the curds. These *pasta cruda* cheeses, as they are called in Italy, are made by preparing a very small curd, which yields a firm cheese; higher water loss during a longer ripening and storage period results in hard cheese and grating cheese (such as Fiore Sardo).

After the curd has been treated as described above, it can be transferred directly to the cheese molds, or undergo further processing first. Common to both options is the separation of the whey from the curds.

The cheesemaker heats the curd–whey mixture to a specific fixed temperature, which affects particular qualities of the curd.

Lifting out the curds in the cheesecloth

The direct method of separating the curds and whey is to lift the curds out of the kettle in a cheesecloth, as is done with Parmesan, Asiago, Bergkäse, and, in some

Even now, many cheeses are still hand-scooped. Ladling the curd by hand is usual where traditional molds are used, as in the case of Brie, goat cheeses, and Romadur.

cases, Emmental. Alternatively, the curds and whey mixture is allowed to flow into the molds (as in the case of Emmental); in this way, a cheese wheel is formed in each mold. It is also possible to place the curds-and-whey mixture in large rectangular vats to drain. The blocks thus formed are pressed, then cut into smaller pieces and salted, and from then on treated as usual and

Using a cloth, the curds are lifted out of the vat. The whey drains out through the cloth, and the curd is pressed into the mold with the cloth. This method is used with Asiago, Parmesan, and many other types of cheese.

ripened. This is how Swiss-type cheese and square hard cheeses are produced.

Gouda: the curd is prepressed

To make Gouda, the curd is molded into raw cheese in two stages. First the curds-and-whey mixture is drained in a prepressing vat, where the curd is only lightly pressed. It is then cut into pieces to fit the molds. This method is still common practice when processing smaller quantities of milk. However, in large-scale manufacture the vats have been replaced by vertical cylinders, in which the curd is lightly pressed and from whose lower end appropriately sized pieces can be cut to slide into the molds below.

In making cheeses that have round holes, the curd is allowed to settle under the whey to prevent air being trapped. If a so-called curd-hole formation is essential (as for Tilsit), most of the whey is removed and the curd is transferred to the molds.

Cheddaring

Cheddar, Cantal, and similar cheeses are made by a different method. Here, the curd is left to sit and draw together. The curd cake is cut into pieces, which are stacked on top of one another for a period of time, and then relayered. This method of pressing, which expels

Prepressed curd is cut into pieces the size of the molds into which it is placed for further pressing. This method is used, for example, with Gouda.

more whey and during which the cheese becomes more acidified, is called cheddaring. It is carried out until the curds acquire a stringy texture, similar to that of cooked chicken breast. A similar process is used to make Cantal. After cheddaring, the curd mass is milled, mostly by machine, into small pieces. Although Colby, which is produced in sizable quantities in the United States, is a well-known cheddar-type cheese, it does not undergo cheddaring. The curd grains are not allowed to unite, but instead are stirred until they reach the right degree of acidity. Sometimes the grains are washed with cold water. The milled curds or grains are then salted, transferred to molds, and pressed.

Pasta filata cheeses

A third method is used to make *pasta filata* (drawn curd) cheese. The first step also consists of letting the curd sit, draw together into a curd cake, and acidify. Then the curd cake is broken up and the pieces are cooked in hot water, or sometimes hot whey, at approximately 149–163°F. The curd mass becomes plastic, and is then kneaded. According to cheese type and regional custom, the curd is made smaller and drier, as for Provolone, or larger and moister, as for mozzarella. Correspondingly, the curd is also acidified to a greater or lesser extent. After molding, the cheeses are cooled to make them firm.

Pressing

When the curd mass is placed in the cheese molds, it expels more whey and draws together. The first and simplest pressing takes place as the upper layer of curds presses on the lower layer. For cheese types that are meant to have a relatively high water content, this inherent pressing is sufficient. Solidification to the desired consistency, which is also necessary to give the cheese its shape, generally occurs within 4 to 24 hours. If more whey has to be expelled to produce a firmer curd mass, and to encourage rind formation, the cheese is pressed mechanically. Pressing is generally reserved for hard and semi-hard cheeses, but semi-soft cheeses in the Saint-Paulin style are also lightly pressed. In modern mechanical presses, the pressure can be adjusted to the size of the cheese and the required whey expulsion. It is important for pressing to begin slowly, and for the pressure to increase gradually. Pressing may also be carried out in a slight vacuum, as is common in the case of Cheddar, for example.

After the curd is transferred to the cheese molds, whey expulsion increases noticeably, a process that is supported by continued acidification. Because of this, the top of many types of cheese, particularly soft cheeses, may become deformed. To counteract this

To make Cheddar, the curd that has drawn together, known as the curd cake, is cut into pieces. These chunks are stacked and pressed by their own weight, and then relayered. This process, during which the curd acidifies further, is known as "cheddaring."

problem, the cheeses must be turned. Cheeses having a soft consistency are turned more often than firmer cheeses. Mainly, however, turning promotes the even distribution of water throughout the cheese and contributes to skin or rind formation.

Salt

Cooking salt, or sodium chloride, is well known as a seasoning and preservative for many foods, and it plays a substantial role in cheesemaking. Each type of cheese has a specified salt content. A salty taste is an important characteristic of some cheeses, while for many others, a fraction more salt would make them unpalatable.

Most sorts of cheese are salted during or at the end of the production process. Sometimes the cheese is salted in the curd — Cheddar and Colby are good examples. In the case of several cheeses with curd-hole formation, such as Tilsit, Maribo, and the Finnish cheese Turunmaa, most of the whey is drained off, then some salt is stirred into the curds, the cheese is shaped, and then the main salting occurs in a salt, or brine, bath. A few cheeses are made by adding salt to the milk (for example, in Egypt), but only part of this salt actually enters the cheese. In so-called dry salting, salt may be strewn over the surface of the cheese, as is common with some types of Brie, or it can be mixed with powdered charcoal, the method used for some goat cheeses. Cheeses are also rubbed with salt, then sprinkled with it. This operation may be repeated during the ripening period, as in the case of Pecorino and German blue cheese.

Salting in a brine bath, usually a solution with a salt concentration of between 15 and 20 percent, is common for many sorts of cheese. This type of salting is more economical and enables the cheese to be evenly salted. The required salting times vary greatly, depending on the type of cheese (shape, surface,

volume and fat level, and water content among other factors) as well as the salt-bath characteristics (such as concentration and temperature). The cheeses remain in the salt bath for anything from half an hour to several days, according to their size and desired salt content.

During the salting process, the sodium chloride is concentrated in the outer layer of the cheese and only gradually penetrates to the interior. The time it takes to achieve balance throughout the cheese varies according to cheese type. Cheeses salted in the curd, as are Cheddar and Colby, have the required balance right from the start; for Camembert, the process is complete after four to six days; it may take larger cheeses a long time (several weeks to several months) to achieve the right balance. For a number of cheeses, especially large ones, salt also serves to solidify the outer layer. Generally speaking, salting puts an end to the free draining of whey.

In the ripening cellar

The environment in which the majority of cheeses are ripened is usually a ripening cellar or a special storage room. As far as possible, its atmosphere imitates the natural atmosphere of the cave, which for centuries has been used to ripen cheeses (the caves of Roquefort are a well-known example). The ripening cellar may be humid and warm, or relatively cool. The climate of the cellar is determined by the ambient temperature and relative humidity, as well as by the natural movement of air in the space. Although the temperature can range from 32 to 77°F, the majority of cheeses are ripened at between 46 and 60°F. The relative humidity can range from 75 to 98 percent, but as a rule lies between 85 and 95 percent. During maturation there is a constant exchange between ripening gases, such as carbon dioxide and ammonia, from the cheese and oxygen in the air, which is crucial for the growth of both aerobic surface flora and interior flora.

For most cheeses, a relatively slow process of achieving a balanced distribution of important constituents (such as water, sodium chloride, lactose or lactic acid) throughout the cheese is set in motion or continued in the initial stage of ripening. This is an important prerequisite for the rest of the process, which must be as even as possible. Ripening, which is also called aging or curing, refers to the process by which the constituents of the milk retained in the cheese (such as protein, residual sugar, and fat) are further broken down to produce the required flavors and qualities of the specific cheese. Enzyme activity is the driving force of this process. It may be initiated by the milk itself, or by various aids (for example, rennet or

The salt or brine bath, immersion in a salt solution, is the most common method of salting individual cheeses. The length of this process varies according to the shape and size of the cheese.

Dry-salting, where salt is sprinkled over the cheese, is usual for some soft cheeses.

ALPINE CHEESEMAKING — a dying art

There are few masters of the art of alpine cheesemaking today, and practitioners are becoming rarer, for, despite its aura of romance, it is sheer hard work. The short growing season in the high alpine meadows has for centuries been used by farmers for the production of milk, and hence cheese, which, despite the relatively primitive production conditions in which it is made, is indisputably of the best quality. This is because the milk is so good; the cows' fodder — the fragrant grasses and herbs of the alpine pastures — flourishes under optimal conditions, generally without artificial fertilizers. This leads to the production of cheeses of a unique character, on which the landscape, the weather of the short alpine summer, and, not least of all, the people have left their mark: each cheese is a unique creation.

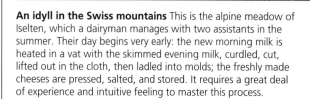

An idyll in the Swiss mountains This is the alpine meadow of Iselten, which a dairyman manages with two assistants in the summer. Their day begins very early: the new morning milk is heated in a vat with the skimmed evening milk, curdled, cut, lifted out in the cloth, then ladled into molds; the freshly made cheeses are pressed, salted, and stored. It requires a great deal of experience and intuitive feeling to master this process.

In the alpine meadows, many people are largely self-sufficient: they make butter too, of course, from the cream from the evening milk. Nor does the whey go to waste: Swiss dairymen heat it to coagulate a new, protein-rich curd to make Zieger, which is similar to Ricotta.

rennet pastes), and it may also be set in motion naturally by microorganisms that have landed in or on the raw cheese through contact with the equipment, the brine bath, or the surrounding air. The main sources of enzymes are the acidifying and ripening cultures that have been used. Very occasionally, it is just the acidifying cultures (such as the lactic acid bacteria in the case of fresh cheeses), but usually the ripening flora are composed of many groups of microorganisms. These may be lactic acid bacteria, propionic acid bacteria (in the case of certain hard cheeses) or cultures such as yeasts and "noble" molds (white and blue molds).

The role of the *affineur*

Ripening, and hence control of the development of specific qualities in the cheese, is usually carried out on the cheesemaker's own premises, but can also be taken over by an *affineur*, a cheese-tender or finisher. The *affineur* carries out the work of tending the cheeses in specialized cheese-ripening cellars or rooms until the desired degree of ripeness for packing is reached. Some of the ripening techniques employed by the *affineur* are very traditional, especially where cheese is made in small quantities and according to traditional methods. In modern cheese factories, the ripening processes at this stage of production make substantial use of technology.

Cheese may ripen from the outside inward, as is typical of soft cheeses with surface mold or red flora, or it may ripen homogeneously on the inside, as do hard, semi-hard and some semi-soft cheeses. The care received during the ripening period depends on the cheese type. Taken into consideration in each case are the size and shape of the cheese; the ratio of cheese interior to surface, especially for surface-ripened cheeses; and the length of the ripening period matched to these. Work in the ripening cellar is limited mainly to tending the rinds or surfaces of the cheeses, and controlling the temperature and relative humidity. The surface treatment consists of regular brushing, rubbing down or "washing" with brine and ripening cultures, as well as coating with salt. It is generally true that as the cheese becomes riper, the temperature is lowered slightly, and that surface-ripened cheeses require a higher relative humidity. For non-surface-ripened cheeses, care is reduced to a minimum, as their surfaces are coated or they are ripened in so-called ripening foil. All cheeses must be turned from time to time, in order to guarantee even development of the surface flora and prevent possible deformities. At the end of the ripening process, each cheese will have acquired its typical character, determined by specific qualities such as appearance, aroma, taste, consistency, and digestibility.

The climate in the ripening cellar is a decisive factor in successful cheesemaking. Different cheeses demand different, and for the most part strictly stipulated and controlled, ripening conditions. In this Montasio-cheese factory each cheese is stamped with its date of production.

Packaging to preserve quality

Packaging is needed mainly to maintain the quality of the contents. It provides protection against environmental factors such as bacteria, light, and air, as well as against drying out and loss of aroma and flavor. It prevents strong-smelling cheeses from tainting the surrounding area, such as the contents of the refrigerator, with their smell.

Packaging also allows cheese to be split into consumer-sized portions cost-efficiently without sacrificing quality, to be handled economically, and to provide information on contents, nutritional value, shelf-life, and preparation. Easy opening of the packaging should be guaranteed.

An urgent matter of concern today is the environmentally friendly disposal of packaging that is no longer needed, which has led to major recycling programs. Glass, paper, aluminum, and some sorts of plastics are now collected and recycled in order to reduce waste of valuable resources. Packaging that could cause difficulties in disposal — materials containing chlorine compounds, for example — is being used less and less

Cheeses with a rind can usually be transported without packaging in wooden cases or crates, corrugated cardboard boxes, or on palettes, since, in principle, the rind provides protection from mechanical, bacterial and chemical factors. Surrounding the cheese with a layer of wax or paraffin, as is common for hard and semi-hard cheeses, limits weight loss during storage, in addition to protecting the cheese from physical damage. After they reach the predetermined degree of ripeness, cheeses with rinds are either sold by the piece or divided into portions and prepackaged.

Prepackaging is the dividing up and packaging of de-rinded or washed hard and semi-hard cheeses into pieces, blocks, or slices ready for sale. It protects the cheese against contamination with unwanted bacteria and prevents it from drying out.

It is clear that packaging is particularly important in the case of fresh, soft and processed cheeses, as well as for portioned hard and semi-hard cheeses. Soft cheeses are traditionally manufactured in smaller unit weights. Because of their sensitive outer skin, and the fact that they ripen more quickly than hard and semi-hard cheeses, they need a protective layer that facilitates the continuation of the ripening process and protects against drying out and loss of flavor.

Soft cheeses that have been surface-treated with red bacteria, such as Limburger, Romadur and Münster, are preferably packaged in varnished or paper-laminated aluminum foil, or in plastic-coated paper. The inner paper layer in laminated packaging material allows for the exchange of moisture and ripening gases. For soft cheeses that have an external mold, such as Camembert and Brie, similar packaging materials are used: varnished or laminated aluminum foil, coated paper, cellophane or plastic wrap. The outer packaging is important for these sorts of cheese, and preferably consists of woodchip or cardboard boxes, which ensure the cheese is not damaged or

The softer the cheese, the more complicated the packaging. The simplest and oldest is the rind; more modern forms include layered paper and foil, paraffin coating, and plastic containers.

broken by handling. An outer wrapping that is too heavy, however, could suffocate the bloomy white rind of the cheese by preventing adequate air circulation.

The preferred packaging for some fresh cheeses and Quark is white-dyed, injection-molded plastic bowls. These are usually sealed with a varnished aluminum foil top that can be peeled off, under a plastic lid that snaps back in place for resealing the container after it has been opened. Various sorts of fresh cheese of higher fat content are still packaged in opaque, varnished and sealed aluminum foil wrappers or plastic-coated paper, while low-fat Quark is also found in transparent polyethylene film or tubes.

Processed cheeses were originally developed with the aim of using heat treatment to extend the storage qualities of hard cheeses over relatively long periods of time. For this reason, hermetically sealed packaging is important. The most common shapes for small portions are the triangle, square, rectangle, or disk. The most common packaging material is heat-sealed, lacquered aluminum foil. These small portions are mostly marketed in round or rectangular cardboard or plastic boxes containing six, eight, or twelve individual portions. Processed cheese in slices is also very common; paper, cellophane or a fine plastic film placed between the slices can prevent them from sticking together. A heavy plastic film is usually used for packaging slices.

Classifying cheese

Cheese holds no secrets in terms of its composition. Everything you need to know to be able properly to classify and evaluate a cheese is clearly stated on its packaging. Of course, you must know the meaning of the mysterious abbreviations Wff, FDB, fdm and m.g.

Classifying cheese according to the firmness of the body

The ratio of dry matter to water content is to a large extent decisive in evaluating the consistency of a cheese. The dry matter is composed of fat, protein, lactose and lactic acid, salts, vitamins, and enzymes: it is the part that is left when the water is removed from the cheese. This means that the more water a cheese contains, the softer it is. Conversely, the higher the proportion of dry matter, the harder the cheese. A number of countries have regulations limiting the minimum content of dry matter and the maximum content of water in their traditional cheeses.

Based on this factor, a new criterion was introduced some time ago for cheese that is not clearly defined but has to be classified for the purposes of

international trade: water content in the fat-free cheese matter, or wff (standing for "water fat-free") for short. The fat-free cheese matter is the total cheese matter including water, but, obviously, excluding the fat. Thus, if a cheese contains 25 percent fat, the fat-free cheese matter is 75 percent, and the wff is the proportion of water contained in this 75 percent. This proportion can be determined by a simple calculation; for this, in addition to the fat-free cheese matter, you need to know only the percentage of the water content or the dry matter. Thus, if the cheese in our example has a water content of 50 percent, it has a corresponding dry matter of 50 percent. By multiplying the water content (50 percent) by 100 and dividing the result by the fat-free cheese matter (75 percent), we arrive at a wff of 66.7 percent.

Cheeses are divided into groups according to this criterion. Standards for the range of wff for individual groups of cheese have been established by the Food and Agriculture Organization of the United Nations and the World Health Organization (FAO/WHO), and independently by a number of countries, because of the nutritional and economic importance of cheese, with a view to protecting the consumer and in accordance with the concept of truth and clarity in trade. The chart below shows the cheese categories established by the FAO/WHO. Some of the ranges for wff vary from country to country, mainly owing to tradition, with the result that the cheese groups may differ somewhat. For example, a number of countries, including France, group hard and semi-hard cheeses according to production characteristics (scalded, pressed or not — *pâte cuite, non cuite, pressée, non pressée*) — rather than on the basis of wff.

Classifying cheese according to fat content

Although a number of other criteria naturally come into play, the fat content of a cheese is of decisive importance when judging its quality. The higher the proportion of fat, the finer and more supple the cheese.

In the first instance, it is the actual, or absolute, fat content that is of crucial importance from a

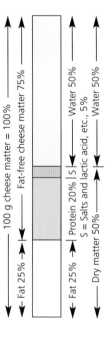

FAO/WHO	
Cheese category	Water content in the fat-free cheese matter (Wff)
Extra-hard cheese	less than 51%
Hard cheese	49% to 56%
Semi-hard cheese	54% to 63%
Semi-soft cheese	61% to 69%
Soft cheese	over 67%

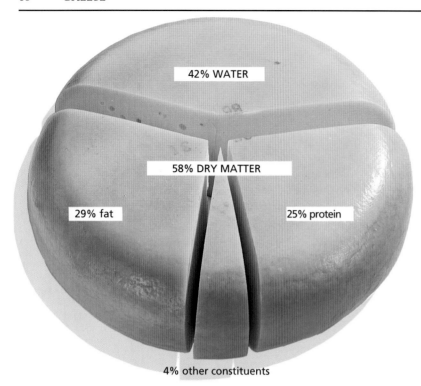

42% WATER

58% DRY MATTER

29% fat

25% protein

4% other constituents

This Gouda wheel illustrates the composition of a cheese: ten days after production, it consists of 42% water and 58% dry matter. The absolute fat content of this cheese is 29%. The remainder consists of protein (25%) and other constituents (4%), such as salt, lactic acid, and minerals. The fat content in the dry matter (FDB) of this cheese is 50%, obtained by the following calculation: 29% fat x 100, divided by the dry matter of 58%.

dry matter. The percentage of dry matter rises or falls according to the type of cheese, but the fat content does not necessarily do the same. This can best be illustrated using the example of cheeses of the same type with differing fat content, such as Camembert with 30 percent, 45 percent and 60 percent FDB. A Camembert with 30 percent FDB is still somewhat tough; the higher fat content of 45 percent makes it substantially more supple; and the consistency of the 60-percent cheese is almost creamy. The art of cheesemaking makes it possible to produce cheese with a low fat content but with a comparatively supple curd.

Increasingly, cheeses, particularly the lower-fat ones, are labeled with the absolute fat content in addition to the FDB. If this information is missing, however, the actual fat content can be roughly calculated by multiplying the FDB percentage by the following figures: 0.7 for hard cheeses, 0.6 for semi-hard cheeses, 0.5 for soft cheeses, and 0.3 for fresh cheeses. The following rule of thumb is an even rougher guide: the absolute fat content is approximately half of the FDB, except in the case of fresh cheese, when it is approximately one-third.

nutritional standpoint, in allowing the caloric value to be calculated, for example. However, all cheeses contain a great deal of water, and since a cheese gives off moisture during storage, the percentage of the dry matter and the proportion of fat increase with age. By contrast, the percentage of fat in the dry matter hardly alters. Because this is a stable figure, it forms a reliable basis for calculating the fat content. This is another fairly simple calculation. When we deduct the weight of the water from the total weight of a cheese, we have the weight of the dry matter. The amount of total fat divided by the amount of fat in this dry matter can then be stated as a percentage.

You will find the statement of this fat content on cheese labels indicated by different abbreviations or terms depending on the country of origin. For example, cheeses made in the United States indicate the percentage of "fat on a dry basis" with the abbreviation FDB, those produced in Britain with fdm (fat in dry matter), and cheeses from France with m.g. (*matière grasse*). The German phrase for fat in dry matter is *Fette in Trockenmasse*, which is abbreviated Fett. i. T. in Austria and Switzerland, and Fett i. Tr. and F. i. T. in Germany.

The FDB is a statement about the suppleness and flavour of a cheese. The chart on page 17 shows how fat, protein, salts, and other solid constituents form the

FDB around the world		
Country	Description	Abbreviation
Australia	fat in dry matter	fdm
Belgium	Vetgehalte in de drogestof matière grasse de la matière sèche	V./D.S. M.G./M.S.
Czech Republic	tuk v susine	tvs
Denmark	Fedt i tørstof	Fedt i t. or F.i.t.
Germany	Fett in der Trockenmasse	Fett i.Tr.
France	% de matière grasse	mat. gr. or m.g.
Italy	grasso sul secco	g.s.s.
Canada	Fat on Dry Basis matière grasse de lait en substance sèche	F.D.B. Gras sur sec/ Gss
New Zealand	fat in dry matter	FDM
Netherlands	vet in droge stof	V.D.S.
Norway	Fett i tørrstoffet	F/T
Austria	Fettgehalt in der Trockenmasse	F.i.T.
Sweden	fetthalt i torrsubstans	fett i. torrs.
Switzerland	Fett in der Trockenmasse	Fett i.T.
Spain	Materia grasa sobre extracto seco	M.G. sobre E.S. or M.G./E.S.
Russia	soderzanie zira v suchom vescestve	
USA	fat in dry matter	FDB
UK	Fat in Dry Matter	FDM

In some countries and in international usage, FDB is also expressed by a plus sign, for example: "Blue 50+," "Edam 40+," "Kaas 48+," "Svecia 45+," "Ost F. 45+," also "28% fat (F45+)."

Cheese quality

How you evaluate a particular cheese depends first of all on what you expect from it. Expectations are influenced by many factors. First, there is a person's own, quite individual taste; then, the experiences he or she has had; and, finally, and most importantly, the intended use of the cheese.

The difficulties of such an assessment can probably be explained most easily by using a particular cheese as an illustration. Let's take Gouda. Like all cheeses, it more or less continuously undergoes a ripening process; it can be eaten from a certain minimum age, and from this point onward it will be bought in the following different stages of maturity by different customers.

As a young cheese, after a ripening period of at least six weeks, it satisfies the modern trend toward mild cheeses with a supple curd, with as inconspicuous a taste as possible.

After a ripening period of approximately four months, the same cheese has lost weight through the evaporation of some of the water content. It has thus developed into a semi-hard cheese, with an unmistakable, pronounced taste, and has become a perfectly acceptable cheese for connoisseurs.

After nine months, it becomes an "aged" Gouda and is just right for cheese-lovers who prefer its now strong, aromatic taste; it has become so hard that it is almost impossible to cut it into slices.

In the case of Gouda, it is mainly the taste at the different stages of maturity that attracts the varied consumer groups. With other cheeses, other criteria play a role. Take Camembert, for example: anyone who has eaten a slightly ripened "Camembert" from, say, Germany and has accepted its taste and outward appearance as typical for Camembert, will surely judge a raw-milk Camembert from Normandy that has been ripened *au point* (to the point of perfection) as too strong; by contrast, its pronounced taste will seem perfect to an experienced cheese-fancier.

An approximately objective judgement, therefore, is possible only if a person is well acquainted with the typical characteristics of a given cheese. Personal preferences aside, there are numerous criteria for judging the quality of a cheese. These begin with the outward appearance: the cheese should have the shape typical of its type, and a smooth rind free from cracks and folds. If the cheese is coated with wax or plastic, the imperfections can be seen only when this layer is removed. The surface of such cheeses must be dry, and never moist, slimy, or moldy. Wax coatings or plastic film and applications of dye should be easy to peel or scrape off. Paraffin must not be brittle, or must be removed before the cheese is cut into, so that it does not get on the cut surface. Although the rind of a very old hard or semi-hard cheese does grow thicker, it should never look rough and crumbly, as this could mean that it is infested with mites.

The interior of a cheese, at least in the case of small soft cheeses, becomes visible only when the consumer cuts into it at home, but with soft cheeses and some wrapped semi-soft cheeses, the degree of ripeness and the consistency can be checked by pressing down on the packaged cheese with a finger.

The structure cannot be assessed by looking or touching. It can be appreciated only in the mouth, by the sensitive tactile nerves there. A fine cheese should seem to slip smoothly off the tongue: it must not leave a rough sensation behind. Descriptions such as supple, sliceable, soft, sticky, or even mushy are particularly important at cheese counters, where the cheese should be cut smoothly without smearing the knife or cutting device. Here it is the semi-hard "cutting cheeses" that show considerable differences. With these, as well as the hard cheeses, the customer can see even over the counter whether the cut is fresh — that the cheese has not dried out where it was last cut — whether the hole formation is typical for the cheese type, and whether the interior of the cheese is of a pleasant color and consistency.

Light has an unfavorable effect on many foods. This applies above all to the cheeses that are higher in fat, such as cream cheese or Quark with 20 percent or 40 percent FDB. If they are packaged in translucent containers, and if they sit too long on an illuminated shelf, they may acquire a certain "taste of light." On the other hand, there is a problem in persuading consumers to accept dark-dyed, and hence opaque, packaging.

Older hard cheeses, and especially grating cheeses, occasionally display what are often referred to as salt crystals. In fact, these are mostly natural agglomerations of amino acids, the building blocks of protein, which have formed during ripening. When buying pre-grated or shredded cheese, it is important to know when the cheese was processed in this way. If stored for too long, it may taste slightly rancid or tallowy because the fat will have begun to break down.

If blue-veined cheeses are heavily salted and the salt is distributed slowly through the cheese, a border of salt ¾ to 1-inch thick may develop, which slows down or even prevents the development of the blue mold. Prepackaged portions of such cheeses exude a salty water if they spend too long in transit. The most sensitive cheeses are the fast-ripening soft cheeses, especially those made from raw milk, which are especially dependent on proper treatment in the store. It is always advisable to shop at cheese counters or specialist cheese stores run by knowledgeable staff.

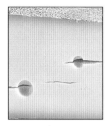

Cracks in the paste. A perfectly ripened Bergkäse dried out and developed cracks because of incorrect storage (refrigeration).

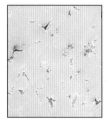

Green mold does not belong in this Cheddar. Hard and semi-hard cheeses must never be penetrated by mold.

Milk mold, or *Geotrichum candidum*, is often desirable or even necessary, but rank growth, as on the surface of this goat cheese, is an undesirable development. This *peau de crapaud* ("toadskin"), as it is called by specialists, may be caused by too little salt or by storage in an atmosphere that is too warm.

Contents per 100g											
Cheese	**Protein**	**Fat**	**Carbo-hydrate**	**Calcium (Ca)**	**Phosphorus (P)**	**Sodium chloride (NaCl)**	**Dry matter**	**Water**	**FDBx**	**kJ**	**kcal**
	g	g	g	mg	mg	g	g	g	%		
Sbrinz 48%	32.0	33.0	+	1200	700	2.0	70.0	30.0	47.1	1833	438
Parmesan 32%	35.6	25.8	+	1290	848	2.0	70.4	29.6	36.6	1634	389
Emmental 45%	27.8	29.3	+	1180	860	0.8	63.6	36.4	46.1	1617	386
German hard cheese 30%	27.0	17.0	+	790	555	1.7	55.2	44.8	30.8	1125	268
Cheddar 48%	26.6	32.0	+	820	540	1.8	63.0	37.0	50.8	1655	394
Gouda 48%	27.0	29.6	+	840	470	2.5	59.8	40.2	49.5	1615	385
Gouda 30%	26.4	16.2	+	800	570	1.9	50.9	49.1	31.8	1112	266
Tilsit 45%	26.3	27.7	+	858	522	1.8	59.4	40.6	46.6	1499	357
Tilsit 30%	28.7	17.2	+	830	580	2.0	53.8	46.2	32.0	1184	282
Bel Paese type 50%	22.0	28.0	+	700	400	1.7	54.0	46.0	51.8	1449	342
Bel Paese type 30%	26.5	16.0	+	900	600	1.8	50.0	50.0	32.0	1095	262
Danbo 45%	23.2	25.4	+	750	500	1.5	55.0	45.0	46.2	1435	343
Saint-Paulin	24.0	29.0	+	650	360	2.0	58.0	42.0	50.0	1527	365
Edelpilz (German Blue) 50%	21.1	29.8	+	526	362	3.5	57.2	42.8	52.1	1542	368
Camembert 45%	20.1	21.8	+	470	380	1.8	47.0	53.0	46.4	1225	293
Brie (French) 45%	17.0	20.9	+	185	190	2.7	43.0	57.0	48.6	1100	263
Munster-Géromé 45%	21.0	24.0	+	222	180	1.9	54.0	46.0	44.4	1347	322
Harz basket cheese low-fat	29.9	0.7	+	125	266	2.6	36.0	64.0	1.9	563	134
Limburger 40%	22,4	19.7	+	534	256	2.2	48.3	51.7	40.8	1156	275
Romadur 20%	23.9	9.2	+	448	325	2.8	39.7	60.3	23.2	773	184
Quark low-fat	13.5	0.3	4.1	92	160	-	18.7	81.3	1.6	323	77
Quark 20%	12.5	5.1	3.2	85	165	-	22.0	78.0	23.2	487	116
Quark 40%	11.1	11.4	3.1	95	187	-	26.5	73.5	43.0	701	167
Petit Suisse 60% (Switzerland)	9.4	20.0	2.9	110	100	-	33.0	67.0	60.6	939	224
Burgos	16.0	24.0	1.6	622	385	0.5	46.0	54.0	52.1	1197	286
Gjetost 35%	11.1	29.6	37.0	520	340	1.0	82.0	18.0	36.1	1928	459

+ = trace amounts of carbohydrates, lactic acid. Sodium content: Sodium chloride value 0.4 = **Na**
Sources: AID - Renner - Souci, Fachmann, Kraut - Peeters

Cheese: a healthy food

Milk and milk products make a substantial contribution to a healthy diet. The nutritional value of cheese is characterized not only by its protein content, but also by its fat, mineral, and vitamin content, and the large variety of cheese available makes it easy to include this nutritious staple in our menus.

The amount of fat in the modern diet is more than sufficient — perhaps even excessive. This is no reason, however, to avoid nutritious milk fat, which is contained in an easily digestible, finely distributed form in cheese, and which is also important in helping to provide the human body with a sufficient supply of the essential fat-soluble vitamins A and E. Since the fat content of cheese is stated, it is possible to control how much is eaten. We are also often warned in particular to control the amount of cholesterol (a component of animal fat and a vital building block of all body cells) we consume because of its contributory effect in the development of arteriosclerosis and other heart ailments. However, only a very small proportion of the average person's intake of cholesterol comes from eating cheese.

High-quality protein, like that available from milk and milk products, is also essential for the human body. Cheese contains all of the essential amino acids, in particular lysine, and is thus superbly suited to complementing plant protein, an important consideration for vegetarians. On average, 35 percent of the adult daily protein requirement can be supplied by about 4 ounces of soft cheese, and 45 percent by 4 ounces of hard cheese. Milk protein is composed of about 80 percent casein and 20 percent whey protein, which is of even higher nutritional value. The majority of the casein remains in the cheese solids, while most of the whey protein passes into the whey. The net dietary value of the protein in cheese is thus, at 80–85 percent, somewhat lower than that of the total milk protein, but higher than for casein alone.

The ripening of the cheese leads to a sort of predigestion, and hence makes it easier for the body to digest the protein. Protein is more than just a building block. Because it is easily digested, milk protein is particularly suited to those activities involving mental exertion; in contrast, protein deficiency leads to a decrease in mental energy and acuity. Amino acids fulfill other important roles in the central nervous system. In addition to glucose and oxygen, they are of particular importance for good brain function in old age. The formation of long-term memory molecules and certain metabolic functions can be ensured just through a sufficient supply of amino acids.

Lactic acid in cheese has a beneficial effect on bowel activity, while the amino acids aspartic acid and glutamic acid are credited with stimulating the secretion of gastric juices. At the same time the protein and minerals in cheese neutralize excess gastric acid. Low-fat fresh cheese has a relatively low protein and mineral content in comparison with other types of cheese, but it is especially important in the diets of invalids and elderly people because of its low fat content and easy digestibility.

The carbohydrate content of cheese is comparatively low, and consists almost exclusively of milk sugar. A minority of people have a lactose intolerance, which causes digestive problems. Cultured-milk products such as yogurt, buttermilk, and cheese, in which the lactose has, to a large extent, been broken down into lactic acid, offer a healthy alternative to milk.

Cheese, like other dairy products, helps to protect against tooth decay because its protein and mineral content bring about a reduction in acid formation in saliva. Many people are not aware that bread can contribute to tooth decay because its starch is split into fermentable sugar levels by the saliva. This is why, for example, eating cheese with whole-wheat bread is particularly sensible.

Calcium takes pride of place as the main mineral in cheese. Four ounces of soft cheese, for example, supply 30 to 40 percent of the daily calcium requirement, and 12 to 20 percent of the phosphorus requirement. Four ounces of hard cheese supply up to 100 percent of the calcium requirement.

The content of other minerals in various sorts of cheese is: sodium (Na), 0.6 to 9.0 g/lb; potassium (K), 0.3 to 1.6 g/lb; chlorine (Cl), 0.7 to 6.8 g/lb; magnesium (Mg), 0.1 to 0.3 g/lb. In addition, cheese contains many prominent trace elements, for example iron (0.7 to 5.3 mg/lb) and copper (0.1 to 1.6 mg/lb).

The amount of fat-soluble vitamin in cheese depends on the fat content. Eighty to 85 percent of the vitamin A in the milk goes into the cheese, while the transfer rate of the water-soluble B-complex vitamins is lower (thiamine, 10 to 20 percent; riboflavin and biotin, 20 to 30 percent; pyridoxine and pantothenic acid, 25 to 45 percent; cobalamin and folic acid, 40 to 60 percent). Some mold-ripened cheeses have a higher vitamin B content than others; for example, blue-veined cheese has up to 13.6 mg/lb of niacin. The ripening process is responsible for sizable variations in vitamin B content, with the B vitamins being both synthesized and consumed by microorganisms.

There are some ingredients in cheese that in other circumstances might be considered undesirable. Strains of mold used in the manufacture of Camembert (*Penicillium camemberti*) and Brie, for example, are related to the types of mold used in the manufacture of antibiotics, to which some people are allergic. According to in-depth tests, the mold cultures used under strict control in the production of cheese do not pose a health risk to humans. Neither does the amount of salt in cheese. Salt is essential to good health, and, normally, the amount of sodium chloride naturally present in a balanced diet is sufficient. Heavy physical exertion, combined with substantial loss of salt through perspiration, may, however, require an additional supply. On the other hand, some people have to follow special diets that restrict the use of salt. The great variety of cheese allows for appropriate selection in such cases.

The addition of sodium nitrate or potassium nitrate in order to prevent "late blowing" is permitted for only a few types of semi-hard cheese, and is subject to stringent control. Compared with the nitrate and nitrite intake from the average diet as a whole, however, the amount contributed by cheese is negligible. Nitrite cannot be detected in cheese.

Biogenic amines (histamine, tyramine, and tryptamine, among others) are formed from free amino acids during the ripening process; however, they are degraded relatively quickly by enzymes in the human body. In cheesemaking, great value is attached to residue-free, high-quality raw materials. Milk is probably one of the most thoroughly investigated foods, and residues of pesticide and heavy metals — if detectable at all — are, as a rule, far below the maximum quantities permissible.

Glossary

Aerobic, anaerobic Metabolic processes take place aerobically or anaerobically, depending on whether the microorganisms, such as bacteria and mold, require oxygen (aer = "air") or not (anaer = "without air").

Affineur (French) The cheese finisher may take over the care of the cheese until it reaches the desired degree of ripeness (*see* page 15).

Almkäse, Alpenkäse, Alpkäse, are German terms for cheeses made in alpine mountain pastures.

Bare is the term used to describe the surface of a cheese with or without a skin or rind, which has no covering or coating such as mold or red flora, oil or plastic.

Bonde is the term used in France for a cylindrically shaped cheese mold with a maximum diameter of $2^1/2$ inches and a height of between 2 and $2^3/4$ inches.

Cacio (pronounced "cah-cho," in dialect also "cah-sho") is derived from the Latin *caseus*, meaning "cheese." It is also spelled Caccio and Cascio, in compounds such as Caciocavallo, Caciotta, Casciotta d'Urbino.

Caraway (*Carum carvi*) and **Cumin** (*Cuminum cyminum*) These two spices are used to flavor cheese, and are often confused with one another. Caraway is the most familiar as a seed used to flavor bread as well as cheese, and cumin is usually found as a ground spice and is used in making chili, curries, and other spicy dishes.

Casein The most important milk protein in cheesemaking.

Cendré (from the French *cendre* , "ash") means "covered with ash." Used to describe cheese, primarily goat cheese, that has been dusted (*charbonné*) with powdered charcoal (French: *charbon de bois, charbon végétal*).

Charbonné see Cendré.

Cheese flora The microorganisms that are present in or on the cheese during manufacture and ripening. Red bacteria (including the important *Linens* bacteria) and yellow bacteria are the main non-acid-forming bacteria used in cheesemaking. Along with various yeasts and micrococci, they are the typical flora of the washed-rind cheeses, and are responsible for the changes in color on the surface of those cheeses during ripening.

Cheese, or vat, milk is the milk provided for cheese production, which is often pre-ripened with lactic-acid bacteria, is either raw or heat-treated, and has had its fat content adjusted.

Chèvre French for goat, and in France used generically for goat cheese.

Close-textured curd describes a cheese with very few or no holes.

Coagulate To cause the milk to clot or curdle through acidification or the action of rennet, or both.

Coagulum Gelled or coagulated milk.

Cooking or scalding The heating of the curd and whey mixture, which encourages the shrinkage of the curd.

Curd The thick curdled milk in which the solid constituents have already begun to separate from the liquid ones (the whey).

Curd hole-formation *see* Hole or "eye" formation.

Curdle *see* Coagulate

Defined cheeses Those cheeses whose characteristics and composition are laid down in law.

Double-curd cheese Cheese from a mixture of milled curd prepared in the evening and left to stand and acidify overnight, and the curd freshly prepared the following morning.

Dry matter All the constituents of the cheese apart from the water.

Enzymes are special proteins formed in living cells, called biocatalysts, which accelerate or bring about biochemical transformations; for example, in cheesemaking they cause the fermentation of milk sugar (lactose) into lactic acid. They play a part in protein coagulation and contribute to the formation of product-specific aromas and flavors, through protein-ripening and fat-ripening transformations.

Farmhouse cheese is the name given to cheese made on farms, usually from raw milk.

FDB Abbreviation for the amount of "fat on a dry basis." Other abbreviations are FDM (Britain, New Zealand), F.D.B. (Fat on Dry Basis) or Gss (*matière grasse de lait en substance sèche*) (Canada) (*see also* page 17 and the table on page 18).

Fermentation The process in which sugar is transformed anaerobically by microorganisms, in order to provide energy for growth and multiplication. Depending on the agent used to stimulate the process, it is called lactic, propionic, butyric, alcoholic or acetic fermentation.

Fermentation hole-formation Holes or "eyes" that are created by gas, mostly carbon dioxide, which forms during fermentation and collects in a number of places in the cheese.

Gel-like mass Coagulated milk, also called the coagulum.

Hole or "eye" formation During the acidification process, the bacteria that live on the lactic acid emit carbon dioxide, which produces bubbles of gas that create round holes. Irregular shaped holes form when curd is drawn off without the whey, causing air to be trapped. Combined hole formation occurs when round holes are formed in addition to curd holes. Slit-hole formation occurs when the cheese is pressed, causing the curd holes to become flatter.

Labeling The supplying of important information on the cheese or on the packaging: trade descriptions (standard type or cheese category), fat-content level or fat content in dry matter, name and address of the manufacturer, list of ingredients, net weight, price.

Lactic acid bacteria ferment the milk sugar, or lactose, into lactic acid and also partly into aromatic compounds.

Late blowing The beginning of bacterial activity when the cheese ripening process is almost complete, which causes gases to develop again and has a negative effect on both flavor and aroma

Legally protected name of origin The names of certain cheeses are protected by law. In these cases the name may be used only for cheeses produced in a, for the most part, precisely circumscribed area that conforms with the regulations laid down there concerning production, characteristics, and composition. They are then allowed to bear the appropriate symbol: in France, AOC (*Appellation d'Origine Contrôlée*); in Italy, DOC (*Denominazione di Origine Controllata*); in Spain, DOP (*Denominación de Origen Protegida*).

Milk mold *see* Mold cultures.

Mold cultures The generic description for selected surface and interior molds, especially the two penicillate molds *Penicillium camemberti/candidum* and *Penicillium roqueforti*, and *Geotrichum candidum* (previously *Oidium lactis, Oospora lactis*), sometimes known as milk mold.

Open-textured cheese A cheese containing many holes or "eyes."

Pasta filata cheeses An Italian term, *formaggio a pasta filata*, it means literally, "drawn-curd cheese" (from *filare*, to pull or draw). It is also known in English as stretched or pulled cheese, and in French as *fromage plastifié*.

Pasteurization Brief heating of the raw milk to 144–162°F.

pH value A measure of acidity, which can be determined by a physical test.

Propionic acid *see* Fermentation.

Red bacteria One of the non-acid forming bacteria used in cheesemaking.

Rennet A substance containing the enzyme rennin from the stomach of calves or other young mammals, and used to coagulate the milk. There are also vegetable rennets and microbial rennets.

Rind closure This is achieved when the curd grains on the cheese surface join up so that the surface becomes as smooth as possible and has no indentations.

Round-hole formation *see* Hole or "eye" formation.

Salt bath Immersion of the cheeses in a 15–20 percent salt solution, in which they are steeped until they achieve the desired salt content.

Scalding *see* Cooking

Seasoning ingredients Herbs, spices, salt, and pepper are common seasonings. In a broader sense, the phrase also refers to other ingredients that add flavor, such as salami and ham.

Slit-hole formation *see* Hole or "eye" formation.

Starter cultures Lactic acid bacteria with particularly favorable acidifying and ripening characteristics, which are "cultured" in milk and accelerate the acidification of the milk that leads to the formation of curds.

Ultrafiltration A process, sometimes used in cheesemaking, whereby very fine membranes are used to allow very small constituents, such as salts and lactose, to pass through with the water, and to hold back large constituents, such as protein and fat droplets. The constituents passing through the filter are known as the permeate, those held back as the retentate.

Vacuum-packed Refers to those cheeses placed in a plastic bag from which the air is sucked out.

Wff Water content in the fat-free cheese matter. The fat-free cheese matter is the entire cheese mass including water but excluding the fat content.

Whey The liquid portion of the milk that separates from the curd after coagulation.

Whey cheese The name given to two completely different products: whey-protein cheese, such as Ricotta, made from recooked whey, on the one hand; and Brunost (brown cheese) and Mysost in Norway, made from evaporated whey, on the other. Whey-protein cheese, which used to be called albumin cheese, contains a great deal of the nourishing milk albumin from the whey.

Cheese encyclopedia

It has not been all that long since the term "cheese" was linked in our minds only with locally made cheeses — and these were relatively few in number. For people everywhere cheese was generally the product of a particular country, a specific region, or even just one village. Only hard cheeses capable of withstanding storage and transportation were sold further afield. Nowadays, however, thanks to the speed of modern transportation, even an expert in the field would be hard pressed to keep track of the variety of available cheeses. Not only cheeses with a long shelf life, but also regional soft cheeses, and even fresh cheeses are marketed far and wide. In addition, traditional cheeses that at one time were typical of a region are now manufactured throughout the world. Large-scale industrial cheesemaking has created brand names that are sold on the world market and peacefully coexist with the well-known, traditional, and in some cases nationally protected types. At the same time there continues to be a multitude of often exciting though quantitatively modest regional variations, and even new creations.

All of these factors explain why the cheeses in this encyclopedia are not grouped according to regional or national origin, but rather according to cheese "families." In this way it is possible to cope with the constantly growing supply, and to assess and classify new cheeses according to the same criteria.

Farmers deliver milk twice daily to the cheese factory. To make Emmental-type cheeses, the fresh morning milk is mixed with the evening milk of the day before.

The term **hard cheese** might make one think primarily of Emmental in Switzerland, possibly Gruyère or Cantal in France, Grana or Provolone in Italy, Manchego in Spain, Cheddar in England, Herrgardsost in northern Europe, Kashkaval in southeastern Europe, and Cheddar and Swiss in America. In fact, the consistency of "hard" cheeses ranges from very firm to hard, from supple and sliceable to grainy and gratable. This extensive group of cheeses can be divided into four families, based on characteristics that are partly the result of common production processes.

Many hard cheeses, such as Emmental, are typified by their holes, or "eyes," which are the result of carbon dioxide emissions — technically called propionic acid fermentation — during the ripening process. Other hard cheeses, such as Parmesan and Sbrinz, are made in a similar fashion, with a small curd that is reheated — technically, scalded — while being stirred, yet they form very few, if any, holes; on the contrary, they are distinguished by an especially firm to hard consistency and a grainy texture, which characterize them as extra-hard or grating cheeses. The other two families stand out by virtue of the special treatment of the curd. Cheddar and related cheeses are characterized by "cheddaring," which means they are "acidified and salted in the curd." These cheeses are shaped in a mold and ripened. The cooked and kneaded cheeses, including the *pasta filata* cheeses, undergo a similar process initially. The whey is drained and the curd is allowed to draw together and acidify, and the curd cake is cut up. Next, however, the broken-up mass is worked in a striking manner: it is cooked in hot water and then kneaded — and in the case of *pasta filata* cheeses, also stretched or pulled, shaped, salted, and ripened.

Among those hard cheeses for which hole formation is an essential part of the ripening process, Emmental, in particular **Swiss Emmental**, is the best known worldwide. Traditionally, this cheese is made from unpasteurized, or raw, milk and shaped into wheels weighing 150 pounds and more. It has a fat content of about 45 percent FDB and a supple interior that is easily sliced. Good-quality cheeses have a beautifully even scattering of holes, which may be large or small, roundish or oval. **Allgäuer Emmentaler** is produced in Germany. It ripens in less time than its Swiss namesake, and thus remains milder tasting.

Special care is taken during the production of Emmental cheese to ensure that exactly the right type and quantity of lactic acid bacteria and rennet are used, and to control the length of the coagulation period, the cutting and size of the curd, the cooking and stirring of the curd–whey mixture, and even the resting time. After the curd, which has settled under the whey, is ladled into the molds, it is pressed, salted, and ripened

This stamp clearly illustrates the importance of cheese in Switzerland. It shows the coagulated milk being cut up with a cheese harp.

1 **Lactic-acid forming bacteria and rennet** are added to the raw milk, which has been heated to 86–90°F.

2 **The milk coagulates** during a 30-minute resting stage at 86–90°F. If the coagulum has the proper consistency — it must "break" smoothly — preparation of the curd begins.

3 **The coagulum is cut up** with a cheese harp or another cutting device, and is stirred until the curd is the size of kernels of corn.

4 **The individual grains of curd** must be sufficiently firm. To achieve this, the curd is "cooked": heated to 125°F in 30 minutes and left to rest for a further 30 minutes.

5 **The cheesemaker** lines the strainers, or "baskets," in the vat with cheesecloth before filling them.

6 **Tubes** transfer the curd–whey mixture from the vat to the baskets, dividing it up evenly.

7 **The cheese curd** is left to settle in the baskets under the whey, which is later drained off.

8 **The cheesecloth**, with the curds inside, is tied together above the basket.

9 **More whey** drains off when the cheesecloth containing the curd is suspended over the basket.

10 **The curd is transferred** in its cheesecloth to a ring mold and pressed in firmly.

11 **Powerful pressure** expels more whey and molds the young cheese wheel into its final shape.

12 **The ring mold** and cheesecloth are removed when the cheese wheel stabilizes in shape.

13 **Excess curd** is trimmed evenly from around the edge of the cheese wheel.

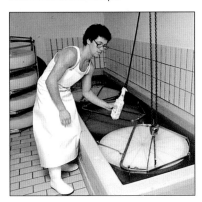

14 **Immersed** in a salt bath for one to three days, the cheese expels water, absorbs salt, and forms a rind.

15 **During ripening** the cheese is carefully tended, washed down, and in some cases sprinkled with salt.

16 **The cheeses** are brought to the curing cellar, where they ripen under strict control in optimal conditions.

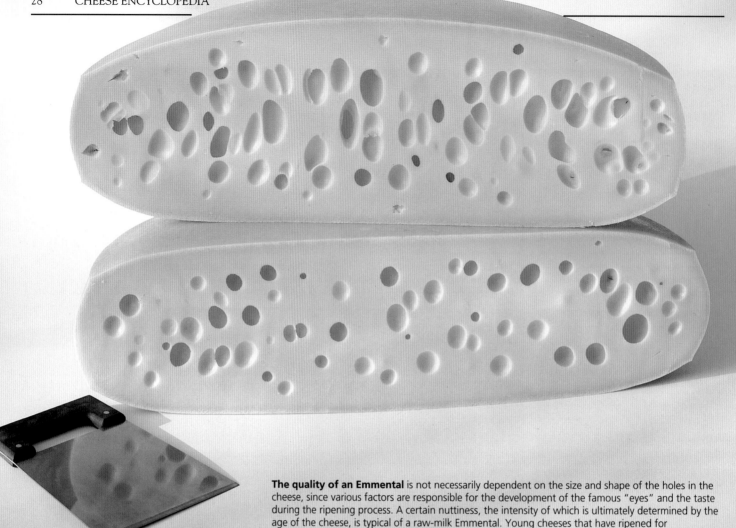

The quality of an Emmental is not necessarily dependent on the size and shape of the holes in the cheese, since various factors are responsible for the development of the famous "eyes" and the taste during the ripening process. A certain nuttiness, the intensity of which is ultimately determined by the age of the cheese, is typical of a raw-milk Emmental. Young cheeses that have ripened for approximately three months have a mild to sweetly nutty flavor while older cheeses, which have ripened for four to five months, such as those from Switzerland, have a strong to piquant taste. Although the strength of flavor in an Emmental cannot be deduced from its appearance alone, a cheese with large, "stretched" holes (such as the top cheese above) is most probably rather mild tasting. Here, the cheese wheel is nicely risen, with a clearly rounded top. The bottom wheel, on the other hand, ripened in a more restrained fashion, remained flatter, and developed smaller, rounder holes. It probably has a full, strong, piquant taste. Swiss Emmental, German Allgäuer Emmentaler, and the French Emmental Français Grand Cru are made only from raw milk, and can be identified by their red stamp.

American Swiss cheese is a hard cheese made from pasteurized milk and with 43% FDB. It is produced in various shapes and sizes: wheel- or block-shaped, sometimes with a rind and a paraffin coating, or rindless and foil-ripened. Ripened for a minimum of sixty days, it is mild and slightly nutty in taste.

Emmental-style hard cheeses produced from pasteurized milk are manufactured in square blocks. Most of them are sold under the brand name of the manufacturer. Good-quality cheeses of this type stand up well to comparison with young raw-milk Emmentals. They are mild in taste and relatively supple.

for two weeks at 50°F, and for six to eight weeks at 68°F. The cheese is then stored at 50°F until fully ripened.

A Swiss specialty is cave-ripened Emmental, which is stored for two months in the fermenting and ripening rooms of the cheese factory, and then kept for approximately six months in caves in central Switzerland. This imparts a special, pronounced note to the typical nutty flavor of Emmental. In some countries, such as Switzerland, the name Emmental is reserved exclusively for raw-milk cheeses. In France, **Emmental** *français grand cru* is produced in the Franche-Comté and Savoie regions from raw milk. However, in Brittany and Normandy several tons of cheese a year are made from pasteurized milk and marketed under the name Emmental. There, cheese from both raw and pasteurized milk is made and sold in the traditional wheel shape. In Germany, the more economic block shape and the name Emmental are now used for both the cheese made from raw milk and that made from pasteurized milk.

Emmental cheeses made from pasteurized milk are generally ripened for about one and a half to two months, and have a softer consistency and a milder aroma than raw-milk Emmental. Internationally, and particularly in English-speaking countries, Emmental-style cheeses are known generally as **Swiss cheese**. American-made Swiss cheese is produced in blocks or wheels, often weighing over 20 pounds, and sometimes as much as 220 pounds. They are ripened for two to three weeks at 60 to 64°F or higher, until their holes are about the size of a penny. They are then stored at a maximum of 40°F before being sold in small blocks or bars, sliced, or shredded. The smaller **Baby Swiss**, which has a higher water content and consequently is softer, is often wrapped in red foil or coated in red wax. It is younger and tastes even milder. Swiss cheese with a lower fat content of 30 percent FDB has a correspondingly less supple consistency.

Emmental-style cheeses made from pasteurized milk and usually with smaller holes are also produced in many other countries. Some examples are Moravsky bochník (Czech Republic), Tal-ha-Emek (Israel), Bohinjski sir (Slovenia), Ementáli (Hungary), and Altaiski syr (Russia). A number of these cheeses bear a greater resemblance to Emmental, others are more akin to Gruyère or American Swiss.

Bergkäse and **Alpkäse** are the generic terms used in Germany and Austria for cheeses produced in the higher mountain regions, in different styles, shapes, and sizes. Many alpine cheeses from Switzerland bear names of origin, such as Brienzer Käse, Grindelwalder Käse, and Urner Alpkäse. (In Italy, mountain cheeses are referred to as *formaggio di montagna*, and in France they are *fromage de montagne*). Mountain cheeses can weigh from 65 to 90 pounds. Their fat levels range

Some time ago, it was discovered that the ratio of temperature to humidity in the caves of central Switzerland helped the nutty flavor of Emmental to develop especially well. The brownish-black rind that forms during storage is the mark of this special cave-ripened cheese.

The good reputation of Emmental demands constant checks during the ripening period. This giant among the not otherwise small hard cheeses is made from raw milk and reacts highly sensitively to the most varied factors. It spends the months until it reaches full ripeness resting in optimal conditions, such as those found in this Swiss cheese storeroom. Its development is checked by experts at regular intervals. Only cheeses of truly perfect quality make it into the stores. Imperfections such as uneven hole formation or holes running lengthwise often have no great impact on the taste of the cheese, but still place it lower down on the quality scale.

The cheese borer is used by experts to check the progress of the cheese during ripening. This knife, in the shape of a tube cut in half lengthwise, has sharp edges and a wooden handle. By simply tapping the cheese with the wooden handle, cheesemakers can tell from the sound to what extent the holes (hollow areas) have developed. By inserting and twisting the borer and drawing out a sample from the interior of the cheese, they are able to judge quite accurately the flavor, hole formation, and consistency.

The castle of Gruyère, in the canton of Fribourg in western Switzerland, gave the spicy cheese its name.

Gruyère is made from raw milk, often with more than 50% FDB. It has a powerful flavor, owing in part to having first a somewhat moist, then later a fine-grained and dry bacterial rub and a four- to eight-month ripening period. It is ideal for grating and melting, and for use in sauces and fondues.

Allgäuer Bergkäse is a German full-fat raw-milk mountain cheese. It is made in the Emmental style, but ripens longer and in a cooler environment, which results in the smaller holes. This is a delicate, aromatic cheese, especially when it hails from one of the increasingly rare alpine meadows where cattle still graze.

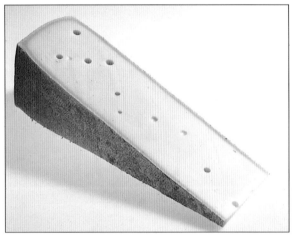

Comté, or Gruyère de Comté, is a French hard cheese from the Franche-Comté region. It is allowed to ripen for four to five months, and has a strong aromatic taste, the result of the surface being rubbed with a bacteria during this period. With a fat content of at least 45% FDB, it is esteemed as a dessert cheese, and can be used in hot dishes in similar ways to Swiss Gruyère.

Beaufort, or Gruyère de Beaufort, is a mountain cheese produced in the French Alps between Annecy and Mont Blanc. Its slightly concave edge is one of its hallmarks. Its high fat content, often over 50% FDB, gives it a fatty, supple consistency, and makes it a good raclette cheese, beautifully creamy when it melts.

The brown Swiss cow is a typical mountain breed found throughout the Alps, especially in the cheesemaking districts. It is also highly esteemed in other countries.

Idiazabal is a good example of Spanish hard cheeses made from sheep's milk, with a typical, very strong, and, when aged, almost pungent aroma. Sometimes smoked, Idiazabal may be kept for up to one year. It is eaten in small chunks with country bread and wine, or used as a grating cheese with rice dishes and pasta. It is salty and distinctively spicy.

Kefalotiri is a Greek raw-milk cheese made from sheep's milk or a mixture of sheep's and goat's milk. The length of its ripening period varies greatly. It is often also sold under the name of the region of production. Used fresh in many Greek dishes, when well ripened it is used as a grating cheese. A variety without holes, called Kefalograviera, is primarily exported.

from low (less than 15 percent FDB) to full (45 percent FDB). They differ correspondingly in the percentage of dry matter, texture, and flavor, which ranges from mild to strong. **Tyrolean Alpkäse** is a well-known mountain cheese in Austria. **Allgäuer Bergkäse** is a full-fat mountain cheese made in Germany. When this cheese is made in an alpine meadow dairy, it remains there for three to four weeks. Warm weather during this time will encourage hole formation and ripening, cool weather will slow them down. The subsequent storage period in the valley until the cheese is fully ripened will partly compensate for the initial climatic differences. The consistency is supple, and the flavor, depending on the provenance and age of the cheese, varies markedly from aromatic to piquant.

    Gruyère, for centuries made in the area of present-day western Switzerland and the French Jura, comes in a number of varieties. It differs from Emmental in its smaller size, fewer and smaller (approximately pea-sized) (or no) holes, and a surface bacterial treatment. The cheeses measure 16 to 25 inches in diameter and 3½ to 5 inches in height, and weigh 45 to 100 pounds. In France, Emmental made from raw or pasteurized milk, as well as the other round-holed hard cheeses Beaufort and Comté, are considered members of the Gruyère family. **Comté** or **Gruyère de Comté** is a raw-milk cheese made in the shape of a wheel or millstone (*meule*). The cheeses are 16 to 28 inches in diameter and 3½ to 5 inches high, and weigh 45 to 130 pounds. According to the season, the cheese is ivory-colored to yellowish, and has hazelnut- to cherry-sized holes. Its high fat content (often over 50 percent FDB) gives it a delicate, supple consistency. **Beaufort**, or **Gruyère de Beaufort**, is produced in the alpine meadows in the summer, when it is called Beaufort de Montagne (mountain Beaufort) or Beaufort d'Été (summer Beaufort). In the winter it is made in the valleys, and is called Beaufort d'Hiver (winter Beaufort) or Beaufort Laitier (dairy Beaufort). Made from raw milk, these cheeses have a concave edge, and after a long ripening period are given a dry surface bacterial rub. The very sparse small holes are known to the French as *oeil de perdrix* (eye of the partridge). Similar cheeses, often made from pasteurized milk, with names derived from the French, are found in other countries, such as Graviera (Greece) and Gruviera (Italy).

    The Swiss cheeses Spalen and Saanen-Hobelkäse represent a link between hard cheeses and extra-hard grating cheeses. Although made from raw milk in a similar manner to Emmental, they are nevertheless quite different. They ripen for one, two, or even three years, and are a combination of two cheese types: cheese with a semi-hard, supple, sliceable and shreddable body that nonetheless is crumbly, and

Mountain cheeses can also be spiced, like this **Ginepro**, from the Valle d'Aosta in Italy, which is flavored with juniper berries. The full name of this cheese is La Tometta di Giain al Ginepro.

A wide variety of **Swiss mountain cheeses** is produced in a range of fat levels from 15% to 45% FDB. From top to bottom: Müstair, Puschlaver, Bergeller, Brienzer Mutschli, Hasliberger, Bündner, quarter-fat Bündner, and half-fat Bündner.

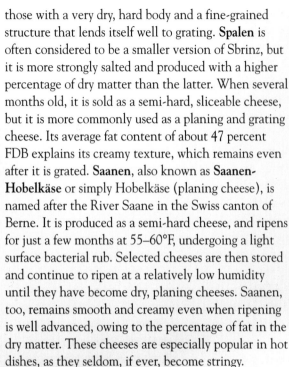

Planes for hard cheeses should be designed not to slip during use. The one shown here has a notched leg that enables it to be held fast against the edge of the table.

Planing cheeses, such as **Saanen** (shown below) or Spalen, are produced as semi-hard, or sliceable, cheeses. Some cheeses can then continue to ripen into hard cheeses. Their high fat content means that they remain supple even when ripening is far advanced: the cheeses can be planed into wafer-thin pieces that won't crumble, which are best eaten straight from the plane or rolled, with wine. Planing cheeses are very popular in hot cheese dishes, melting without, or virtually without, becoming stringy.

those with a very dry, hard body and a fine-grained structure that lends itself well to grating. **Spalen** is often considered to be a smaller version of Sbrinz, but it is more strongly salted and produced with a higher percentage of dry matter than the latter. When several months old, it is sold as a semi-hard, sliceable cheese, but it is more commonly used as a planing and grating cheese. Its average fat content of about 47 percent FDB explains its creamy texture, which remains even after it is grated. **Saanen**, also known as **Saanen-Hobelkäse** or simply Hobelkäse (planing cheese), is named after the River Saane in the Swiss canton of Berne. It is produced as a semi-hard cheese, and ripens for just a few months at 55–60°F, undergoing a light surface bacterial rub. Selected cheeses are then stored and continue to ripen at a relatively low humidity until they have become dry, planing cheeses. Saanen, too, remains smooth and creamy even when ripening is well advanced, owing to the percentage of fat in the dry matter. These cheeses are especially popular in hot dishes, as they seldom, if ever, become stringy.

Extra-hard cheeses are produced in a similar way to Emmental types, but because little or no propionic fermentation occurs, they do not develop many holes. In most cases, they contain substantially more than 65 percent dry matter. Their piquant, extra-hard body, which is crumbly and flaky, makes them excellent for grating. The three main types are, represented by Sbrinz, Grana, and Pecorino. **Sbrinz** is made in Switzerland from raw milk. It is produced as wheels weighing 45 to 100 pounds, with a diameter of 20 to 28 inches and a height of 4 to 5½ inches. Young cheeses are used like Spalen and Saanen as planing cheeses, but most are ripened for one and a half to two years, and are then used as grating cheeses. An FDB of 45 percent and above means a good fat–protein ratio, so even the grated grain retains a fine supple quality.

Grana, which literally means "grain," is the generic term for two types of cheese from Italy: those made in a specified production area, such as Parma and Reggio Emilia, which since 1934 have been bracketed together as **Parmigiano Reggiano**; and those produced elsewhere in northern Italy and called **Grana Padano** ("granular cheese from the plain of the River Po") and **Grana Trentino**. They are large, drum-shaped cheeses weighing 40 to 55 pounds, with a rind about ⅓ inch thick, and at least 32 percent FDB. Fine-grained and leafy in structure, with a few small holes, they are spicy but in no way pungent. The details of production for the different types vary. For example, Grana Padano ripens for ten to eighteen months at 59–68°F; Parmigiano Reggiano for at least two years, first at 60–64°F, later at 50–54°F. The length of time the cheese is aged is indicated by the terms *nuovo* (one year), *vecchio* (two years), *stravecchio* (three years), and

Parmigiano Reggiano is an Italian cheese with a legally protected name of origin. The seal of the consortium, with which the cheese is branded, guarantees impeccable quality.

Grana Padano is another name-controlled cheese, and bears a clover-leaf brand.

Grana Trentino, a raw-milk cheese, carries the quality seal of its regional consortium.

The best-known seasoning cheeses come from three classic cheese-producing countries. Their extra-hard curd makes them excellent for grating, and they are ideal for rounding out sauces, soups, pasta and rice dishes, as well as tasting superb on their own with wine. Some extra-hard cheeses are manufactured as such from the outset, others start life as semi-hard cheeses and are ripened into grating cheeses by virtue of especially long storage. **Parmigiano Reggiano** (Italy, extreme top) is the most famous. For this cheese, as well as for **Grana Padano** (Italy, center left) structure and consistency are established in the kettle. The Swiss **Schabziger**, or Sapsago (center right, with its typical conical shape), is an especially piquant seasoning cheese. It is made with dried, ground honey-lotus clover. **Aged Gouda** (Netherlands, bottom left) is made from semi-hard cheese. The well-known **Sbrinz** from Switzerland (bottom right) is a particularly fine-melting extra-hard cheese.

The seal branded on the rind of this Asiago Vecchio not only guarantees high quality but also gives the exact production date.

Asiago Vecchio (Asiago Piccante) becomes an extra-hard grating cheese after ripening for eight months to two years.

Montasio Vecchio (Montasio Piccante) ripens for over a year from a semi-hard cheese into an aromatic grating cheese.

Provolone Piccante develops within six months into one of the spiciest and most popular grating cheeses in Italy.

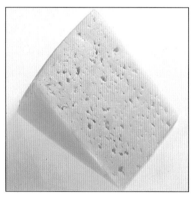

Västerbotten is a quite hard, very aromatic cheese from Sweden. It ripens for at least eight months.

Tyrolean Alpkäse is a well-known Austrian mountain cheese. It is spicy, almost a bit harsh, and slightly salty.

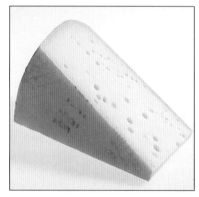

Favorel, an example of a new hard-cheese type from the Netherlands, has a delicate, spicy taste.

Mimolette Vieille is sometimes produced in the Netherlands and ripened in France. It is used for shredding and grating.

Pecorino Romano may be produced only in strictly specified regions. Its ripening period is at least eight months.

Pecorino Sardo has a basket-weave rind. The cheese shown here is medium-matured.

Many cheeses, such as this young Pecorino Toscano, are sold as table cheeses after only two months' ripening time.

Pecorino Toscano has a tempting *dolcezza* or slight sweetness when medium-matured.

Fiore Sardo, shown here as a well-aged, ripe cheese, is a Pecorino variant made only in Sardinia.

Pecorino Pepato is a Pecorino made with whole or, as here, crushed black peppercorns.

stravecchione (four years). Seals are branded onto the cheeses after stringent quality testing by the consortium responsible in each case, and are a guarantee of quality for the buyer. Similar style extra-hard grating cheeses are often called simply **Parmesan** elsewhere. That made in Brazil is Parmezao, and those from Argentina are Parmesano and Reggianito.

Pecorino cheeses are produced in central and southern Italy as well as on the islands of Sardinia and Sicily, and differ widely in character throughout Italy. The variations result from the type of milk used, as well as the mixtures of cow's milk, sheep's and goat's milk; the use of calf, lamb or kid rennet; and the production methods in each case, with different curd size, scalding times, and ripening periods. Fresh, unripened **Pecorino** *fresco* or the slightly ripened **Pecorino** *semifresco*, and the only slightly salted **Pecorino** *dolce* are enjoyed mainly as very mild table cheeses. The hard cheeses and grating cheeses, however, are far more important. The best-known of these are Pecorino Romano, Pecorino Sardo or Fiore Sardo, and Pecorino Siciliano or Canestrato. They too are often used as table cheeses when they are only several months old, but as they become riper and firmer they are used as grating cheeses. **Pecorino Romano** is a DOC cheese in Italy: only cheeses produced in specific regions may be sold under this name. Sixty percent of the Pecorino Romano produced in Italy is actually made on Sardinia, which has the most sheep of any region in Italy. The production of Pecorino Romano and some of its close relatives is more varied and labor-intensive than for other Pecorino cheeses. The milk is heated and coagulated at 102°F with lamb rennet, and the coagulum thus formed is cut into curds the size of wheat grains. Next, the curd is scalded by heating to about 118°F while being stirred, and is then transferred into molds. The cheeses ripen at 54 to 61°F for a minimum of eight months, during which time they are repeatedly salted, turned, washed with salt water, and cleaned. The combination of sheep's milk and lamb rennet to coagulate the milk produces the characteristic, piquant flavor of Pecorino Romano. The white to straw-colored interior is very firm to hard. The full-fat cheeses are layered, scaly, supple, and sliceable; the low-fat cheeses are rather granular and interspersed with the tiny "salt crystals" typical of aged cheeses. Only occasionally do small holes form, and a ripening liquid, called *lacrima* (teardrops) is found in cheeses that have been stored for a long time. Pecorino Romano must have at least 36 percent FDB, but often contains more than 40 percent. The smooth rind of the cheese is usually light yellow to straw-colored, and is rubbed with oil, tallow or clay (*terra gialla*, yellow earth). More and more, however, the

Ragusano, the Sicilian *pasta filata* cheese, ripens over a long storage period into a grating cheese. A spicy variant is **Ragusano Pepato** (top cheese in photo), whose interior is studded with whole black peppercorns.

manufacturers are turning to plastic coatings of varying shades of dark brown. The cylindrical cheeses are 8 to 12 inches in diameter, 5½ to 12 inches high, and weigh 17 to 48 pounds.

The **Romano** made in the United States, Canada and other countries is a popular grating cheese produced from cow's, sheep's or goat's milk, or mixtures thereof, and derives its typically piquant flavor from lamb or kid rennet. Romano made in the United States must contain at least 38 percent FDB and 68 percent dry matter; similar specifications apply to its manufacture in Canada, Australia, and New Zealand. Fat-ripening enzymes are often added. Other Pecorino cheeses bear the name of the relevant region of production. Pecorino di Norcia from Umbria (made from absolutely freshly milked milk), Pecorino di Crotone from Calabria, Pecorino di Moliterno or Canestrato di Moliterno, named after a village in the Basilicata, Pecorino Abruzzese, Pecorino del Frignano from the Apennines and Canestrato di Foggia from Apulia are just a few examples. In Tuscany, numerous cheeses are produced under the names **Pecorino Toscano** and **Toscanello** (as well as Pepato, which contains black peppercorns), using different processes and different sorts of milk and milk mixtures. Occasionally, you can find **Pecorino Toscano Sotto Cenere** (under ash). Like Pecorino Romano, **Pecorino Fiore Sardo** (also called Pecorino Sardo or **Fiore Sardo**) is made in Sardinia. The cheeses weigh between 3½ and 9 pounds, and are distinguished by a slightly convex rim, the so-called mule's back. This is formed when two young, conical cheeses are laid one on top of the other to ripen. Sheep's milk, lamb or kid rennet and at least 40 percent FDB are prescribed, and the interior of the cheese is whitish or pale yellow, and firm to hard and piquant to sharp when ripened for a period often in excess of nine months.

Another hard cheese made in Sardinia is **Pecorino di Macomer**, named after an important sheep's-cheese center. A popular eating and grating cheese is **Formaggio Sardo Pepato**, studded throughout with black peppercorns and coveted by *buongustai* (gourmets) for its individual, rich taste. The best-known hard cheese and grating cheese of Sicily is **Pecorino Canestrato Siciliano** (also called **Pecorino Siciliano** and **Canestrato Siciliano**), which is a DOC cheese. Its name derives from the basket (*canestra*) of woven reeds that gives it its typical shape and structure. This cheese has at least 40 percent FDB, often even more. Here, too, there is a **Pepato**, which has black peppercorns mixed into its milk curd.

La Mancha, the region of Spain occupying the plateau of New Castile, made famous by Cervantes in his novel *Don Quixote*, is the home of **Manchego**, Spain's best-known hard cheese. It is made from the

An example of the numerous ways in which Pecorino is used in Sicilian cooking is the dish *Sarde a beccafico*. Fresh sardines are filled with a mixture in which aged Pecorino and garlic predominate, and then cooked with bay leaves.

Farmers in the mountains of Sicily still make Pecorino in the traditional manner. Sheep's milk is heated in copper kettles over a simple wood fire. The curdled milk is cut up and the curds ladled into baskets, which give their shape and texture to the finished cheeses, to drain.

Handmade in the traditional manner

The pride and joy of Sicilian farmers is their **Pecorino Canestrato Siciliano**, which they still produce traditionally by hand, and the use of whose name is legally restricted to their island. The name is derived from the woven-reed basket (*canestra*) in which the curds are filled to drain, and which gives the cheese its typical shape and texture. By law, the cheese must be made with full-fat sheep's milk, use lamb or kid rennet for coagulating the milk, and have at least 40% FDB; in fact, the fat content is usually higher. The cylindrical cheeses, which range from 9 to more than 44 pounds in weight, are 10–12 inches in diameter and between 4 and 7 inches in height. Their hard rind is characterized by the basket-weave pattern. At first whitish-yellow in color, they acquire an ever more golden-brown hue from a treatment with oil and a sludge-like substance called *morchio*. The close curd, whitish to straw-colored according to age, has only a few holes. It contains 4–5 percent salt or even more, although there is also a **Pecorino Dolce** with a lower salt content (*primo sale*) made in Sicily, which is eaten quite fresh, when only slightly ripened. Even spicier, on the other hand, than the already piquant "normal" Pecorino, **Pecorino Bianco** (or Pecorino Calcagno), is the **Pecorino Siciliano Pepato** (also called Pecorino Col Pepe, or Canestrato Pepato), whose interior is strewn with whole black peppercorns. After four months' ripening it is regarded as a table cheese; it is used as a grating cheese when six to eight months old. A cheese of this sort from the vicinity of Messina is **Piacintinu**, which is sometimes dyed yellow with saffron.

Sheep rearing is now, as ever, an important economic factor in the mountainous regions of Sicily. Every evening the ewes are driven into the pen, from which they are released after they have been milked. The quantity of milk produced is small, but it is especially flavorsome, owing to to the abundance of herbs in the pastures where the sheep graze.

In the Italian marketplace, Sicilian Pecorino, with its typical basket weave appearance, is easy to distinguish from Pecorino Romano, which has a dark painted rind. Produced in various sizes, Sicilian Pecorino can weigh between 6½ and 26 pounds. Its highly piquant flavor makes it particularly suitable for hot cheese dishes, for example risottos and pasta dishes.

A wide variety of Spanish cheeses

The types of cheese that have been produced in Spain for centuries are as numerous as the Spanish landscape is varied. Relatively few, though, are widely known within Spain, let alone beyond the country's borders. The reason for this is simple: throughout the country, dissemination of the more than forty types and varieties of cheese is limited to the close environs of the place of production, and quite a few cheeses are only made in a single village. What cheese is produced where is also dependent, above all, on the features of the landscape. In the north, including Galicia and Cantabria, cow's-milk cheeses predominate, since the lush pastures of these regions are ideal for raising cattle. The semi-hard cow's-milk cheese **Formatge de La Selva** (fourth from top), for example, comes from the mountainous country of Catalonia in the northeast. Cows are also raised on the Balearic Islands, where the well-known, strong-tasting cow's-milk cheese **Mahón** (the cube-shaped cheese in the center of the photo) is made on the island of Minorca. By contrast, Andalusia as well as Extremadura and other mountainous areas are famous for goat's cheeses, such as **Los Ibores** (second cheese from bottom) **Tietar** (very top of photo) and **La Breña** (very bottom). However, it is mainly sheep that are raised in Spain, and so sheep's cheese is produced throughout the country. The best known, most widely produced is **Manchego;** the typical wavy pattern formed by the molds can be seen on the side of the cheese at the top left.

San Simón is a cow's-milk cheese from the province of Galicia in northwest Spain. It is often smoked over birchwood, which not only imparts a special aroma and flavor to the cheese, but also improves its keeping qualities.

milk of the undemanding and adaptable Manchega sheep, which gives it its characteristic, very pronounced "sheepy" aroma. The Manchega is the most widespread and economically most important breed of sheep in Spain. For Manchego, a DOP cheese since 1984, there is a series of requirements: the cheese may be produced only in the provinces of Alicante, Ciudad Real, Cuenca, and Toledo, which form part of the region of La Mancha; it may be made only from sheep's milk with at least 6 percent fat, 4.5 percent protein and 16.5 percent dry matter; the milk must be pasteurized, raw milk being used only for artisanal production; the cheese must contain at least 50 percent FDB and 55 percent dry matter (though both are often considerably higher); and it must ripen for at least two months at 54 to 59°F, followed by storage at under 50°F. In addition, the name Manchego and the week of production must be printed on the cheese. The hard, straw-colored to dark brown, lightly furrowed rind of the cylindrical cheeses, which weigh from 4 to 9 pounds, is either left bare or covered with wax, plastic wrap, or olive oil. A young Manchego cheese no more than a few days old is referred to as *fresco*; a few weeks older, as *semifresco*; and one ripened for one to two months is referred to as *tierno*. In Spain, cheese made from unpasteurized milk cannot be sold for consumption less than two months after production. After the minimum ripening period of two months and up to three months, the cheese is described as Manchego *semi-curado* or Manchego *medio curado*; Manchego *curado* or *viejo* has been ripened for three to six months, and a one-year-old cheese is characterized as Manchego *añejo*. Many cheeses are allowed to ripen for up to two years in olive oil; the grayish-black rind that forms during ripening is characteristic of this **Manchego en aceite**. Nowadays, other sheep's-milk cheeses similar to Manchego are made in a multitude of varieties and under different names throughout Spain. Among these is the very firm to hard **Grazalema** from Cadiz. Other Manchego types are **Los Pedroches** and **Serena** from Córdoba in Andalusia, both prepared with vegetable rennet. However, cheeses made from mixtures of sheep's, cow's and goat's milk, especially medium-matured cheeses, garner virtually the same approval both inside and outside Spain as the Manchego-type cheeses produced from sheep's milk alone.

The sheep's-milk cheese **Roncal**, from Navarre (at least 60 percent FDB and 60 percent dry matter, ripened for over four months), and the smoked cheese **Idiazabal**, from the Cantabrian Basque country, with its many, locally restricted variants such as Gorbea, Orduña, Urbia, Aralar, Urbasa, both possess a hard to very hard body, suitable for grating, with a piquant taste and a characteristic aroma.

Manchego (below) is Spain's best-known and most important sheep's cheese. Most of the sheep's milk produced throughout the country is made into this and similar cheeses, such as the very firm **Roncal** (pictured at the very top). **Queso de Huerte** (immediately below) is a comparable cheese made from sheep's, cow's and goat's milk.

This agreeably piquant Manchego-style cheese is a good example of optimal inherent qualities (supple curd, even hole formation) and painstaking tending.

The **Cheddar** family is distinguished by the special treatment of the curd. Prepared in the normal manner, it is allowed to settle, draw together into a "cake," and acidify, while being repeatedly relayered. The curd is then milled, the resultant yield (also called curd) salted, and the cheese molded, pressed, and finally ripened at 45 to 50°F. The method is somewhat different for the stirred-curd cheese **Colby**, a variant of Cheddar found throughout the world, but especially in America. The curd is stirred, causing it to acidify further and become sufficiently firm. It is then salted and ladled straight into the molds; the cheddaring process is omitted. This shorter process, used for a number of cheeses, means that they develop qualities that make them particularly attractive for various uses. They are popular as table cheeses at different degrees of ripeness, and, especially in the "Cheddar countries," are indispensable as a cooking ingredient.

Considering the quantity produced, Cheddar must be the most widely available of all cheese types. The majority of worldwide production is in large factories, which produce cheeses of uniform quality that satisfy the requirements of most consumers. The principles by which Cheddar is produced are very old, but have been and are applied very differently from region to region. As a result, cheeses of different type, shape, size, and quality are sold under the same name. **British Cheddar** is made from cow's milk. The cylindrical cheeses measure 14 to 15 inches in diameter and 13 to 15 inches in height, and weigh 60 pounds. Their fat content is at least 48 percent FDB, their dry matter at least 61 percent, and their maximum water content, correspondingly, 39 percent. Smaller cylindrical Cheddar cheeses weighing 9 to 13 pounds are known as **truckles; cheddlets** are those weighing approximately 2 pounds. Blocks of Cheddar packaged in plastic wrap weigh between 40 and 42 pounds, or sometimes less. The interior of the cheese, usually undyed but sometimes dyed yellow with annatto, is supple to crumbly, according to its degree of ripeness. It is usually quite close in texture, but quite open-textured cheeses containing many cracks are still often found on the market. Scottish Cheddar is usually firmer and dyed darker with annatto. **Farmhouse Cheddar**, which has a nutty, buttery taste, is considered a specialty.

Numerous other British cheeses are similar to Cheddar. Most of these are traditionally considered to be hard cheeses in their country of origin, but are ranked as semi-hard (sliceable) cheeses in the international classification. Their minimum fat content is 48 percent FDB. **Derby** is a regional cheese type from Derbyshire in the Midlands, where the first cheese factories in England were established. Its curd is never dyed, and is thus always light and honey-

Obtained from the seeds of the annatto tree (*Bixa orellana*), the reddish-yellow extract annatto is used to dye a variety of foods, chief among these cheese. Bixin, the pigment in annatto, is related to carotene.

Two traditionally made Cheddars with different ripening times: sixteen months (below) and three months (bottom).

Longhorn is the name given to cylindrical Cheddar-style cheeses similar to Colby; this one is 13 inches long, 6 inches in diameter, and weighs 13 pounds.

Not all Cheddars are alike. Only rarely are they still made in the traditional manner, bandaged in cloths, like the example in the photo above and to the left, which is ripened for five months. Cheddar cheeses produced according to modern methods are mostly foil-ripened or dipped in wax (as on the right in the photo), and are often also dyed orange with annatto.

Cheddar: the pride of Britain

The village of Cheddar, located at the foot of the Mendip Hills in Somerset in England, gave its name to this cheese, whose origins can be traced back to the twelfth century. Since then, it has been produced in the region south of Bristol and in the southwest of Scotland, and has become the most widespread cheese type in the world. From America to Australia, from Britain to New Zealand, Cheddar is as well known as it is well loved. There are still some cheesemakers in the Cheddar-producing countries who use the labor- and staff-intensive methods developed in the middle of the nineteenth century on English estates; however, it is the large cheese factories that are now responsible for the majority of world production.

Traditionally made Cheddar cheeses in a wide variety of sizes ripen in this storeroom under the best conditions. Giant cheeses such as the one shown above are also made to order.

How Cheddar is made

After the approximately pea-sized curd has been prepared and has drawn together into a cake, "cheddaring," a step specific to the Cheddar-making process begins. The cake is cut into slabs, which are repeatedly stacked and restacked on top of one another. At the same time as the whey is expelled, more lactic acid forms. When this acidification is far enough advanced, the curd, which has become fibrous, is cut into pieces. The rest of the production process is illustrated in the photo sequence.

Cheddar curd is a popular snack in some regions of Canada and the United States. These scraps or shavings, produced when the curd is milled, are eaten fresh, just as they are, salted or unsalted.

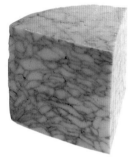

Sage Derby is unmistakable: the herb to which it owes its name is mixed into the curd, giving it its characteristic green veining.

1 **Manageable-sized pieces** are cut from the acidified curd and milled.

2 **Salt is sprinkled** into the small curd and distributed evenly by relayering.

3 **The salted curd** is transferred to cylindrical molds, which are lined with cloths.

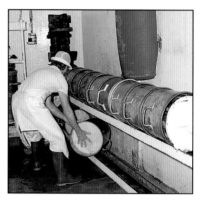

4 **Cheddar is pressed** in two stages, here in the horizontal press, for 12–16 hours each time.

5 **Each young cheese** is very carefully turned out of its mold after the first pressing.

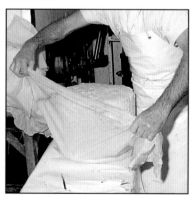

6 **The cloth** is carefully removed. The surface is slightly uneven, with furrows and troughs.

7 **Dipping the cheese** in hot water encourages the rind to contract, or close, and smoothes the surface.

8 **Greasing the cheese**, a labor-intensive procedure, reduces the adhesion of the cloth to the cheese.

9 **Before the second**, very hard pressing, the cheese is wrapped in cloth — first, the top and bottom.

10 **The cheese** is precisely wrapped all around. After the second pressing, the cloths are removed.

11 **The finished cheeses** are stored together at 43°F, or, for faster ripening, at 50°F.

colored. Waxed or packed in foil, it ripens for three to four months at 57°F. Like **Dunlop** cheese from Scotland, Derby, with its somewhat moister and hence less firm curd, is considered to be a pleasantly mild Cheddar variant. Fully ripened cheeses are sometimes covered with a grayish-green mold. Ground sage leaves and other herbs are added to the curd to produce **Sage Derby**. They are either evenly distributed throughout the curd, or layers of specially produced "green" curd are placed between layers of white curd. The flat sides of the cheese may also bear a pattern of sage leaves. **Double Gloucester** comes from the grazing areas of Gloucestershire, but is nowadays predominantly produced in the southwest of England. The cheeses weigh approximately 62 pounds, are 6 inches high and measure 14 inches in diameter. Their height and weight are about twice that of **Single Gloucester**, which, however, is no longer produced. Traditionally made cheeses ripen for four to six months at 50 to 55°F, foil-packaged cheeses for a shorter time at 39 to 43°F. Gloucester, which previously was rather similar to Cheddar, is today more often considered to be a hybrid cheese. **Cheshire** is reputed to be even older than Cheddar. The cylindrical cheeses weigh about 48 pounds each, with a height and diameter of 12 inches. When cut into, Cheshire has an open appearance, characterized by numerous fissures; its curd is crumbly, slightly flaky, and silkily lustrous. The cheese is now often produced with a firmer, more closed curd as "cheddary Cheshire" for sale in portion-sized packages. **Wensleydale** was first made in the Yorkshire Dales by monks who came over with the Norman conquerors, bringing with them sheep-rearing as well as cheesemaking methods. At first they produced a **Blue Wensleydale**, similar to Roquefort; but today **Wensleydale** or **White Wensleydale** is produced almost exclusively. **Leicester**, also referred to as **Red Leicester** because of its dark reddish-yellow coloring, has a firm curd with an open, flaky structure. **Caerphilly**, like Lancashire, stands out from the rest of the cheeses acidified and salted in the curd by virtue of the clearly softer consistency of a semi-soft cheese. **Lancashire** is considered to be particularly suited to toasting. A farmhouse cheese, Lancashire is also referred to as a **double-curd cheese**: the acidified curd of the previous evening is combined and processed with the morning curd. Ground sage leaves are mixed into the milled curd to make **Sage Lancashire**.

American Cheddar resembles the British cheese, but is described as waxy and less crumbly. Its fat content is at least 50 percent FDB, its dry matter at least 61 percent (maximum water content 39 percent). The cheeses are produced with a wax covering, some cylindrical (longhorn), others block-shaped (loaf) or in the form of a wheel. In labeling the degree of

Cheshire, shown here in block form, is considered to be an excellent basis for processed-cheese products.

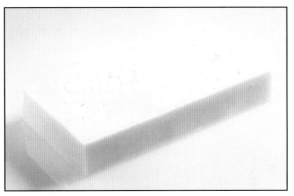

Jack, or Monterey Jack, was first made in California. This undyed cheese is often used as a pizza topping, while the well-ripened, hard Dry Jack is used as an eating and a grating cheese.

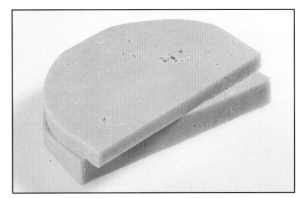

Colby, a milder variant of Cheddar that originated in America, is also available in New Zealand and other countries. It is a stirred curd cheese with a relatively soft, orange-yellow interior.

The acidity of the Cheddar curd is measured and remeasured many times; the pH value has a great impact on the exact course of the manufacturing process.

Double Gloucester has a fine, silky structure, and is either undyed or dyed orange. Similar in taste to Cheddar, it is milder and less sharp.

Dunlop is well known on the Scottish market. Its creamy white curd tastes mild when young, but grows stronger with increasing ripeness. It is well suited to *au gratin* dishes.

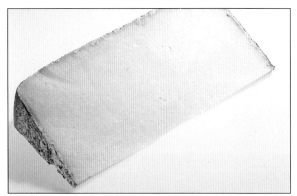

Laguiole, or Laguiole-Aubrac, mentioned in writings as early as 1560, is similar to Cantal. It ripens into a cheese with a very strong, assertive flavor, and is a cheese for gourmets.

Cantal, also referred to in France as the Dean of cheeses, is related to Cheshire. Its characteristic taste ranges from mild to fruity and piquant. Nowadays the trend is towards Cantal Jeune or Cantal Doux; a good 70% of the quantity produced is sold as young Cantal.

ripeness, "mild" means a ripening period of just a few months, with the cheese not yet having much flavor. "Medium" or "mellow" refers to cheeses ripened for up to six months, with a developed flavor, and cheeses labeled "aged," "sharp," or "extra sharp" have been ripened for more than six months and have a very pronounced smell and taste. **Coon**, a "vintage Cheddar," ripens for a year or more. **Cheedam** is the name given to an Australian combination of Cheddar and Edam, like **Egmont** from New Zealand, which is a combination of Cheddar and Gouda. **Low-sodium Cheddar** may contain no more than 96 mg of sodium per pound. In the United States, Cheddar, Colby, and **Monterey Jack** may be bought freshly cut, or in small packages, in slices, or shredded. Monterey Jack most likely got its name in the 1880s from David Jacks, a Monterey businessman whose dairies produced a cheese that was shipped to San Francisco with his name on it. At some point the "s" was dropped, and the place of origin added. **Jalapeño Jack** is Monterey Jack seasoned with jalapeño peppers. There are also varieties of Jack seasoned with caraway, habanero pepper (the hottest pepper known), green chile, and smoked salmon. **High-moisture Jack cheese** is a young, very soft, creamy cheese with a relatively high water content, and is used a great deal in spicy dishes, and **Dry Jack** is a low-fat cheese made with skim or partially skim milk, and aged from nine months to several years.

In terms of production method and qualities, Cheddar, and in particular Cheshire, are very similar to **Cantal**, also called **Fourme de Cantal**, one of the oldest French cheeses, from the Massif Central. Cantal, which has a legally protected name of origin, or AOC, is produced in a cylindrical form and in various sizes, in weights ranging from 37 to 99 pounds. Smaller versions are **Petit Cantal**, in weights of 44 to 49 pounds, and **Cantalet**, 18 to 22 pounds. **Cantal** *fermier* is a farmhouse Cantal made from raw milk; **Cantal** *laitier* is produced in cheese factories from pasteurized milk; the prepackaged cheese is also made in blocks. The cheeses ripen for between one and twelve months. Fresh, unripened cheeses, known as **Tomme Franche** or **Aligot** are used primarily for cooking. At one month, Cantal is considered to be young (Cantal *jeune* or Cantal *doux*), aged between two and six months, medium-mature (Cantal *entre-deux*, Cantal *demi-vieux* or Cantal *doré*), and over six months old, aged (Cantal *vieux* or Cantal *caractère*). Gourmets particularly like cheeses ripened longer — one year or more — from higher regions (over 2,800 feet), such as **Salers** or **Salers Haute Montagne** and **Laguiole** or **Laguiole-Aubrac**, named after the village of Laguiole in the Aubrac mountain range. The milk must come from cows of the Aubrac breed, and the

Cheshire is highly esteemed in the Midlands and the north of England. A number of varieties are available there.

This Cheshire owes its yellow color to the addition of the vegetable dye annatto. Like many British cheeses, Cheshire is available as a white or colored cheese.

Wensleydale, from the Yorkshire Dales in the north of England, is slightly tart to mildly aromatic.

Red Leicester has a firm, bright reddish-orange dyed curd. It is usually strong tasting and is well suited to melting.

A young Caerphilly from South Wales. The curd is white and very soft, the flavor fresh and slightly tart.

This aged Caerphilly also has a soft curd. It tastes somewhat sharper and, when ripened through, also slightly bitter.

Farmhouse Lancashire, a double-curd cheese, is still manufactured according to the old method. When fully matured, it is ideal for cooking. In England it is very popular for melting on toast and on top of casseroles.

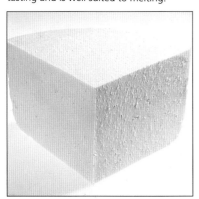

Lancashire has a semi-firm, crumbly curd. It has a slightly nutty flavor.

How Provolone is made

The curd has drawn together and set as a cake, and is roughly cut up.

The pieces remain piled on top of each other to acidify further, until the typical, fibrous structure develops; they are then cut into small pieces.

The cut up pieces have been "cooked" in hot water, and are worked into an elastic, malleable dough by continuous kneading.

Here, the dough, which has been pulled into ropes and then cut into pieces the size of the mold, is being placed in the mold to be pressed.

Freshly molded, the now-firm cheeses are removed from their molds, immersed in a salt bath, then tied and hung up.

Suspended by strings, the cheeses are dipped in a paraffin or wax bath. Cheeses that are intended to ripen longer are not dipped.

The cheeses are suspended from a special apparatus to ripen. The length of the ripening period and the temperature depend on the desired degree of ripening as well as other factors.

Cheeses of differing shapes and sizes festoon this ripening room. The most typical shape for Provolone is that of the truncated cone (center of photo).

Pasta filata cheeses from Mozzarella to Provolone

The cooked, kneaded cheeses of Italy are referred to as *formaggi a pasta filata*. The best-known representatives of this group are Mozzarella, Provolone, and Caciocavallo, around which another entire series of cheeses is grouped. Common to all of them is the typical structure of the curd, but in other respects they can be very different. According to method of production and age, they are available fresh and unripened, soft to firm; ripened and firm to hard; smoked or unsmoked; with a mild or piquant flavor; and in the most varied shapes and sizes.

Cutting into this Provolone (right) reveals that the ripening process is quite advanced. The layers in the curd, originally formed by kneading, are scarcely still visible. By contrast, they can still be seen clearly in the photo above.

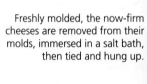

cheeses may be ripened and stored only in the alpine dairy huts (*burons*) or the cellars of the district.

In producing cooked and kneaded cheeses, including *pasta filata* cheeses, the curd is first allowed to draw together into a cake and acidify, as for Cheddar. The soured cake is also then cut up again, but the rest of the process is quite different: the small pieces of curd are then "cooked" in hot water, kneaded, and in some cases drawn out into strands. This treatment renders the curd malleable, giving it a typically streaky, fibrous to layered texture, which disappears as ripening progresses and the body of the cheese becomes fine-grained.

In southeastern Europe, the kneaded mass is mostly placed in round molds, as for **Kashkaval**. The cheeses are salted and nearly always ripened for several months. In Romania, the cheese is called **Cascaval**, Cascaval Dobrogea (Dobruja Kashkaval) when made from sheep's milk, Cascaval Dalia when made from cow's milk, and Cascaval Penteleu when a mixture of cow's and sheep's milk is used. The **Cas** (Kash) that is produced during the cheesemaking process is also consumed fresh. It is a curd mass obtained from the the curd cake by crumbling it and pressing it together again. In Bulgaria, the cheese is called **Kaskaval** or Balkanski Kaskaval; in Slovakia, **Kackavalj**. In Greece, the similar **Kasseri**, available in wheels or blocks, is often produced from young Kefalotiri cheese; in Turkey, it is called **Kasar peyniri**.

In Italy, the *pasta filata* cheeses are scalded and kneaded as described above, but the kneaded, plastic mass is then drawn out into bands or strands. One of the best-known cheeses of this sort is **Provolone**, as a hard cheese; at two to three months old, it is sold as a table cheese, after six to twelve months as a grating cheese. A distinction is made in terms of taste between the mild **Provolone Dolce** and the piquant **Provolone Piccante**, in which kid rennet is also used in order to accelerate ripening and intensify the distinctive taste. Provolone is made from cow's milk, has a fat content of at least 44 percent FDB and consists of over 62 percent dry matter. Traditionally, it is hung from ropes, and made into numerous shapes. Best known of all is the classic truncated cone, 14 to 18 inches long and weighing 9 to 16 pounds. Smaller cheeses in the same shape are called Calabresi and Silani; larger ones, Gigantini. According to their size, cylindrically shaped cheeses are offered as Pancettoni, Pancette, Salami or Giganti: spherical cheeses are known as Mandarini or Melloni. **Caciocavallo**, roped together in familiar fashion and hung in pairs, is made like Provolone and considered to be a delicate eating cheese and a piquant grating cheese. The cuboid **Ragusano**, 11 to 22 pounds in weight, is a Caciocavallo from the Sicilian town of Ragusa.

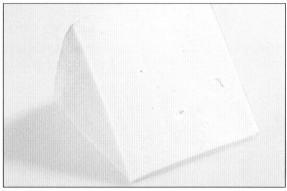

Kaskaval, a cooked hard cheese from Bulgaria, is usually made from raw sheep's milk or sheep's and cow's milk. It has at least 50% FDB and tastes piquant and slightly salty.

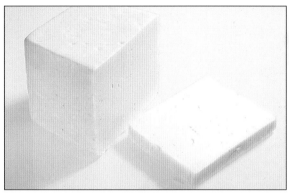

Kasseri is from Greece. This cooked hard cheese (40% FDB) is produced from fresh Kefalotiri, a sheep's cheese, and closely resembles Provolone and Kaskaval.

Ostiepok, is a Slovakian cooked cheese. Carved wooden molds give it a beautifully decorated surface, which is brown from smoking.

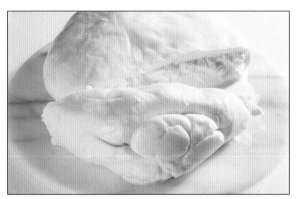

Burrata is a specialty cheese produced mainly in southern Italy. A piece of butter or butter-and-sugar paste is enclosed in the cheese curd.

Burrata di Andria is wrapped in fresh asphodel leaves (*foglie di asfodelo*). The asphodel is a plant of the genus *Asphodelus*, in the lily family, which is widespread throughout the Mediterranean.

Mozzarella di Bufala is a *pasta filata* cheese traditionally made from the milk of water buffalo, which produces its distinctive mild flavor.

Mozzarella-style cheese is increasingly made in blocks. This cost-efficient marketing format is preferred primarily by restaurants and supermarkets.

Little Mozzarella balls, or *bocconcini*, are yet another variety of this *pasta filata* cheese. The portion-sized tidbits are ideal as an appetizer, and are handy for slicing for salads.

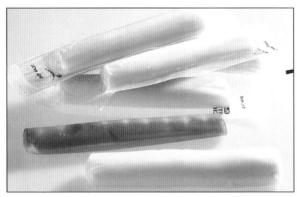

String cheese is a popular party food. Smoked or unsmoked, with garlic or onion, this packaged cheese is equally popular as a snack.

Treccia Pugliese Affumicata is a smoked, firm Mozzarella-type cheese from Apulia in Italy. The ease with which the cooked, elastic curd can be shaped facilitates the highly imaginative, decorative shapes so popular for these cheeses.

Cow's-milk Mozzarella is now more common than the original kind; the increasing demand could not begin to be met by the genuine Mozzarella, made from the milk of water buffalo.

American Provolone is made from cow's milk, with at least 45 percent FDB and 55 percent dry matter, and hence is softer than the Italian version. **Provola,** or **Cicillo,** is a small, spherical *pasta filata* cheese made from water buffalo's milk or cow's milk, or from a mixture of the two. It ripens for a shorter time than Provolone, and has a somewhat higher moisture content. **Provolini, Provolette, Topolini,** and **Bocini** have in common a smaller shape, a whitish, semi-soft curd, and a mild taste.

One of the best-known *pasta filata* cheeses is **Mozzarella.** During manufacture, its curd is subjected to a less marked treatment than is the case for Provolone. Mozzarella is marketed fresh and unripened, virtually as a fresh cheese, and is meant to be consumed quickly, even when stored in a cool place. Buffalo-milk Mozzarella must have at least 50 percent FDB and 35 percent dry matter, while cow's-milk Mozzarella must have at least 44 percent FDB. Traditional Mozzarella is made from water buffalo's milk (**Mozzarella *di bufala***) in Campania and Latium; nowadays, however, the cow's-milk cheese, also referred to as **Fior di Latte**, is more common. Mozzarella is traditionally sold in a light brine, but a factory-made version is also sold commercially unbrined in blocks. According to the area where it is produced, Mozzarella is given additional designations or other names, such as **Bocconcini, Ciliege, Nociolini, Nodini,** and **Ovaline**, depending on size and shape. The similar **Scamorza** from Abruzzi is also ripened and frequently smoked. In Denmark, Mozzarella is produced from cow's millk with 30, 40 and 45 percent FDB and a dry matter of 40 percent in each case. In the United States, in addition to Mozzarella with 45 percent FDB and 40 to 48 percent dry matter, usually sold unbrined in plastic film, there are varieties, used especially for topping pizza, with less fat and more dry matter. In Canada, one variety of this sort is simply called **Pizza** cheese. Smoked *pasta filata* cheeses from Italy are labeled *affumicato*, and those produced in the United States, "smoked." A special variety of *pasta filata* cheeses are products in which the cheese is formed in a layer around a piece of butter or butter-sugar paste. In another cheese, made mainly in Apulia and Calabria, small pieces of *pasta filata* cheese are enclosed with fresh cream in the Mozzarella, and the outside of the cheese is covered with interwoven green leaves. When pear-shaped, they are called **Butirl,** in the form of small balloons they are referred to as **Burrate** and **Palloni**. Other names are common to a particular region: Burrini, Occhi di bufala (buffalo eyes), and Uova di bufala (buffalo eggs). When these products are ripened for one to two weeks, their otherwise sweetish taste acquires a piquant note reminiscent of Provolone Dolce.

Leerdamer, a Goutaler belonging to the Maasdamer group from the Netherlands, has become one of the best-known representatives of this new type of cheese. The cheeses come in 13 or 26–30-pound sizes, have 45% FDB, and are supple. With their mild, nutty taste, they are well suited to eating plain and to cooking.

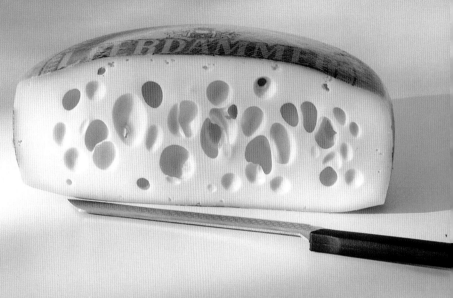

The Goutaler cheeses

Goutaler is a new cheese type with an interesting pedigree. It has inherited its sliceable consistency and suppleness from Gouda, and its fine flavor from Emmental. In fact, it was modeled on Emmental cheese, although it is less labor-intensive and time-consuming to produce, and has a higher water content and a shorter ripening period. Originally, all Goutaler cheeses contained approximately 45% FDB, but lower-fat versions with only 30% FDB are also manufactured now. The size of the holes can vary greatly. Cheeses of this new type are currently produced in varying qualities in a number of European countries.

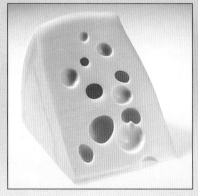

Jarlsberg is the prototype for Goutaler cheeses. Made in Norway, its sliceable curd tastes mild and slightly sweet.

Alpsberg, as well as Felsberg, one of the German cheeses of this type, is produced in two fat levels: 45% and 30% FDB.

Raw-milk Gouda is still produced in the way farmers in Holland have made it for centuries, as well as in factories. Its flavor, ranging from mild to strong and piquant, is often underscored by additional seasonings — garlic, onions, caraway, cumin, nettles or other fresh herbs — that have been mixed into the curd.

The **semi-hard cheese** category is characterized by its best-known representatives: Gouda, and other cheeses with round holes, such as the Italian Fontina; Tilsit and Havarti, which have curd-holes; and Cheshire and Derby from the Cheddar family. They are also described as **sliceable cheeses**. Both terms refer to the consistency of these cheeses and to their dry matter or water content. Sliceable or semi-hard cheeses contain less dry matter and correspondingly more water or moisture than hard cheeses. This also explains why semi-hard cheeses require a shorter ripening period than hard cheeses. However, the distinctions between softer and firmer cheese categories are blurred: some cheeses, such as Colby, a number of Appenzell cheeses, and some versions of Gruyère, can be considered to be either semi-hard or hard, depending on whether they are produced with a little more or less moisture. Other sorts, such as small Gouda-types and a number of Trappist cheeses, may, similarly, be considered either semi-hard or semi-soft. Because of the continuing evaporation of moisture during ripening and storage, semi-hard cheeses can become hard cheeses or extra-hard grating cheeses, as is the case with, for example, Asiago, Gouda, and a number of Pecorinos.

One of the most famous cheeses in this group is **Gouda**. It has been known in Holland, where it was originally made on farms in the environs of the village of Gouda, since before the sixteenth century. In the twentieth century, the factory-produced **Goudse Kaas**, made from pasteurized milk, became more and more widespread. **Goudse Boeren Kaas**, the farmhouse cheese made from raw milk, nevertheless again has a great many devotees, not least because of the various seasonings that are added to it. Today, Gouda made in the Netherlands has a fat content of 48 percent FDB. The wheel-shaped cheeses weigh from 5½ to 33 pounds, and in the case of farmhouse cheeses even up to 60 pounds. It is increasingly common for Gouda to be foil-ripened and sold in blocks. The mini-version **Baby Gouda** weighs from about 4 ounces to 2 pounds. A comparable German cheese is **Geheimratskäse**, with its soft, sliceable consistency and 40, 45, and 50 percent FDB. **Mai** or **Gras Kaas** is a young Gouda, made in spring from the first pasture milk, whose high carotene content contributes to the cheese's yellow color. In the past, farmers made cheese twice daily, immediately after milking, with milk fresh from the cow. Nowadays, evening milk, cooled in most cases to 46°F or lower and mixed the following day with fresh morning milk, is made into **Dagkaas**, the "day's cheese." Most Goudas ripen for one to six months, and are sold as young, medium-aged, or aged or ripe cheeses, depending on their exact age. About one in ten cheeses is carefully selected for its predisposition to

This Dutch **Minell** is a reduced-fat Gouda-type cheese (29% FDB); nevertheless, it has a supple consistency.

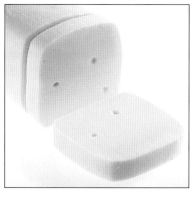

Vitadam is a German Edam-type cheese. It has a quite low fat content of only 20% FDB.

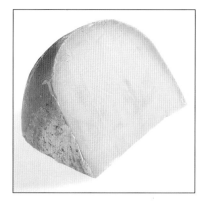

Mimolette has a reddish-orange interior. Depending on its degree of ripeness, it is supple to firm and crumbly.

Baby Gouda tastes creamy, and is milder than Gouda.

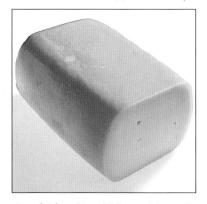

Bread Edam (Brood-Edammer) is usually sold in the Netherlands with a yellow paraffin coating.

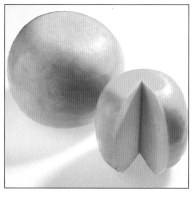

These Edam balls have a natural rind, which, depending on the age of the cheese, is light yellow to mid-brown in color.

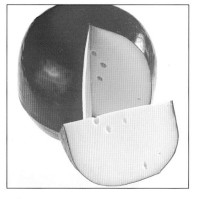

Edam balls are almost always coated with a protective layer of red or yellow paraffin.

Geheimratskäse (Privy Council cheese) has a buttery, supple structure. The small foil-coated cheeses weigh 1 pound each.

Gouda changes in taste, consistency, structure, and color as it ripens, Young, very mild cheese (top) has a supple, light yellow interior. The much stronger-tasting medium-aged Gouda (center) is suitable for shredding. After a one-year ripening period (below) Gouda finally has the flaky, crumbly consistency of a grating cheese; the color is then dark yellow.

Cloves and cumin impart an assertive flavor to **Friesian Clove Cheese** (Friese Nagelkaas).

Leyden is always flavored with cumin and has 20% or 40% FDB.

Consistently good: Dutch Gouda

Modern, standardized production methods in the large cheese factories guarantee the constant quality of Gouda from Holland, which is exported throughout the world. In order to illustrate the principles of Gouda production, however, the photographs on this page were taken in a relatively small cheese dairy; the production process would be difficult to depict in a large mechanized factory.

1 **A cheese harp** is used to cut the coagulated milk into curds the size of corn kernels.

2 **Hot water** is added, and the curd–whey mixture is scalded and lightly "washed."

3 **The curds** are prepressed and the whey, which has separated, drains out through a pipe at the bottom of the vat.

4 **Rectangles are cut** from the curd, which has already drawn together slightly.

5 **The blocks of cheese** are placed in plastic molds, which are lined with a cloth or (as here) strainer .

6 **The cheeses are pressed** for 1½ hours, turned, and pressed again for 1-2 hours.

7 **The strainer** is removed, the cheeses are taken out of the molds and then placed back inside them.

8 **The cheeses remain** in their molds until the following morning. During this period they are turned several times.

9 **The cheeses** sit in a salt bath for a few days. Their flavor develops, their body becomes firmer, and their rind hardens.

10 **As soon as the cheeses** are sufficiently dried, the protective layer is applied with a sponge.

11 **The cheeses are stored** in the ripening room, carefully tended, for one month to one year or more.

a long ripening period and the transformation into cheeses for shredding and grating. Such cheeses are ripened for longer than six months, and some for even longer than a year. During this time they develop an ever-firmer consistency and an increasingly strong taste. Gouda is available throughout the world, either under its original name or under others, such as Drabant and Gårda in Sweden, Norvegia in Norway, Kol-Bi in Israel, and Prato in Brazil.

Nearly as well-known as Gouda is **Edam** or **Edammer Kaas**, named after the village of Edam in the province of Noord-Holland. For centuries now it has been made on the farms there from full-cream milk processed in the evenings right after the milking. At the same time, it has also been made from a mixture of ripened, part-skimmed evening milk, and fresh morning milk. Edam is produced in many countries, in the typical ball shape, but also in block or loaf shapes (the latter known in Holland as Brood-Edammer, or Bread Edam). The cheese comes in a great variety of weights, foil-ripened or with a rind covered with red or yellow wax. Edam is supple, with a minimum FDB of 40 percent in the Netherlands and between 30 and 50 percent in Germany. The Finnish **Lappi**, mild and aromatic, has 45 percent FDB. **Bola**, a spherical cheese in the Edam style with 45 percent FDB, is highly regarded in Spain, Portugal (where another variety is called **Flamengo**), and South America. **Mimolette** is related to the large, spherical **Commissiekaas**, a cheese that used to be supplied to France in response to an order, or commission, for a large Edam. A large proportion of the Mimolettes produced in Holland are ripened in France, under the care of *affineurs*, while others, weighing 4–9 pounds and with a minimum FDB of 40 percent and a dry matter of 54 percent, are manufactured in France. The sliceable to hard body, with few holes, is yellowish-orange to reddish in color. Different varieties are available, depending on the production and ripening processes. The young cheese (Mimolette *jeune* or Mimolette *tendre*) tastes best as a sandwich filling; the riper, approximately six-month-old cheese (Mimolette *demi-vieille* or Mimolette *demi-étuvée*) and the approximately year-old, very ripe cheese (Mimolette *vieille* or Mimolette *étuvée*) are good as a snack with wine, as canapés, or as a seasoning in hot dishes. From Switzerland comes **Appenzell,** or **Appenzeller**. It is made from raw milk, with at least 50 percent FDB and 58 percent dry matter. The fatty, sliceable cheese has a sparse, even sprinkling of cherry-sized holes. The wheels, weighing 13 to 18 pounds and measuring 12 to 13 inches in diameter, have a slightly convex rim and a firm rind with a yellowish-brown coating. This is created by washing the rind during ripening with *Sulz*, a liquid made from wine, yeast, salt, and spices, which

Semi-hard cheese from eastern Europe. From the wide range of cheese types made locally, here are three that are increasingly exported: **Rossisky** (above, 50% FDB) is a semi-hard cheese with a vivid curd hole formation and a full-bodied taste, reminiscent of Tilsit; **Estonsky** (center, 45% FDB) is a mild, well-ripened, cylinder-shaped Gouda-type cheese; **Bausky** (below, 50% FDB) is a semi-firm cheese with a lovely *Linens* bacteria growth, a soft, sliceable consistency and an agreeably sharp taste.

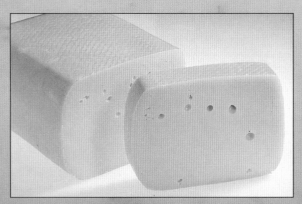

German Steppe cheese has a mild to full-bodied taste and a supple interior. It is available with 45 and 50% FDB, and in lower-fat versions with 30 and 40% FDB.

Swiss Tilsit has nothing in common with the original Tilsit other than its name. In Switzerland, raw-milk cheeses bear a red label, those made from pasteurized milk carry a green label.

Appenzell is a traditional, highly aromatic Swiss raw-milk cheese. A reduced-fat version, which is spicier, is known as Appenzell Rässkäse (sharp cheese).

Danish Cave Cheese, a well-ripened Danbo-type semi-hard cheese, is ripened in caves at 46°F.

Danbo, a Danish Steppe cheese, varies in taste from aromatic to spicy, depending on whether or not it is ripened with the aid of bacteria, and age. It is also made with caraway seeds.

Geltinger, a German Steppe cheese from Schleswig-Holstein has 45% FDB. Depending on its age, it tastes aromatic to slightly piquant. It is manufactured in blocks weighing 13 pounds.

Samsø is named after a Danish island. It is made in disks or blocks with 30 and 45% FDB. It tastes mild, slightly tart to sweetish.

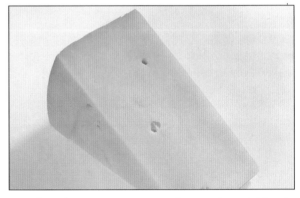

Herrgårdsost, the Swedish "manor cheese," also available in its country of origin as a hard cheese, is mildly aromatic in taste. It is highly rated as a sandwich filling and in hot dishes.

Finished Asiago wheels leave the storeroom. The DOC quality seal, branded onto the cheese, is clearly visible.

Asiago Pressato, also known simply as Pressato, comes from the Veneto, where Asiago originated. It is eaten quite fresh, after about four weeks.

After three to six months' ripening, **Asiago d'Allevo** is a mild to spicy eating cheese. Selected cheeses are ripened for up to a year, sometimes longer, and then used as grating cheeses.

also contributes to the typical taste of the cheese. Appenzell is ready for consumption after a minimum of three months of ripening, and is sold, according to its degree of ripeness, as "mild" and "recent," and as "extra" when it is six months old. A low-fat version with only 20 percent FDB, marketed as "Appenzell quarter-fat Räss," has a really strong taste, but now there is also a mild version.

Steppe cheese is well known in the countries of southeast and eastern Europe, and in Scandinavia. When made according to traditional methods, it has a well-dried-on, reddish-yellow surface bacteria; however, this is often washed off, and the cheese dried and then waxed. Danbo is a Danish steppe cheese that has round- or curd-hole formation, and 30 and 45 percent FDB. Its taste varies in strength according to the age of the cheese, and whether or not it has been bacterially ripened. Samsø (spelled Samsoe for export), named after a Danish island, was originally modeled on Swiss Emmental, but now is a cheese with its own distinctive character. Quite firm, with 30 and 45 percent FDB, and sprinkled with a few pea- and cherry-sized holes, it has a mild, slightly sharp to sweetish taste. Related cheeses are Elbo, Fynbo, and Tybo. Herrgårdsost (manor cheese) and Svecia (Sweden) are widely available in Sweden.

Asiago is an Italian semi-hard cheese. The name, however, refers to two entirely different cheeses. Asiago d'Allevo, or Asiago d'Allievo, is produced mainly in the Veneto region and the adjoining areas. Its fat content is at least 34 percent FDB, but is often as much as 40 percent and above. The flat wheels weigh between 18 and 31 pounds. The smooth, reddish-yellow rind conceals a firm, light straw-colored interior with a few small holes, which in older cheeses becomes increasingly close-textured, grainy, crumbly, and dark. The taste alters accordingly from the mildly spicy, several-month-old Asiago *dolce*, to the strong Asiago *medio*, to the hard Asiago *piccante*, which is suitable for grating. Asiago Pressato is a cheese of similar size with a fat content of 44 percent FDB and over, but with a soft, sliceable interior, and vivid curd-hole formation. It is used as a table cheese when still quite young, after only a few weeks. Along the edge of the Alps up to Piedmont, there are similar, as well as different, sorts of cheese called *pressato*, which means that they have been pressed during production and should be eaten quite young. There are those comparable to Fontal, as well as ones lower in fat, called simply Magro d'Alpe or Semi-grasso d'Alpe. There is also an American-made Asiago, which even when young is stronger tasting than Asiago d'Allevo *piccante*.

Monte Veronese types and the Lombardy Alp cheeses Bitto and Branzi correspond to Asiago Grasso

From left to right: The curd–whey mixture runs into a prepressing vat, where the curd is evenly spread and the whey drains off. After the curd is lightly pressed, pieces are cut out, placed in molds and pressed for 24 hours. The cheeses are then turned several times and the cloths arranged afresh. The cheeses sit in a salt bath for one to two days; first flat, then standing on end close to one another. They are then stored at 57–61°F at a relative humidity of 80-85%.

Montasio is produced using modern methods, but according to the old principles. It is made primarily in the provinces of Udine and Gorizia, and, like Asiago, mainly in cooperative cheese factories.

Montasio Mezzano (medium-aged Montasio) is enjoyed as a table cheese after ripening for approximately two to four months. This one is six months old, and already looks almost like a grating cheese.

Montasio Fresco at four weeks old. Like Pecorino, which is likewise known primarily as a ripe, piquant cheese, Montasio is also enjoyed in Italy when young and barely ripened.

Firm cheeses produced from sheep's milk, such as **Yolo** (in the foreground) and **La Bergère** (Prince de Claverolle) from the Massif Central, have a fine, sliceable consistency, a mild aroma, and a full-bodied taste from long ripening.

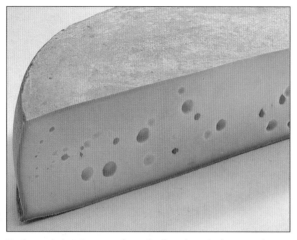

Raclette derives its name from the French *racler* (to scrape). Thanks to its ability to melt without immediately turning runny, it is superbly suited to the Valais dish of the same name. The cutting surface of the cheese is heated next to an open fire, and the melted cheese is scraped off and eaten with dill pickles and potatoes boiled in their skins.

The name **Fontina** may be used in Italy only to designate a raw-milk cheese produced in the Valle d'Aosta. Between June and September it is made in the alpine meadows themselves, and during the other months in the cheese factories in the valley. With its spicy, pleasantly sweetish flavor, it is a superb eating cheese, but it is also well suited to cooking, as it melts easily.

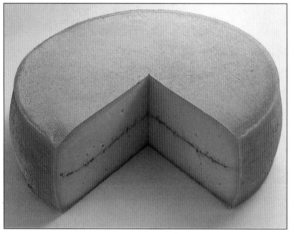

Morbier, a firm French semi-hard cheese with 45% FDB, has been produced for over a century in the environs of the village of the same name, in the Franche-Comté region. Just why it has always had an internal layer colored traditionally with soot, but nowadays with charcoal, is not known for sure.

Fontal is made in the same style as Fontina but from pasteurized milk. It is produced not only throughout Italy, but now also in other countries, including Denmark and France, and is even exported to Italy. This popular, mild table cheese with a white to straw-colored curd contains at least 45% FDB.

In Portugal, cheese is often still produced on the farm, but increasingly in modern factories. **Monte Verde** from the north, has 40% FDB (top left of the photo); Queijo castelões (top right) has 50% FDB; Alvorca (left), with 50% FDB, is a semi-hard cheese made from sheep's, goat's and cow's milk; in the foreground is **Queijo Serra da Estrêla**, a hard sheep's cheese with 45% FDB. that has been ripened for ten to twelve months, making it a *queijo velho* (aged cheese), There are legal regulations laid down in Portugal for Queijo da Serra (made mostly in the Serra da Estrêla). Other Serra-type cheeses are, for example, Serpa and Queijo da Ovelha.

di Monte, the high-fat mountain Asiago that has at least 45 percent FDB, in all stages of ripeness.
Montasio takes its name from a mountain range in the Alps of Friuli-Venezia Giulia in the northeast of Italy. This raw-milk cheese with at least 40 percent FDB is produced in a flat wheel weighing 13 to 20 pounds, with a smooth, slightly reddish rind. Montasio is sold young, as a mild eating cheese, as Montasio *fresco*; when several months old, as Montasio *mezzano*; and is highly esteemed at a year and over as Montasio *vecchio*, an aromatic to piquant grating cheese.
Fontina Val d'Aosta may be produced only in the Valle d'Aosta, and only from raw milk. The wheel-shaped cheeses, with a minimum 45 percent FDB, weigh 122 to 40 pounds and are ripened for three months. The thin, yellowish to light-brown rind encloses a very light-colored, supple, soft body, which contains a few small holes and tastes pleasantly sweet to spicy. Fontina-style cheeses made from pasteurized milk are called Fontal.

Raclette is produced mainly in Switzerland and France, and is used primarily for the cheese dish of the same name. In France, Fromage à Raclette or Raclette and Petite Raclette are produced with at least 45 percent FDB and 53 percent dry matter, and have a ripening period of eight weeks. In Switzerland, cheesemakers distinguish between Raclette and Valais Raclette. Raclette may be produced from raw or pasteurized milk in the form of flat wheels or blocks weighing 10½ to 16½ pounds. The name "Raclette" must be stamped on the side of the cheese. Valais Raclette (Fromage à raclette Valaisan, Formaggio Valesano da Raclette), made from raw milk, is produced in more than fifty designated regional and local places, such as Bagnes, Forclac, Gomser, the Valais, and Wallis. These names are stamped on the rind. It contains at least 50 percent FDB and 57.5 percent dry matter. The ivory-colored to light-yellow interior is suitable for slicing and melting, the taste is mild, becoming more aromatic as ripening advances. Raclette is ready for consumption after a minimum of sixty days, Valais Raclette after ninety days.

The mild Swedish Gräddost, which has 60 percent FDB, is soft but sliceable, and is considered to be good for topping pizzas, just like the German Prälat Pizza with 40 percent FDB. Dietmarscher Landkäse (55 percent FDB) with paprika, Diplomat (55 percent FDB) with various seasonings, Oldenburger Maurice (50 percent FDB) with herbs and spices, and Molfseer Büttenkäse (60 percent FDB) with chives, dill or garlic, are among the spiced cheeses in this category.

Tilsit owes its name to the former East Prussian town of the same name. Today it is produced in various countries, with a relatively soft to compact consistency and restrained to obvious curd-hole

Cheeses have been smoked since time immemorial. It is mainly hard and semi-hard cheeses, such as **Cave** (top), **Bruder Basil** (left) and **Caram** (right), that are smoked, but other types, even some fresh cheeses, are sometimes treated this way. Not only can this make the cheeses more attractive, it also affects their flavor and shelf life.

Queso Ahumado is a smoked cheese from the Spanish province of Navarre. The cheese, made from a mixture of cow's, goat's and sheep's milk, with 50% FDB, has a brownish rind from the smoke. The curd is sliceable, and the aroma and taste have a pleasantly smoky note.

formation; it is either surface ripened or foil ripened. Its aroma and taste range from mild to typically strong and spicy. In Finland it is known as **Kreivi**, and when spiced with caraway as **Kesti**; in Norway it is **Edda**; in Sweden it is called **Ambrosia** (with 55 percent FDB); in Germany it is also known as **Tollenser** and **Stangenkäse** (bar cheese); and in Austria and the southern Tyrol, Tilsit is often used in connection with a regional name, such as Schlanderser, Brunecker, or Eisacktaler. With its round holes, **Swiss Tilsit**, also exported as **Royalp**, resembles Appenzell. Tilsit made from raw milk has at least 45 percent FDB and is ready for consumption after fifty days, that made from pasteurized milk (Past-Tilsit) has at least 52 percent FDB and is ready to eat after only twenty-one days.

Havarti is named after an estate in Danish Zealand, but until 1952, when cheese names specific to a particular country were introduced, it was referred to as Danish Tilsit. It is marketed in 30, 45, and 60 percent FDB versions (Havarti mild). It has a soft, sliceable body and well-developed, in some cases relatively large, curd-holes, and tastes mildly sharp to strongly aromatic. Piquant versions of this cheese are the green-paraffin-coated Havarti seasoned with dill, and caraway Havarti. Similar to Tilsit is **Wilstermarsch**, which has a traditionally fine-pored, even curd-hole formation. Its fat content is 45 or 50 percent FDB, and it is ripened for four weeks, after which it tastes mild, or often slightly sharp. **Maribo**, with a fat content of 30 or 45 percent FDB, is made with or without red bacteria. The non-bacterially ripened version has a mild flavor, the bacterially ripened variant is quite spicy. Related to it is the Finnish **Turunmaa**.

Fromage des Pyrénées was originally a generic term for cheeses produced in this area, but now often refers only to cow's-milk cheeses (**Pyrénées Vache**), which are often exported, in many cases coated with black wax. **Pyrénées pur Brebis** is made only from sheep's milk, mostly with more than 45 percent FDB. **L'Ossau-Iraty-Brebis-Pyrénées,** with a name of origin legally restricted to Béarn and the Basque country in the Pyrénées Atlantiques and a small portion of the Hautes-Pyrénées, contains at least 50 percent FDB. The wheels usually weigh 9 to 11 pounds, with the exceptions of **Fromage Fermier** (farmhouse cheese), which weighs 15 pounds, and **Petit Ossau-Iraty**, which is only about 4 to 7 pounds. The thick rind ranges from yellow-orange to gray; the body is firm, supple, and nutty tasting. Cheeses made from mixtures of cow's and sheep's milk are marketed as **Iraty** or **Pyrénées Fermier**. Cheeses produced by a similar method and having similar characteristics are found in the mountainous areas of Spain south and southwest of the Pyrenees.

Havarti is the Danish Tilsit. Its white to light-yellow curd is evenly interspersed with numerous holes of irregular shape and size. In the foreground is a Tilsit of German origin, very similar to Havarti.

German Tilsit, which is made with an FDB of 30, 40, 45, 50 or 60%, has the red surface flora typical of its kind, even curd-hole formation, and a compact yet supple consistency.

Maribo, from the Danish island of Lolland, has a lively, small curd-hole formation, and a tart, strong taste.

Wilstermarsch, a cheese type from Holstein that is not very widely available even there, is similar to the original Tilsit.

Svecia is produced in many versions, young and ripened, as well as spiced; most have 45% FDB.

Prästost (Priest cheese), a traditional Swedish cheese with 50% FDB, has a tangy, aromatic to strong taste.

Kryddal is related to Prästost. The addition of caraway seed makes it very aromatic. It has 50% FDB.

Hushållsost is a mild, soft-slicing cheese with 30 or 45% FDB from Westgotland in Sweden.

Pyrénées Pur Brebis, is made in the Pyrenees exclusively from sheep's milk.

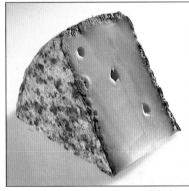

Haute Pyrénées has an unusual rind and a pronounced sheep's milk taste.

Pyrénées Vache is increasingly becoming the brand name for all cow's-milk Pyrenees cheeses meant for export.

Tourmalet, named after the Col du Tourmalet in the Parc National des Pyrénées Occidentales, is ripened in the Vallóe d'Ossau. A firm sheep's-milk cheese with 50% FDB, it has a mild to aromatic taste.

Semi-soft cheeses are those that, because of their ratio of dry matter to water, are softer than semi-hard cheeses and firmer than soft cheeses. The cheeses in this group are extremely varied. Their surfaces (with or without a rind) may be bare, or covered with moist or dried-on red bacteria, yeasts or molds, or enclosed in wax, paraffin, or plastic film. Their colors range from yellowish (similar to that of the interior of the cheese) to reddish, brownish and black, from light to dark, with a dark hue not infrequently intended to convey the impression of long-standing tradition. Semi-soft cheeses have a soft, supple consistency and slice well. **Esrom** was developed in Denmark in the 1930s, and was called Danish Port-Salut in those days. It was given its present name in 1952, when all Danish cheeses were named according to Danish regions and towns. The bricks weigh approximately 3 pounds on average, but also come in smaller and larger sizes. The thin, yellowish skin is covered with a light bacteria or waxed. The yellowish interior, with 45 and 60 percent FDB, has numerous small, irregular holes and a strong to piquant flavor.

Bel Paese (beautiful country) is a popular cheese from Italy. A similar cheese is produced in the United States. It is made in the shape of a disk, weighs four pounds and has an FDB of 50 percent. The name **Italico** was created in Italy for comparable cheese types. In Canada, the description "Butter cheese" (with 50 percent FDB) gained currency; in Germany and Austria, **Butterkäse**. Depending on the fat content, the interior is supple to creamy and melting; the taste and aroma are mild, but with a special note.

The mild, soft, sliceable **Bonbel**, with 50 percent FDB, comes from France; the Bonbel "light" variety has only 25 percent FDB. Bonbel is made in loaf shapes weighing 5 pounds. **Babybel** comes in small disks weighing 7 ounces, and Mini-Babybel are disks weighing less than 1 ounce, both covered with a thick, easily removed layer of wax.

Brick is a semi-soft cheese that originated in Wisconsin, and contains at least 50 percent FDB. It is now also made in other countries. After a ripening period of three weeks at 59°F, traditionally made, surface-molded Brick is mild in taste; if left to ripen for an additional one to two months at 44 to 50°F, it develops a strong flavor and aroma.

Trappist cheese is a special sort of semi-soft cheese. One famous place of production was the Maria-Stern Abbey in Banja Luka in Bosnia. From there, this type of cheese spread to other countries of the former Austro-Hungarian Empire. Today, Trappist style cheese, although admittedly of quite varied nature, is found in many countries. Its surface may be dry, covered with dried-on red bacteria, or waxed. Only those cheeses produced in Entrammes, France,

Esrom was rediscovered and redeveloped in 1937–38 by employees of the state-run Danish Dairy Farming Institute. This highly aromatic cheese, originally produced by monks from the abbey of Esrom in northern Zealand, had fallen into obscurity.

Seasoning ingredients are especially popular in Esrom. The most popular ones are caraway (top left), pepper (top right), red pepper (above left) and Herbes de Provence (above right).

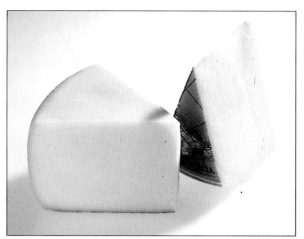

Bel Paese owes its unmistakable character to its soft, supple, straw-colored curd, and its quite distinctive, slightly tart, delicate taste. In Italy, the name is protected for the original producer, although a domestic version is produced in the United States; the name Italico was created in 1941 for a similar type of cheese

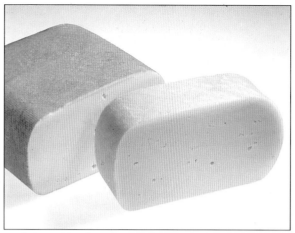

Bonbel, a mild, soft, slicing cheese from France, originally made only in the shape of a small wheel, is now also produced in the more efficient loaf or block shape. The different-colored surfaces are a key to fat content: cheeses with a reddish rind contain 50% FDB, those with a light yellow rind 25% FDB.

Babybel and **Mini Babybel** are the names given to the small and individually portioned wax-covered wheels of Bonbel, which have a consumer-friendly tear-strip for easy opening.

German Butterkäse made in the traditional manner has a fine, yellowish-brown to reddish skin, a creamy, supple interior with few holes, and a mildly sharp flavor. More widespread nowadays, however, is a cheese type without a skin, with a firmer interior, and in some cases with more holes.

Brick derives its name from its shape. It was created in Wisconsin in about 1875. Traditionally made with reddish-brown, slightly dried-on surface bacteria, it is now nearly always foil-ripened without the aid of red bacteria. It can be mild or strong in taste, according to its ripeness.

Swabian Country Cheese is a relatively new type, which combines different features. It is covered with a rather dry, red-brownish flora, and has a slightly yellowish, fine, supple body (50% FDB) with a scattering of small holes. Mildly tart in taste at the outset, it becomes aromatic and spicy with age.

Almkäse has a full, distinctive taste, which becomes hearty and spicy as ripening advances, and a light surface flora.

Bianco, like the Almkäse just to the right, represents an entire group of cheese types developed recently in Germany. These cheeses are distinguished by a soft, sliceable body, usually with plentiful curd-hole formation. Bianco, with 55% FDB, has a smooth, light-colored rind and a mildly sharp to strong taste.

Trappist cheeses

When Trappist monks, forced into exile during the French Revolution, returned to their monasteries after the reign of Napoleon, those at the Abbey of Notre-Dame du Port-du-Salut, near Entrammes, began making an agreeable tasting cheese that soon became know outside the abbey as Port-du-Salut or simply Port-Salut. Today, there are over ten similar types of this cheese in France alone. Trappist cheeses are also known in other countries, although with different qualities, in different sizes, and with different fat levels.

Port-du-Salut, or **Port-Salut** for short, refers only to cheeses produced in Entrammes under license of the Abbey.

Echourgnac is a small Trappist cheese from the Périgord. It has an agreeably strong taste.

Trappiste de Belval is made in Picardy, traditionally with surface bacteria.

German Trappist cheese is produced in block or loaf shapes. It has a mild to strong taste.

Mondseer, also known as Schachtelkäse (box cheese), is made in Austria. It is strong and spicy.

Loo Véritable, a slightly domed cheese from Belgium, is covered with black plastic film. It is mild to strong.

Ridder from Norway, is soft, supple, and easily sliced. It tastes creamy and aromatic.

Brigand, a Belgian cheese from Flanders, tastes mild; with increasing ripeness, the taste is strong and slightly bitter.

Steinbuscher, an old German cheese type with golden brown to reddish skin and a light covering of surface bacteria, tastes mild to spicy.

Tamié, or Trappiste de Tamié from the Savoie, has a full-bodied aroma and a strong taste.

Pavé d'Auge, or Pavé de Moyaux from Normandy, is a piquant cheese with a long tradition.

Pont l'Evêque is one of the great cheeses of Normandy. It has a soft, fatty paste, and tastes spicy.

Nantais is also known as Curé. With its red surface bacteria and fatty interior, it resembles Herve Kaas and Romadur.

Saint-Paulin is sometimes still ripened, or part-ripened, with red surface flora, then washed with salt water, dried, dyed, and covered with a plastic coating.

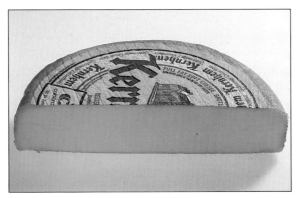

Kernhem, named after a Dutch estate, is a fine dessert cheese. It is supple and creamy, and may be very piquant.

Reblochon, made in a strictly delineated area in Savoie and Haute-Savoie, is typically packaged in boxes into which a thin woodchip disk is inserted.

Tomme de Savoie, originally made only in Savoie, today is produced over a much wider area. The surface is gray and brownish with russet spots, the taste pronounced.

under license of the Trappist abbey may be marketed under the name **Port-du-Salut** or **Port-Salut**. This ruling led to the development of a cheese of the same type with a new name: **Saint-Paulin**. Its wheel shape, diameter of 7¾ inches and height of 1½ to 2 inches, as well as its FDB of at least 40 percent, are prescribed, as are a diameter of 3–5 inches, a height of 1 to 1¾ inches, and the same fat content for **Petit Saint-Paulin**. **Echourgnac** is a small cheese from Périgord weighing only about 10 to 11 ounces; similar is **Mont des Cats** from French Flanders. Both cheeses have a semi-dry, yellowish-red surface mold, and are pleasantly strong in taste. Other small Trappist cheeses are **Chambarand** from the Dauphiné, **Campénéac** from Brittany, **Citeaux** from Burgundy, **Igny** from Champagne, **Oelenberg** from Alsace, **Beaumont** and **Tamié** from Savoie, and the somewhat larger **Bricquebec** from Normandy. Similar in style are the British **Penbryn**, and **Oka** from Canada. **German Trappist cheese** is produced with a dried-on red surface bacteria, or bare. It has a lively curd- and fermentation-hole formation and is often as firm as a semi-hard cheese, and mild-to-strong tasting. Well-known types are **Castor**, **Porta Prälat** and **Tegernauer**. A widespread name for different variants with a distinctive style is **Monastery cheese**. A famous cheese in Norway is **Ridder**, known as **Riddar** in Sweden. Under its orange-gold skin is a creamy interior with 60 percent FDB. Another type of cheese is the Belgian **Passendale**, with 50 percent FDB, characterized by its sliceable, supple interior with numerous curd-holes, and a flavor ranging from mild to discreetly piquant. The domed wheels of cheese have a hint of mold on their rind.

The Pays d'Auge area in Normandy is the home of **Pont l'Evêque** and **Pavé d'Auge**, also known as **Pavé de Moyaux**, which resembles a number of predecessors of the present-day Camembert. Ripening with dry flora ranging from yellowish-gray to reddish-brown and orange, as well as a milk mold, the soft, fatty cheese tastes mild to strong and full-bodied, depending on age. A similar type of cheese, which has a golden-brown-reddish skin with a sparse surface bacteria and a mild to slightly spicy taste, is known as **Steinbuscher** in Germany. According to tradition, **Nantais**, also called **Petit Breton** or **Fromage du Curé**, was first made by a parish priest near Nantes. The square or wheel-shaped cheeses weigh only about 7 ounces, have a red surface bacteria and a soft, fatty consistency. The Dutch **Kernhem** is ripened with a surface mold at 59°F in humid cellars, which gives it a piquant aroma and a strong nutty flavor. With more than 60 percent FDB, the cheese is particularly supple.

Reblochon is a legally protected name of origin in France. It is reserved for cheeses made in the

Swiss Mutschli are small Alpkäse from the high Swiss alpine valleys, which may be young or ripe, soft or firm.

This Tomme de Savoie is shown with its characteristic gray bloomy rind, which is removed before eating.

Vacherin Fribourgeois is made in softer and firmer versions, for fondue or for eating as is. Depending on its degree of ripeness, it is slightly sharp to aromatic.

A typical curing cellar for Vacherin and Gaperon on the premises of the Parisian *affineur* and cheese expert, Pierre Androuët.

Vacherin Mont d'Or is made in the Swiss Jura, where the cheese shown here is from, and in the French Jura. The mildly aromatic cheese has a reddish-brown surface mold.

Saint-Nectaire, from the Massif Central in France, has a rich, colorful, and rather dry surface flora. The aroma and taste are correspondingly strong.

Pavin, which comes from the Auvergne in France, is closely related in appearance and taste to Petit Saint-Nectaire.

Banon, formerly only a small goat cheese, sometimes with herbs, is now also made as a delicate, mild cow's-milk cheese, but still retains its typical packaging.

département of Haute-Savoie and in part of Savoie from raw full-cream milk that have at least 45 percent FDB, although they often have 50 percent and more. The flat disk-shaped cheeses weigh approximately 1 pound, or 8 ounces in the case of **Petit Reblochon**. The dry rind is pale pink to yellowish and brownish, often with a hint of whitish mold; the interior is straw-colored and soft to supple, with few holes. The well-ripened cheese has a strong flavor. There are similar cheeses made from pasteurized milk. Reblochon is also made in western Switzerland, as well as in some alpine meadows of the Italian mountain slopes. There, the name **Reblosson** is traditional. Similar round cheeses with varying characteristics and in some cases a lower fat content are called Tomme (formerly Tome) in France and Toma in Italy, in combination with local names. **Tomme de Savoie** comes in many different sizes, from about 3 to 12 pounds. Originally this cheese was made only in Savoie, but it has also spread south into the adjacent mountain regions and the Massif Central. Both similar and quite different cheeses are known under the name **Vacherin** in western Switzerland and eastern France. The town of Fribourg gave its name to **Vacherin Fribourgeois**. This cheese, made from raw milk or a mixture of raw and heat-treated milk, and which is ready for consumption after a minimum of sixty days, comes in two distinct versions: the firmer Vacherin *pour la main* for eating as is, and the soft Vacherin *pour fondue*, which, as its name indicates, is made exclusively for fondue. The wheels, which weigh between 12 and 22 pounds, have a thin skin with a yellowish-brown surface bacteria, and a yellowish interior, which tastes slightly sharp to aromatic, depending on its degree of ripeness. An entirely different sort of cheese is made in Switzerland, at the foot of the Vaud Jura, between September and March: **Vacherin Mont d'Or**, which actually ought to be considered a soft cheese. The flat disks weigh between 1 and 6½ pounds and have a reddish-brown rind. The interior, often with over 50 percent FDB and 42.5 percent dry matter, is whitish and, when well-ripened, very aromatic and strong tasting. Occasionally, owing to ripening in a mold made out of pine bark, it tastes faintly of pine. A cheese produced in the Lac de Joux area is called **Vacherin de Joux**. In addition to the Swiss variety, there is a French Vacherin Mont-d'Or, also called **Vacherin de Haut-Doubs** when made in the *département* of Doubs at an altitude of over 2,300 feet. The surface of the cheeses, which weigh 1 to 2 pounds and are packaged in boxes made from spruce or pinewood shavings, is wavy and yellow to light-yellow, and the ripe curd is very soft to runny. A close relative from Savoie, **Vacherin de Beauges**, is sometimes so soft that it can be eaten with a spoon. During ripening, it is washed with a mixture

Tomme de Brebis, a French sheep's-milk cheese with a mild taste, in the round *tomme* shape.

Tomme de Beaujolais, from the area between Lyons and Mâcon, which is famous for its wine, has a discreet flavor.

Crimlin is made in Ireland in the style of Port-Salut, with 45% FDB.

Plateau d'Herve from Belgium has a pronounced cheese aroma. It is strong but not sharp-tasting.

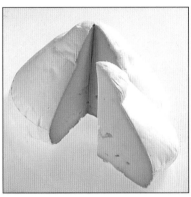

Airiños, a Spanish cow's-milk cheese with a bloomy white mold from Asturias, has a creamy, mildly spicy body.

Marzolino, made in Tuscany from sheep's milk, or a mixture of sheep's and cow's milk, tastes mild to slightly piquant.

A peculiar characteristic of **Murol** is the hole in its center. This cheese from the Auvergne is mild to strong.

Trous du Murol, which is the central portion of the Murol, is covered in red wax, and is mild in taste.

Robiola Valsassina is available in mild and piquant versions. This one is a mild *tipo dolce* with a sparse red surface flora.

Passendale from Belgium, here with a light, whitish surface flora, tastes mild at first, and strong with increasing ripeness.

Gaperon is produced in the Auvergne. Additions of pepper and especially garlic impart aroma and taste to this cheese.

Tête de Moine is a very tasty cheese from Switzerland, well suited to shaving, as shown right.

The *girolle*, a special cutting device, is used to plane circular shavings from the Tête de Moine. First, a "lid" is removed, which is later replaced, so that the remaining cheese does not dry out.

Taleggio, named after a valley to the north of Bergamo, has long been produced in the valleys of the foothills of the Alps in Lombardy. Previously known as Stracchino Quartirolo, this cheese, which comes in many varieties, is ripened at only 41–43°F, sometimes in caves, where it develops its characteristic spicy flavor.

Quartirolo is similar to Taleggio and, like it, is marketed at different stages of ripeness. The cheese shown here is still quite young, has only a light surface mold, and a consistency typical of young, tart cheeses. The slight lactic-acid tang changes during ripening to mild and aromatic, and the curd becomes more supple.

Pannerone, from northern Italy, is a cheese with a very strong fermentation brought about mainly by gas-forming bacteria and certain yeasts.

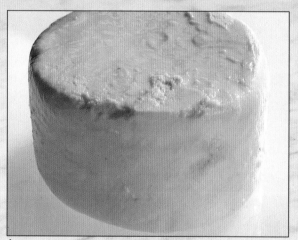

Évora, named after a town in the south of Portugal, is made from sheep's or goat's milk, or mixtures of the two. A favorite way of storing this small, firm, well-salted cheese with 45% FDB, often without a rind, is in oil. Évora is frequently ripened into a hard cheese; it then tastes sharp, sometimes salty.

Aragón, also called Tronchón, is made from sheep's milk or a mixture of sheep's and goat's milk. This Spanish cheese, which has 50% FDB, has a whitish-yellow interior with many small holes. The cheese mold imparts the characteristic shape shown here. Ripening for only one to two weeks, its taste is mild.

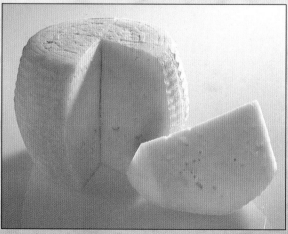

Corsica, made according to old Corsican pastoral tradition, is a sheep's-milk cheese with a bloomy white rind on which a light brownish-red bacteria develops as ripening advances. The supple body, with small curd-holes, is initially mild in aroma and taste, becoming strong and full-flavored with increasing ripeness.

Bambolo is an Italian cheese made from a mixture of cow's and sheep's milk. The impression left by the cheese mold can be seen on its surface. The interior is quite supple. Bambolo is sold after little ripening, with a hint of mold (as seen here), or in a riper state. Its taste is slightly tart.

Two examples of new types of cheese from Austria: **Steirischer Hirtenkäse** (shepherd's cheese) (above), with a flavor characterized by the sheep's-milk forming part of its makeup; and **Steirischer Bauernkäse** (farmhouse cheese) (below), a further development of the cheese made from a mixture of cow's and sheep's milk from the Koralm area, with a delicately sharp to tangy aromatic taste. Both cheeses have at least 45% FDB and are made from a mixture of 55% sheep's milk and 45% cow's milk.

of white wine, salt, and spices, and is always sold packaged in boxes made from wood shavings.

A Swiss specialty is **Tête de Moine** (monk's head), which was formerly made in the shape of a truncated cone. The origin of its name is unknown; it may have been a derisive nickname from the time of the French Revolution, or the term for a type of stockkeeping (only one cheese per head — that is, per monk — remained in the abbey; the rest were sold). Its second name, **Bellelaye**, points to the estates of the Premonstratensian abbey in Bellelaye near Berne. The cheeses are cylindrical in shape, measure 3 to 8 inches in diameter, and weigh 1½ to 9 pounds. Their rind is covered with a reddish-brown mold, the interior has only a few holes, is ivory-colored to light yellow, fine, shaveable, sliceable, and according to age, mild to strong. **Banon**, with a fat content of 40 to 60 percent FDB, may be made from goat's milk, from a mixture of goat's, sheep's and cow's milk, or from pure cow's milk. Cow's-milk Banon weighs up to 2 pounds; the others between 3 and 4 ounces. It is wrapped in chestnut leaves and tied with raffia or plastic strips. Two cheeses are created at once when **Murol** from the Auvergne is made: the Murol itself, with its characteristic large hole in the center, and **Trous du Murol**, the central portion that is cut out before ripening and covered in red wax. The Murol, also called **Grand Murol**, measures about 5 inches in diameter and about 1½ inches in height, and weighs about 1 pound; the hole in the center is 1 to 1½ inches in diameter. The surface of the cheese is covered with red bacteria, the interior is supple, and at the outset mild, but thanks to the surface bacteria, becomes typically pronounced as ripening advances. Cheeses with the name **Saint-Nectaire** come from a specified area in the departments of Cantal and Puy-de-Dôme in the French Massif Central. They are sold in two sizes, weighing either 1¼ or 3¾ pounds. The fat content is at least 45 percent FDB. The cheeses are ripened for three to eight weeks in natural cellars, and have a pronounced, very dry surface flora composed of various bacteria, yeasts, and molds. Sometimes they have brown, yellow or reddish spots, and a grayish-white or ocher-toned surface mold. The farm-produced **Saint-Nectaire Fermier** can be recognized by its oval green label, and the factory-produced **Saint-Nectaire Laitier** by its square green label. Closely related to Saint-Nectaire are **Pavin** and **Savaron**. The French **Gaperon** from the Auvergne owes the somewhat tough consistency of its interior, which is scattered with many small curd and fermentation holes, to its fat content of 40 percent FDB and the use of buttermilk or, in some cases, skim milk. Its aroma and taste are determined by the addition of crushed peppercorns and garlic, as well as by its ripening with white mold.

Franken-Rolle, a bloomy white mold cheese lightly seasoned with garlic, is a specialty from Bavaria.

Latvysky sir, or Latvijas Siers, from Latvia, is characterized by its strong rind with red surface flora. Its supple interior contains at least 45% FDB, and is very tasty.

Cushlee is a Port-Salut-type Irish cheese with a light, dry red surface flora, soft, slicing body with clear curd-hole formation and a mildly spicy taste.

St. Achatz, a sliceable cheese with 55% FDB, is spicy and expressive in taste.

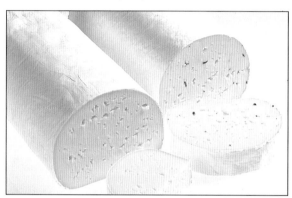

Comtesse (left) and **Coburg Knappenvesper** with garlic and chives (right) both have 56% FDB and a bloomy white rind, and are slightly tart in taste.

Mainauer, a German cheese made with 45% and 50% FDB, and in lower-fat versions with 30% and 40%. The creamy hued, supple interior is mild to full-bodied in taste.

Wasserburger Bauernkäse (Wasserburg farmhouse cheese), with the ocher-yellow surface, has 45% FDB and tastes mild to spicy, depending on its degree of ripeness. **Rahmkäse** (cream cheese), with the white surface, contains 55% FDB, and is tart but mild.

The different types of Caciotta cheese — there are about three dozen in all — are produced primarily in the regions of central Italy (Tuscany, Umbria, Latium, the Marches) as well as on Sardinia. They are predominantly made from cow's milk, sometimes still from sheep's milk, and often, too, from mixtures of cow's milk with sheep's and goat's milk. The delicate interior can be soft to firm, and depending on age, may have a buttery consistency. Aroma and taste are pleasantly mild and slightly sweetish.

An Italian cheese from Lombardy with varied surface flora is **Robiola Valsassina**. A distinction is made between the mild Robiola *tipo dolce* and Robiola *tipo piccante*, with its distinctive red surface bacteria, and hence its stronger taste. The shape and size of the different types vary. It is also available as a fresh cheese similar to Caciotta.

The name **Caciotta** stands for a large number of very diverse cheeses, which differ above all in the type of milk used and the length of the ripening period. For the most part, fresh, unripened or only slightly ripened cheeses made from sheep's milk (for example, unripened Pecorinos) are designated as Caciotta, but the name can also cover cheeses ripened for a longer period, and ones made from mixtures of sheep's and cow's milk, or from cow's milk alone. **Taleggio**, from northern Italy, is sometimes still made in the traditional manner from raw milk, but is increasingly produced from pasteurized milk, with a minimum of 48 percent FDB. These rectangular blocks of cheese have a brown-greenish, white or reddish, sometimes slightly wavy, skin with a hint of surface mold. There are several versions, determined by different production methods. Other examples of the great variety of cheeses made from various mixtures of sheep's, goat's and cow's milk are the Italian **Bambolo**, the Spanish **Aragón (Tronchón)** and the Portuguese **Évora**, which ranges from semi-firm to hard. **Corsica**, which contains 50 percent FDB, is made exclusively from sheep's milk.

Many countries have a tradition of marinating cheeses in brine, olive oil, wine, or vinegar. This stops the cheese from drying out and prevents the growth of bacteria and molds on its surface as ripening continues. The cheeses can be stored for a few weeks or several months, often into the season when milk is scarce. They are preserved fresh or after ripening for several days, in small casks or large canisters, often now in individual consumer portions. There are three different types of brined cheeses called **Feta**: Feta from sheep's milk, if need be with a little goat's or cow's milk mixed in; Feta-style cheeses from cow's milk, made in the traditional manner; and cheeses with the name Feta but produced using modern ultrafiltration methods that differ from the traditional type in terms of composition and curd structure, and are largely a breed apart. The following are well-known traditional brined cheeses of southeastern Europe and the Middle East, often made according to the methods of old pastoral and nomadic cultures: in Bulgaria, **Bjalo salamureno sirene** (sheep's-milk cheese); in Israel, **Brinza** (up to 25 percent cow's milk is permitted); in Bosnia and Croatia, **Beli sir** and **Bijeni sir** ; in Romania, **Telemea**; in Egypt, **Kareish** (buffalo milk and/or cow's milk); and in Turkey, **Beyaz peiniri**.

Feta, here a sheep's milk variety from Greece, is the best-known brined cheese. Containing 50% FDB, it is semi-firm to soft in consistency, and typically white.

Brined cheese in the Feta style is produced in many varieties in numerous countries. Increasingly, it is also made from cow's milk, like the Feta in the photo below.

Halloumi is a brined cheese from Cyprus. It is "cooked" and kneaded, and often spiced with mint. Similar cheeses are Halloum from Lebanon, and Hallomy from Australia.

Well over half a million sheep graze on the Causses, the barren chalk plateaux southwest of the Massif Central. They provide most of the milk for the famous Roquefort. In addition, sheep's milk is made into cheese on Corsica and in the Pyrénées Atlantiques. The young, fresh cheeses are then brought to the Roquefort area, where, together with the cheeses produced locally, they are ripened in limestone caves. Here, the desired conditions of constant temperature, high humidity, and optimal air circulation are to be found.

Roquefort: the blue with a history

If legend is to be believed, Roquefort was created by sheer chance: A young shepherd had retired to a cool rock grotto to consume his supper of bread and fresh cheese made from the milk of his sheep. When a beautiful girl came along, he forgot his hunger and followed her. It was not until several weeks later that he returned to the grotto. In the meantime, the bread and cheese had gone moldy, but the shepherd was so hungry that he bit into the now blue-green veined cheese. It tasted so good that from then on he left each of his cheeses for some time in the grotto. Since then, these cheeses with their unique flavor, coveted the world over, have been ripening in the caves and grottos of the village of Roquefort and its environs.

The use of the name **Roquefort** is legally protected in France. Only cheeses that contain at least 52% FDB, are made from raw sheep's milk, and are ripened in the caves of the area around Roquefort may bear this name.

There is a large family of cheeses with interior molds, which may have very different surfaces and be produced from different types of milk. Based on their consistency, most can be regarded as semi-soft cheeses, and some as soft cheeses. The mold may be found in the curd-holes and in the veins between them, or in the inoculation channels. The molds are mostly dark blue, blue to blue-green, and green to dark green strains of *Penicillium roqueforti*. The intensity of the cure, and hence the cheese's aroma and taste, depends on the type of mold and its ripening activity, but also on the shape, size, composition, and surface of the cheese, as well as, in particular, the microclimate of the curing cellar and the length of the ripening period. In English-speaking countries, the penicillum cheeses are described as **Blued-veined** or simply **Blue cheese**. In German-speaking countries the name Edelpilzkäse (noble mold cheese) has gained currency. In Germany itself, however, **Edelpilzkäse** is not only the generic term for all cheeses with blue veining in their interior, but it also describes a specific variety in this cheese group, whose qualities are laid down in laws governing cheesemaking. In France, these cheeses are referred to generally as **Fromage bleu** or **Bleu**, and **Fromage persillé** or **Persillé** (literally "parsleyed," that is, speckled with green). In Italy, these cheeses are also described as "herbed" — **Formaggio erborinato**; in the Spanish-speaking countries, they are called **Azul, Queso Azul** or **Pasta Azul**, and in the case of sheep's-milk cheese, **Azul de Oveja**.

By far the best-known blue cheese is the French **Roquefort**. Laws to protect the name and quality of this cheese were enacted as long ago as 1411. Originally, its production was limited to the area around Roquefort-sur-Soulzon, a village in the *département* of Aveyron on the southern edge of the Cévennes. As demand increased in the 1870s, however, the area of production was extended to include even Corsica and the Atlantic Pyrenees. In each of these areas, full-fat raw sheep's-milk is used, and the mold *Penicillium roqueforti* added to the milk or the freshly formed curds. Traditionally, the mold is grown on a special type of rye bread, and is then carefully dried and ground to a powder, which, in turn, is mixed with the curd. Today the mold is often used in the form of an easily controlled liquid culture. The cheeses produced in the vicinity of Roquefort, as well as on Corsica and in the western Pyrenees, are taken a couple of days after their production, as *fromage blanc* (white cheese) to the multistoried caves in the Cambalou Massif of Roquefort. Accordingly, the name Roquefort implies that the cheeses may be produced from milk from other areas but are always ripened under controlled conditions in the Roquefort area. After repeated salting by hand during the first three to

"Piercing" is a crucial process in the manufacture of blue-veined cheeses. The cheeses are pierced with needles, so that oxygen, required by the molds for even growth, can penetrate through the channels created.

Piercing machines have been around for a long time. Here is an old model, which pierced each Roquefort cylinder with thirty needles.

The blue mold grows first on the inside, then diffuses outwards. The conditions for the outward growth of the blue mold improve as the salt, at first concentrated in the outer layer, spreads throughout the cheese. Here, the mold can clearly be seen growing in the holes in the curd, and along the channels pierced in it.

These photos illustrate clearly how the surfaces of blue cheeses with bloomy white rinds are gradually covered by an even, fine down of white mold.

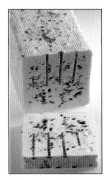

Blue-veined cheeses also come in a rectangular loaf shape, like this one with 50% FDB and showing good mold growth. This style is particularly suitable, sliced, as a topping for toast.

German blue-veined cheeses, such as this **Bergader**, are produced in a similar fashion to Roquefort, but from cow's milk. These cheeses are rindless, with a bare, whitish surface. A flaky to crumbly but supple body is an indication of quality. The flavor is quite pronounced, and grows piquant as ripening progresses.

Bleu d'Auvergne, from the Massif Central, is made from cow's milk. Although still made on the farm, it is now more often produced in factories, and is sometimes still ripened in caves. The yellowish-brown rind has a sparse covering of mold. The interior is well marbled and supple, and tastes strong to piquant.

Blue Castello is a **Danish blue-veined cheese** with 70% FDB — a very high fat content — and a relatively soft consistency. The surface of the horizontally cut cheese shows the inoculation channels. The cheese is usually ripened for two weeks, but sometimes longer. It tastes particularly creamy and mild.

Bleu des Causses is an AOC cheese from the southern Massif Central. It is a cow's-milk cheese with at least 45% FDB and a very strong taste. The mold is added when the curd is packed into the forms. The cheeses, which weigh 4–7 pounds, are ripened for two to six months in humid caves.

Bleu de Laqueuille has been made in the village of that name, southwest of le Puy-de-Dôme, since 1845. It is somewhat milder than Bleu d'Auvergne.

Bleu de Gex, like the similar Bleu de Septmoncel, is an AOC cheese produced in the *départements* of Ain and Jura. This raw-milk cheese, with at least 50% FDB, ripens for one to four months, and its taste ranges from mild to strong and piquant. The rind is dry and slightly rough, and the word "Gex" is stamped on the bottom of the cheese.

Danish Blue, internationally the most widely available blue cheese, is made from cow's-milk. The cylinders weigh 7 pounds and are rindless. The interior is slightly crumbly, but sliceable and vividly veined. Danish Blue is produced with 50% FDB, in which case its taste is strong, almost sharp, and with 60% FDB, which imparts a milder flavor.

five days, the cheese are pricked, so that the oxygen essential for the growth of the mold can penetrate them. They are then brought into the ripening cellars, which have a temperature of 44 to 50°F and a high relative humidity, a climate naturally maintained by the gentle currents of air, known as *fleurines*, that flow constantly through the numerous cracks in the limestone mountain. Here the cheeses remain, standing on end on shelves for three to four weeks. Once the first green flecks appear on the surface of the cheeses, they are ripened, under constant checks, for a further three to four months. The result is a cheese with a unique aroma, spicy to piquant according to its degree of ripeness, and a fat content of 52 percent FDB and above. The flaky, crumbly structure of the interior of the fully ripened Roquefort is a sign of quality, even if the cheese cannot be cut up easily.

Similar to Roquefort is **Bleu de Corse**. Made on Corsica, it too is ripened in caves, as is the Spanish **Azul de Oveja**. Nowadays, the overwhelming majority of blue-veined cheeses are no longer produced from sheep's milk, but from cow's milk. Here too, it is primarily *Penicillium roqueforti* cultures that are used, and ripening takes place in humid caves. A well-known example of these cheeses is **Bleu d'Auvergne** (50 percent FDB), whose AOC status ensures that the production and ripening of the cheeses is restricted to the region of the same name. Similar cheeses from the Massif Central are **Bleu de Causses** and **Bleu de Laqueuille**. **Bleu de Gex**, from the French Jura, with at least 50 percent FDB, and **Bleu de Septmoncel**, also referred to as **Bleu du Haut-Jura**, have a long tradition. Related to them is **Sassenage**, which comes in a wide variety of shapes. **Fourme d'Ambert** is made in the alpine meadows of the northern Massif Central, at heights of 2,000 to 5,300 feet. There are several local names for very similar cheeses, such as Monts du Forez, Fourme de Pierre-sur-Haute, and Fourme de Montbrison. They are all now officially called **Fourme de Pierre-sur-Haute dite d'Ambert ou de Montbrison**. The cylindrical cheeses weigh around 4 pounds, are 7¾ inches high, and 5 inches in diameter. They contain at least 50 percent FDB. During the manufacture, salt, preferably coarse sea salt, is added to the curd as early as the molding stage. The whey must drain thoroughly; for this, in the case of traditional farmhouse production, the molds are placed in the warm cow shed. German blue cheeses can be made from cow's milk, sheep's milk, or a mixture of the two. Examples are **Bergader** and **Paladin**, both with 50 percent FDB, and **Montsalvat** with 60 percent and 65 percent FDB. There are also versions with a lower fat content. Danish blue cheese, called **Danablu** for short, is internationally the most widely available blue-veined cheese made from cow's-milk. The 50 percent

Blue Bayou is a Bavarian blue cheese with 60% FDB. These cheeses weigh 2 pounds, have no surface mold, and develop an agreeably piquant flavor. The cut shows how the cylinders were pierced for even ripening: the channels are strung together like a chain of pearls.

Bleu Termignon was named after the village lying at the foot of the Col du Mont Cenis. The blue mold grows in the numerous small curd holes. When well ripened, like the cheese pictured above, it has a balanced, strong taste.

Bayerhofer Blue, another blue cheese from Bavaria, has a red mold on the surface. This makes it ripen from the outside inwards, the interior — with 60% FDB — becoming increasingly creamy and soft. Aroma and taste change from fine and piquant to full-flavored and spicy.

Fourme d'Ambert has been made in the northern Massif Central for over a thousand years. It has a very pronounced taste, owing, among other things, to its four- to five-month ripening period and to its surface flora.

Fineform Blue, a blue cheese from France with a light, white surface mold. The low fat content of 20% FDB means that the consistency is somewhat tougher than that of higher-fat types.

Cabrales, or Cabraliego, from the mountainous countryside around the Picos de Europa is the *campeón* among the blue-veined cheeses of Spain. A hard cheese with 44% FDB, it weighs 2–11 pounds, and is made from cow's milk, sometimes mixed with sheep's and goat's milk. It ripens for six months, wrapped in plane-tree leaves, in the well-ventilated caves of the limestone mountains of Asturias.

FDB version tastes strong and sharp, the 60 percent version, mild. **Mycella**, another mild Danish blue cheese, is close to Gorgonzola.

Gorgonzola, the great cheese from the north of Italy, is a type with numerous varieties, all having at least 48 percent FDB. First-class Gorgonzolas owe their unique aroma and taste to a successful interplay of their inner mold with the strong bacteria on their rind. The great variety is a result of different manufacturing and ripening conditions, although two basic types came to the fore some time ago: the mild **Gorgonzola Dolce** and the spicy to strong **Gorgonzola Piccante**, with different ripening-mold strains and a salt content of about 2 percent for Gorgonzola Dolce, and 3 percent for Gorgonzola Piccante. The name Gorgonzola comes from a town northeast of Milan where the herds of cattle coming down from the mountains in the fall used to winter, and where the forerunner of Gorgonzola, Stracchino or Stracchino di Gorgonzola, was created. Increasingly, a method of processing the milk was introduced that made use of selected cultures and lactic-acid bacteria, as well as controlled strains of mold; the latter are referred to in Italy as *Penicillium gorgonzola*, in individual cases still as *Penicillium glaucum*, but are otherwise described today in scientific terms as a strain of *Penicillium roqueforti*. An especially mild Gorgonzola-type is **Dolcelatte**. Another Gorgonzola variant is a product based on Gorgonzola with layers of Mascarpone: a cheese composition with very limited keeping qualities because of the combination of a high-fat fresh cheese and a ripening mold. As is the case with several traditional blue-veined cheeses, Gorgonzola Verde (the traditional name for Gorgonzola in Italy) is also marketed unripened or only slightly ripened, before the veining develops, as **Gorgonzola Bianco**, also known as **Pannerone**, but with greatly varying quality. A regional *formaggio erborinato* from western Piedmont is **Castelmagno**.

Some blue cheeses have a bloomy white rind: their surfaces are covered with a white mold, and they develop a light, red bacterial coating, usually from the edge inwards, as ripening progresses. Sometimes they are called **Blue Brie**. Examples of these cheeses are **Bavariablu, Cambozola,** and **Ramee Blue**, which vary considerably in terms of consistency and flavor. The French **Bresse Bleu** or **Bleu de Bresse**, developed in the 1950s from Saingorlon, a variant of Gorgonzola, has 50 percent FDB and a white surface mold. With increasing ripeness, an orange-reddish brown bacteria displaces the external mold, and the aroma and flavor become stronger and stronger. The British **Lymeswold** is shaped like a flat disk. **Montagnolo** is produced by hand in an expensive process, and contains at least 70 percent FDB. At the outset it has a whitish-gray

With their white Camembert mold on the outside, and their interior permeated by blue-green mold, here are three examples of typical blue-veined cheeses with bloomy white rinds: **Bavariablu** (above) and **Cambozola** (below) are soft cheeses with a creamy, mild aromatic paste; both have 70% FDB. The French **Bresse Bleu,** or Bleu de Bresse (center photo below), with 50% FDB, was developed in the 1950s as a variant of Gorgonzola with a bloomy white rind. Depending on its degree of ripeness, it tastes mild to strongly aromatic.

Gorgonzola, the classic Italian blue-veined cheese, has become one of the best-known cheeses in the world. It takes its name from a town in northern Italy, in the fields around which the migratory herds from the Como and Bergamo area would in the past spend the winter. Manufacture of this cheese later spread to the neighboring provinces, which are the only ones legally entitled to use the name Gorgonzola. In the foreground of the photo is a Gorgonzola Dolce; behind it, a Gorgonzola Piccante.

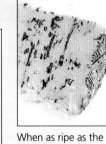

When as ripe as the cheese shown here, **Saint Agur,** from France, tastes strong and spicy.

Mycella is a Danish version of Gorgonzola with blue-green mold, 50% FDB, and a mild aromatic taste. Its name derives from the Latin word for fungal filaments (*mycelium*).

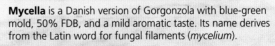

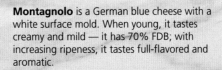

Montagnolo is a German blue cheese with a white surface mold. When young, it tastes creamy and mild — it has 70% FDB; with increasing ripeness, it tastes full-flavored and aromatic.

The London cheese specialists Paxton & Whitfield not only sell cheese, but also enjoy a good reputation as "maturers." They are particularly committed to the nurture of traditional English cheeses, including, of course, Stilton, which they sell in 12-ounce ceramic jars — a very popular gift — as well as by the piece or whole cylinder.

Stilton: "king" of English cheeses

At one time, the Great North Road, which linked London with Scotland, ran through the village of Stilton in the Midlands. In the mid-eighteenth century travelers who broke their north–south journey in Stilton stopped off at the village pub, the Bell Inn, and fortified themselves with bread and a creamy, blue-veined cheese. Many found this cheese to be so tasty that they took some with them on the rest of their journey, thus spreading its fame beyond Stilton. The cheese was actually being made long before this on Leicestershire estates (where it was also called Leicester cream cheese or simply cream cheese) and in the neighboring counties of Derbyshire and Nottinghamshire. Today, the center of Stilton production is still in this region.

Blue Stilton is marketed in two versions: either evenly marbled with blue (with clearly visible blue to brownish veins in a creamy white interior), or with dark blue veins in a chalk-white interior. Depending on production methods, degree of ripeness, mold growth, and surface flora, Stilton tastes mild to strong, or sharp to salty and piquant.

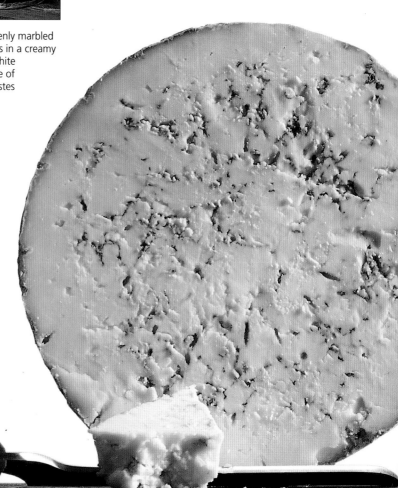

Shropshire Blue comes from the area south of Cheshire. With its reddish-brown surface flecked with whitish-gray spots, and its frequently highly pronounced aroma, it resembles an aged Stilton.

surface, which later becomes dark gray and light brownish in color; its creamy, spicy taste becomes stronger as ripening progresses. The French **Saint Agur** has 60 percent FDB and a vigorous blue mold growth on its surface.

The most famous English blue cheese is **Stilton**. It is now produced primarily from pasteurized milk and has a 48 percent FDB. The color of the internal veining and the qualities of the rind vary from one cheese factory to another. Raw milk cheeses often develop distinctive reddish-brown surface molds. Young cheeses that have been ripened only for a brief period and have not yet developed any veining are sold as **White Stilton. Wensleydale**, a cheese brought to Britain in Norman times by monks of the Cistercian order, now refers to two completely different cheeses: **White Wensleydale**, which in most cases has been ripened for only a few weeks, and **Blue Wensleydale**, a distinctive cheese, aromatic to strong according to its ripening time of two to six months. **Shropshire Blue** does honor to the name of an old county adjoining Cheshire south of Chester, and is similar to **Blue Cheshire**. Thanks to the traditionally open structure of their curd, both cheeses offer a good climate for mold development, and develop a strong to penetrating taste. A cheese from Ireland that is similar in shape, rind characteristics, and vein-marbling is **Cashel Irish Blue**, a farmhouse cheese that is full-bodied in taste. **Dorset Blue**, **Blue Vinny**, or **Blue Veiny** is made from milk that is skimmed by hand and left to stand overnight.

Other countries produce comparable cheeses. American-made blue-mold cheese from sheep's milk must have at least 50 percent FDB. **Nuworld** is a cheese with a white interior mold, a mutant of *Penicillium roqueforti*. In some states **American Blue** includes blue-veined Roquefort-style cheeses, made from cow's rather than sheep's milk, with at least 50 percent FDB. The interior paste is semi-firm with blue-green veining and a strong to slightly salty taste. Blue Cheese must be at least sixty days old. **Oryzae** is a Japanese blue cheese with a special mold. Other national blue cheeses are **Ermite** in Canada, **Blue Vein** in New Zealand, **Aedelost** in Sweden, **Aura** in Finland, and the strong **Normanna** and the milder **Norzola** in Norway. Austria produces **Österola**, Israel makes **Galil**, Spain has **Cabrales**, and the Hungarians prize **Marvany sayt**. In Russia **Syr rokfor** is produced from cow's, sheep's or goat's milk. A very sharp blue cheese made from sheep's milk in Tunisia is called **Numidia**.

Very different sorts of cheese are grouped together in the **soft cheese** category. By virtue of their composition and their consistency, they range from very soft fresh cheeses to semi-firm sliceable cheeses.

Blue Wensleydale was first produced in the Yorkshire dales by Cistercian monks. Nowadays, cow's milk, rather than the sheep's milk, is used to make this cheese. A well-made cheese is creamy and full-bodied and can certainly compete with a Stilton, the aroma of which is, however, somewhat more pronounced.

Galil, an Israeli Roquefort-type blue-veined cheese with 42% FDB, is normally made from sheep's milk, but up to 25% cow's milk may be added. The taste is agreeably piquant and slightly salty.

Blue Cheshire is a blue version of Cheshire. The blue-green mold contrasts sharply with the orange colored interior. The cheese contains 48% FDB and tastes strong, owing to a relatively long ripening period. During production, a cheese permeated with a light mold is crumbled and mixed into the new curds.

Beenleigh Blue, a sheep's-milk cheese from south Devonshire, is very similar to Roquefort in terms of flavor, consistency, and texture.

Cashel Irish Blue is a variety of Irish blue with a grayish-green mold growing primarily in the mostly large curd holes. The cheese, with 45% FDB, is made in cylinder shapes weighing 3 pounds. It tastes spicy, sometimes slightly salty and bitter. It is used like German blue-veined cheeses or Danish Blue.

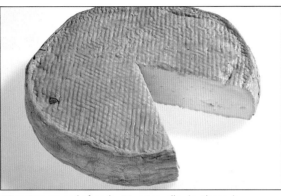

Munster, named after the Munster valley in Alsace, is characterized by a bright orange-red, moist skin, a supple interior, and a distinctively strong aroma.

Géromé is made in Lorraine. Today Géromé and Munster are no longer considered to be separate cheeses, but are both called Munster-Géromé.

Dauphin is produced in the Thiérache in northern France. In addition to the usual bar shape, "fantasy" shapes, such as hearts, fish, crescent moons, and coats of arms are common.

Baguette Laonnaise, one of the numerous versions of Maroilles, is made in the shape of a rectangular loaf, but also in cubes. It is ripened for up to three months, and can taste strong.

Les Beaux Prés has the features of the Belgian Herve family: Its thin skin is covered with a moist red flora, which contributes substantially to ripening and to its strong aroma.

Their surfaces may be bare and dry, or covered by bacterial flora. The surface flora of more than a few varieties of soft cheese consists of a colorful mixture of milk mold, different types of yeast, *Linens* bacteria, micrococci, and strains of mold. Their composition changes as ripening progresses, under the influence of the microclimate in the ripening cellar and the treatment the cheese receives. Many soft cheeses are rather firm when young. As ripening progresses, their consistency may range from soft and supple to flowing. Many cheeses are also dusted with ash or charcoal or covered with hay, in order to protect them from drying out or from mold attack.

An important subcategory of soft cheeses are those treated with red, or *Linens*, bacteria. Depending on the strain, these can also be yellowish or golden yellow in color, and according to the method of treatment and the humidity of the cheese cellar, they can be more or less moist to dry. Two cheeses of this type are **Munster** from Alsace, and **Géromé** (or **Gérardmer**, from the town of the same name) from Lorraine, which served as prototypes for many varieties in other countries, either with their name or of their type. The special style of the French Munster and Géromé is brought about by a substantial preripening of the cheesemaking milk. Munster comes in two sizes: the full-sized 1 pound and the 5-ounce **Petit Munster**. The cheeses ripen for one to two months at 59°F. Their light-yellow interior is creamy to soft, supple, and, when fully ripe, slightly flowing; it contains 45 to 50 percent FDB, and has a strong aromatic taste. Munster with cumin is called **Munster au cumin**. Today, Munster and Géromé are considered to be two variations of a single type, rather than the two separate cheeses they were deemed to be in the past, and they share a legally protected area of origin. German **Münster** has a reddish-yellow mold and a whitish-yellow, supple interior with a mild aroma. American Munster, or **Muenster**, is somewhat firmer, and produced with a golden-yellow surface. It contains at least 50 percent FDB.

Maroilles, from France, is the prototype for several cheeses of different shapes and sizes, some of which are not known outside their region of production. Examples of these are **Sorbais** and **Mignon**. Maroilles itself is a square cheese. Its skin is covered with brownish-yellow mold, its interior is soft and sliceable, and contains at least 45 percent FDB. During the two- to five-week ripening period, the cheese is rubbed repeatedly with salt water. Depending on their degree of ripeness, the cheeses are given different names: freshly formed, they are known as *blancs*, semi-ripe they are called *blondins*. The *vieux*, or old, ones, such as Vieux Gris, Vieux Lille, and the picturesquely named Vieux Puant (Old Stinker) are varieties that

Saint Rémy, in the shape of a Carré de l'Est, ripens with a reddish-brown flora, and is strong tasting.

Herve Kaas, or Fromage d'Herve, is one of the best-known Belgian cheeses. It is strong to piquant in taste.

Weisslacker, often known in Bavaria as Bierkäse, tastes strong and gutsy. It is also made in portion-sized cubes.

During ripening this Limburger is repeatedly rubbed with a red mold to encourage its development on the rind. Cheeses treated like this are called washed-rind cheeses.

Knappenkäse (squire's cheese) is a highly ripened cheese with strong, brownish aroma-forming flora and a spicy taste.

Langres is shaped like a truncated cone with a depression in the top when young. As it ripens, the top sinks in.

Tartufella, owing to its surface flora, is a cheese that ripens from the outside inwards, with a slightly piquant flavor.

Schlosskäse, an Austrian cheese with red flora and a fine, soft interior, tastes mild to piquant, depending on how ripe it is.

Andechser, the monastery cheese from Andechs, a Bavarian place of pilgrimage, has a light red flora and tastes spicy.

Three of the most popular cheeses in Germany are shown in the photo on the right, in a still largely unripened state: **Weinkäse**, on the left of the cheese board; **Romadur**, center; and **Limburger** right. The typical manner of ripening can be seen in the photo above: a ripe, soft zone around the outer edge, and a firmer, whitish core inside.

The ripening of a Livarot is an intricate matter whether it takes place on the premises of the manufacturer or the finisher (who is called a *caviste*, not an *affineur*, in Normandy). First, the freshly shaped pieces are dry-salted and left to sit at 61–64°F, so that the whey drains off. Then, after three to four days, the cheese wheels are brought into a drying room with a temperature of 61°F, where they stay for two weeks. During this period they are rubbed down or "washed" with a weak salt solution two or three times a week, which encourages formation of the characteristic surface flora. Further ripening takes place in a humid cellar for two months at 54–57°F. The cheese may also be stored for longer, during which time it continues to ripen and further develop its strong taste.

This Livarot is wrapped around with reed-mace leaves that have been split lengthwise — a custom practiced in the past to prevent the ripe cheese from running.

Even today, Livarot is still wrapped around its side with a number of bands, which are usually made of special green or red paper.

are especially ripe and sharp. **Baguette Laonnaise** is also a variant of Maroilles. The 1-pound loaf-shaped cheeses have a brick-red surface flora and a soft interior with 45 percent FDB. The round **Rollot** and the heart-shaped **Rollot Coeur** have a thin, light ocher-colored skin, as does **Coeur de Thiérache**. **Dauphin** was named after the son and crown prince of the Sun King, Louis XIV. It is prepared by grinding fresh cheese — Maroilles Blanc — and mixing it with tarragon and pepper, and sometimes also with whey powder and chives, then shaping it by hand and letting it ripen for two to three months. The interior paste is soft and supple, and contains 45 to 50 percent FDB. **Herve Kaas** or **Fromage d'Herve** comes from the area around Herve, near Lüttich in Belgium. The squares or bars weigh 7 to 14 ounces; smaller cheeses are known as *bouchées* (mouthfuls). Herve has a brownish-yellow to pinkish-orange colored, moist surface bacteria, and contains 45 to over 50 percent FDB. Cheeses ripened for longer and salted more heavily yield the hearty variants Le Piquant and Remodou. A southern German specialty is **Weisslacker** or **Bierkäse** (beer cheese). Sold mostly in small, portion-sized cubes, it is also produced in 2 to 4 pound weights. Its rindless surface is moist and has a whitish, lacquer-type bacterial covering (hence the name, which means "white lacquer"), the interior is slightly flaky to fatty, and contains 40 to 50 percent FDB. A similar cheese in the Czech and Slovak Republics is **Krkonossky pivní syr** (Giant mountain-range beer cheese). **Weinkäse** (wine cheese), **Romadur** and **Limburger** have a delicate skin with yellowish, brownish-yellow to reddish, moist flora. The interior of these cheeses is meant to be matte and whitish in the unripened core, light-yellowish and soft to sliceable in the riper marginal area, and especially supple in the case of Weinkäse. The latter is produced in a loaf shape with 40 to 60 percent FDB, Romadur and Limburger in bars of different sizes and with different fat contents, from 20 to 60 percent FDB. The higher the fat content of the cheeses, the softer their interior, of course, and the fuller-bodied the taste. According to size and ambient temperature, Weinkäse and Romadur are ripened for one and a half to two weeks, Limburger for two to four weeks. Limburger is also called **Backsteinkäse** (brick cheese) or **Stangenkäse** (bar cheese) because of its shape. In the United States it is made with a less distinctive red bacterial growth, and called **Liederkranz**. After manufacture, it is ripened for a short time at 53 to 61°F, then ripened further and stored at just 39 to 43°F. **Langres**, named after a town north of Dijon that was an important cheese market in the Middle Ages, has a strong, spicy, creamy flavor and a 50 percent FDB content. **Chaumont, Epoisses, Pierre-qui-vire,**

Maroilles, a well-known French cheese, is the prototype for numerous local and national variants.

Rollot, from Picardy, is round or heart-shaped (Rollot Coeur, above). It tastes strongly aromatic.

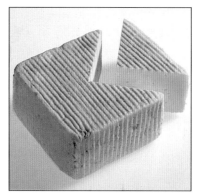

Vieux Lille, thanks to its relatively long ripening period and red flora, is an especially spicy variant of Maroilles.

Soumaintrain, like the similar Saint Florentin and Epoisses, when ripe is usually very soft, almost flowing.

Pierre-qui-vire is related to the other cheeses of Burgundy. It has a yellowish to reddish surface bacteria.

Epoisses, whose red surface bacteria gives it a strong, but not sharp, aroma and taste, has a soft, flowing interior.

Olivet Cendré, an Olivet coated with ash. Sometimes the ash is permeated by blue-green mold.

Aisy Cendré is washed with Marc de Bourgogne during its two-month ripening period, and is later rolled in ash.

Rigotte weighs only 1¾ to 2½ ounces. These little cheeses, which are red-flora-ripened, are often also treated with wine.

Rougette is a delicate cheese with a soft, supple curd, which with increasing ripeness tastes spicy and piquant.

Chaumes, a soft, supple cheese, with 50% FDB and a delicate, light red surface flora, tastes mild.

Saint Albray has a reddish-orange and white surface mold that partly determines its mild taste.

L'Ami du Chambertin has a very soft interior (hence the box). When fully ripe, its taste is very strong.

Boscaiola is one of several variations of Robiola. When ripe, its interior is soft to melting, and spicy.

Soumaintrain, and the similar **Saint Florentin**, as well as **Aisy Cendré**, are other cheeses from Burgundy. They are rubbed down during the ripening period with Marc de Bourgogne or wine, and are, when ripe, mostly very soft, and sometimes flowing. **Rigotte** from the Lyon region is made from cow's milk, as is **Rigotte de Condrieu**. The small cheeses are ripened for about two weeks with a red bacteria, rubbed down with wine or tinted orange-yellow with annatto, or put up in oil and ripened as **Rigotte Blanche**. A spicy red-bacteria-ripened cheese is **Livarot**, named after a town in Normandy. It is produced in two sizes, 12 ounces and 1 pound. A special characteristic of the cheese is that it is wrapped around its sides, which in the past served primarily to stop the ripe cheese from running. A red paper band has also earned the cheese the nickname "the Colonel." The paper is a substitute for the strips of leaves of the reed mace used in the past. The flat, slightly domed **Chaumes** wheel is covered with a light red bacteria and a layer of paper over this. The interior, with 50 percent FDB, is soft and sliceable, with a small curd-hole formation. Aroma and taste are mild to spicy. A similar, though firmer, cheese is **Vacherol**. **Saint Albray** has a distinctive shape, resembling a garland with a crimped outer edge. Its surface is reddish-orange, and covered with a delicate milk mold. Its interior has an obvious curd-hole formation, and is soft and supple. Aroma and taste are mild to aromatic, in part determined by the surface bacteria. **Rougette** ripens with a layer of red bacteria and a light white mold.

The white-mold cheeses form a second large subcategory in the soft-cheese family. The surface of these cheeses is covered with a fine, short growth of mold or a downy, bloomy Camembert mold; gray or bluish molds can also occur. The most important cheeses within this group are Brie and Camembert. Both are originally from France, and had a reddish-brown surface flora, occasionally with a bluish mold. Both types have now also been developed in other countries.

Brie takes its name from the area east of Paris; in the past it was renowned as the "Jewel of the Ile-de-France," and often in addition labeled with the name of its place of origin, such as Meaux, Melun, or Coulommiers. Nowadays, Brie is legally defined in France as a soft cheese with a surface mold, and at least 40 percent FDB and 44 percent dry matter. The wheels, in the shape of a flat cake, must have a diameter of 8½ to 14 inches; smaller wheels measuring 5½ to 8½ inches are described as **Petit Brie**. A wedge cut from the wheel is called **Pointe de Brie**. Two types of Brie are AOC-protected in France: Brie de Melun and Brie de Meaux. Both are made from raw milk with at least 45 percent FDB. **Brie de Melun** ripens at 50°F

Brie de Meaux is an AOC brie with a long tradition.

How Brie de Meaux is made

The milk, whose fat content is standardized, is pumped into 27 ½-gallon vats and coagulated.

The gel-like coagulum in the vats is cut into fairly large-sized pieces with a metal rod.

The delicate curds are removed from the vat with a flat ladle — the *pelle de Brie*, or Brie scoop — and packed into the molds.

The perforated molds are stacked on top of one another and left until evening to drain. The cheeses are then put into adjustable locking hoops, called *éclisses*.

Salt is now sprinkled over the curd mass, which has drained, drawn together, and been molded. The Camembert mold culture is sprayed on at this point.

The sides of the cheeses are also rubbed with salt. For this procedure, the hoops must be removed carefully.

The cheeses remain in the drying room for a week at about 50°F and 80%–85% relative humidity, or sometimes for only one to two days at 57–59°F.

The finished cheeses are laid on hygienic plastic mats (instead of the straw mats commonly used in the past). They then ripen, individually or stacked on top of one another, on wooden shelves.

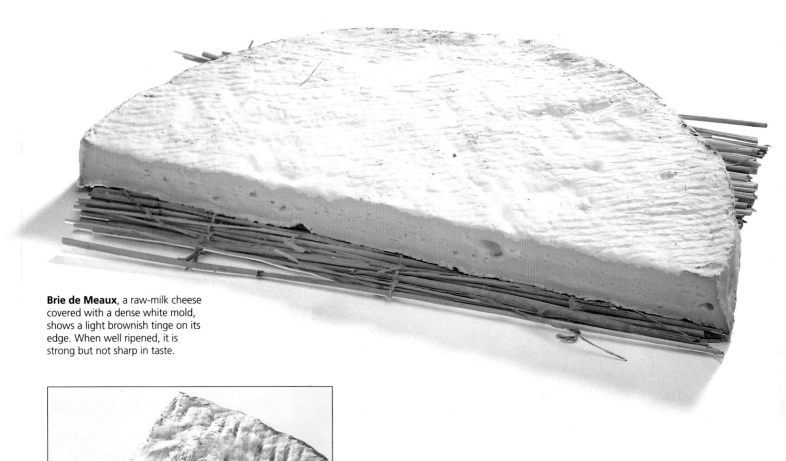

Brie de Meaux, a raw-milk cheese covered with a dense white mold, shows a light brownish tinge on its edge. When well ripened, it is strong but not sharp in taste.

Fully ripened Brie de Melun has a soft interior and a brownish surface flora permeated with white spots of mold. Its smell and taste are penetrating to sharp.

Brie: a classic soft cheese

This cheese originates in the area of the same name in the Ile-de-France. Until the latter half of the nineteenth century, Brie was made exclusively on the farm, where it usually ripened with a reddish-brown surface bacteria, and sometimes a bluish mold. Triggered by ever-increasing demand, however, factory production became more and more the norm. However, Brie with an even, bloomy white rind, as we know it today, has existed only since the beginning of the twentieth century.

On ripening shelves such as these, Brie de Melun is aged for four to six weeks, or for eight weeks until it is fully ripened, at about 50°F and at a relative humidity of 90%–95%.

This **Brie de Melun** has a typical white mold and a clearly developed red surface bacteria. Ripening is advanced, but, as can be seen from the light core, not yet complete.

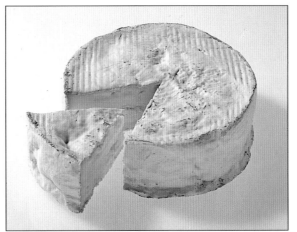

Coulommiers is ready to eat as soon as the layer of mold first appears on its surface. The cheese shown in the photo is fairly well ripened and also has a light, reddish-brown flora.

German Brie is made in a similar fashion to Camembert. It has an even white surface mold, and a delicate mold aroma, and tastes mild to discreetly spicy.

Brie with alpine herbs is one of the flavored varieties of Brie. Herbs and spices are either distributed evenly throughout the curd, or are scattered on the surface.

Camembert, originally from Normandy, has spread worldwide. Some other countries have developed Camembert-type cheeses with their own local character.

for at least four weeks, and in some cases for more than two months. During this period, an unmistakable reddish-brown flora grows over the original white mold, and a strong flavor develops. Cheese-lovers search out the extremely well ripened wheels, which taste and smell of ammonia. **Brie de Melun Frais**, also called **Brie de Melun Blanc**, is unripened and has a bare surface, without skin or rind. **Brie de Meaux** ripens at 50°F for over four weeks, during which time the layer of white mold is permeated to an ever-increasing extent by a brownish flora. As this happens, aroma and taste alter from fruity and spicy to distinctly strong, yet mild. The cheeses are still frequently sold in the classic style on straw mats, but increasingly on plastic imitations of these. In the past, and still in some cases, **Coulommiers** was regarded as a member of the Brie family (**Brie de Coulommiers**); for some time now, however, it has been defined as a cheese in its own right. The 1-inch high cheeses weighing 1 pound were at one time also called **Brie Petit Moule**, to distinguish them from **Tarte de Brie**. Coulommiers is now often produced with an unmistakable Camembert mold, but it is also sold very young with only a light surface mold. It must have at least 40 percent FDB, and may be very soft and moist, or firm. Also from the Ile-de-France is **Brie de Montereau**. Brie from other regions or countries generally has a well-developed to thick bloomy white rind, a soft, supple interior, and the characteristic flavor of a fine Camembert mold. Mild at the outset, the taste becomes stronger as ripening progresses and a red surface flora develops, usually beginning at the edges. **German Brie** is made with 45 percent, 50 percent, or 60 percent FDB. It is meant to taste aromatic, slightly sharp to slightly piquant. **Melbury** is a Brie from Britain. Brie made in the United States must have at least 50 percent FDB. The creamy, firm interior is ivory to gold colored, and may be seasoned with herbs, pepper, or mushrooms. Canadian Brie likewise contains at least 50 percent FDB; its surface is described as a bloomy rind.

Another classic among French soft cheeses is **Camembert**, which also originated in Normandy. Traditionally, it was manufactured with a reddish-brown surface flora, like Livarot, Pont l'Evêque, and Pavé d'Auge. Depending on the surrounding conditions, mold, often bluish mold, would also colonize the surface. Closely connected with the history of Camembert is Marie Harel, a farmer's wife from the village of Vimoutiers in Normandy, who was apparently the first to succeed, in around 1790, in supplying the markets of the vicinity with a uniform cheese. Whether she can therefore be considered to be the inventor of Camembert is a moot point — the truth about the origins of Camembert will, never be known. Nonetheless, Madame Harel has become

Fresh raw-milk Camembert delivered by the cheese factory is stored under optimal conditions on the premises of the Parisian cheese specialist Pierre Androuët.

The different stages of ripeness with Camembert can be seen in this photo. The top wedge is fresh, about one day old, white all the way through and with only a very sparse layer of mold. The bottom wedge is completely ripened through after five weeks.

French Camembert from Normandy is an AOC cheese. It is made from raw milk and has an even white bloomy rind and a light red surface flora. It is favored by many gourmets when fully ripened, as its taste is then strong and spicy.

Gratte-paille, from the Ile-de-France, has a white mold and a distinct *Linens* bacteria, and a spicy taste.

Tomme Vaudoise, made in Switzerland in the Camembert style, is produced with 25% FDB (above) and 45% FDB.

Pierre Robert has 75% FDB, a white Camembert mold and, as it ripens, a brownish-yellow surface flora at the edge.

As a young cheese (top), **Saint Marcellin** has a slight lactic tang; when largely ripened (above), it tastes strong and spicy.

Romans, the "big brother" of Saint Marcellin, is mild to spicy, depending on ripeness. There are also seasoned varieties.

Coeur de Neufchâtel is the heart-shaped version of this famous cheese from Normandy. It tastes mild to full-bodied.

Oreillier de Ciboulette (chive pillow) gets its unique, strong taste from the flora on the surface and the chives inside.

Feuille de Dreux is a very ripe cheese with whitish and dark-gray mold, and a brownish flora.

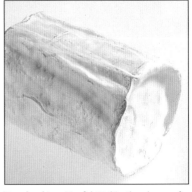

Bondard is a Neufchâtel in the shape of a cork, whose light red bacteria contributes to its delicate flavor.

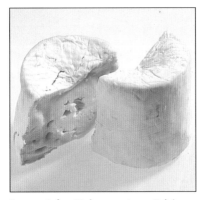

Bouquet des Moines, a strong Belgian cheese with a bloomy white rind, is substantially ripe and flowing at its edge.

Frinault comes from the Orléanais. Lightly dusted with ash, it has a very strong taste.

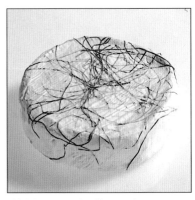

Pithiviers au Foin, like Bondaroy au Foin, is decorated with hay, and has a pronounced taste.

Fougeru, decorated with a fern, resembles Coulommiers both in appearance and taste.

famous owing to a statue erected by Americans in Vimoutiers in 1928, which was destroyed during the war in 1944; after the war, a new statue was put up. Today, Camembert is known and loved worldwide. Two developments were largely responsible for this. The first was the introduction of the box made of wood-shavings by a Monsieur Ridel around 1890. This new packaging gave Camembert its definitive shape, but above all it meant that it could be transported over long distances without coming to harm. The second major step was taken in 1910, when the Laboratoires Roger managed to propagate a white mold (*Penicillium candidum*), which gradually gained currency. A specialty is **Camembert de Normandie**, which has a legally protected name of origin. It may be made only from raw milk and must have 45 percent FDB. Its thin skin is covered with a light mold with reddish-brown to yellowish spots showing through. The wheels are about 4 inches in diameter, 1 inch high, and weigh 8 ounces. As in the past, the cheeses are still typically packaged in boxes made from wood shavings. As with Brie, Camembert is made from well-ripened milk. The wheels are cured for at least twenty-one days, during which time the supple interior becomes softer, but not fluid. Aroma and taste are fruity to distinctly pronounced. Cheeses from outside the Camembert area in Normandy, manufactured from raw or heat-treated milk, are esteemed for their spicy but less piquant style than the original Camembert. In addition to the AOC Camembert from Normandy, there are many variants in France. Two sizes are prescribed for these: 4 inches for the full size, and 3 inches for **Petit Camembert**. They both must contain at least 40 percent FDB. Camembert must contain at least 110 g (about 4 ounces) of dry matter per cheese, and Petit Camembert 60 g (2 ounces). Camembert of uniform quality has also been manufactured for some time now in other countries. In Germany, it is made with a range of fat levels. A similar cheese with only 20 percent FDB is called **Weichkäse mit Schimmelbildung** (soft cheese with mold formation). Round soft cheeses with bloomy white rinds, which are similar to Camembert, are likewise found in many countries. Examples are **Tomme Vaudoise** from Switzerland, **Weisser Prinz** (White Prince), a sheep's milk cheese from Austria, and **Bonchester** from Jersey in the Channel Islands. **Neufchâtel** from the Pays de Bray in Normandy includes cheeses with 45 percent FDB at different stages of ripeness; fresh and lightly salted, with a light hint of mold, and ripened, with a full mold growth. They are made in the shape of corks (**Bonde, Bondon,** and **Bondard de Neufchâtel**) and hearts (**Coeur de Neufchâtel, Coeur de Bray**), as small flat disks (**Malacoff**), square (**Carré**), and rectangular (**Briquette**, similar to **Grattepaille**). In the

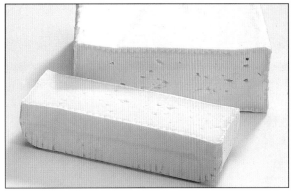

Carré de l'Est is produced mainly in Lorraine and Champagne, and is shown here with a bloomy white skin. It tastes mild with a lactic-acid tang, and spicy with increasing ripeness.

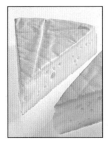

Weisser Prinz (White Prince), a sheep's-milk cheese from Austria, with 50% FDB, has a mild, characteristic flavor.

Weisse Lady (Lady in White) is a rectangular bloomy-rind cheese from Bavaria with a delicate, supple interior (60% FDB), which sometimes contains herbs or horseradish.

A selection of fine soft cheeses: They all have a well-developed, delicate, aromatic bloomy skin and an evenly ripened interior, but each is unmistakably individual. Clockwise: Le Carré, Géramont, Val des Moines, Crème des Prés, Champignon de luxe.

Butte de Doue is stored on racks in the curing room. After less than a week, a light layer of mold starts to form; after about two weeks, the cheese is ripe and ready to eat.

Butte de Doue has a light, white surface mold and, with 70% FDB, a supple, soft, fresh cheese-type interior.

Paglietta is an Italian soft cheese from the Piedmont, with an evenly ripened interior containing 50% FDB.

Lucullus is the name Pierre Androuët gave this delicate, creamy cheese with 75% FDB and a white surface mold.

Explorateur is covered with a thick white mold, contains 75% FDB, and has a lactic tang.

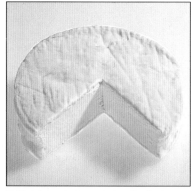

Brillat-Savarin is made in a fresh-cheese style with 75% FDB, with a light bloomy rind, and a lactic tang.

Pavé d'Affinois has a very delicate interior in the style of a fresh cheese. With 45% FDB, it is very mild and creamy.

Vignotte, is a French "vineyard" cheese with a light, white surface mold, a creamy, melting body, and 75% FDB.

Brillador has a dense surface mold. Its interior, containing 75% FDB, is creamy and soft, and mild in flavor.

Bresso is a soft-cheese torte with a strong, spicy taste. It has 60% FDB, and may be spiced with pepper or garlic.

Prestige de Bourgogne, ripened with a whitish or reddish surface flora, has 75% FDB, and tastes fresh, with a lactic tang.

Boursault, with 70% FDB, is very soft and supple, like a fresh cheese, and has a light white or reddish-brown surface flora.

Ramee Royal has an evenly ripening interior, and a slight lactic-acid, aromatic taste.

United States, Neufchatel is a fresh cheese, similar to cream cheese but lower in fat and somewhat softer.

For connoisseurs, the names **Saint Marcellin**, or simply **Marcellin**, and **Romans** or **Tomme de Romans**, its bigger cousin, from the *département* of Isère, bring to mind goat cheeses with the same names. Nowadays these cheeses, made primarily from cow's milk, are prized as fresh cheeses, or cheeses ripened with white and bluish molds. Some are strewn with herbs or spices such as pepper, paprika, rosemary, or savory, or are wrapped in chestnut leaves. An old tradition of applying a decoration of hay, leaves, or ferns has endured; originally this was a method of ripening the cheese, keeping it through periods of low milk production, and preventing it from drying out. Dusting the cheese with ashes (*cendré*) serves to dry off the cheese and also sometimes to counteract acidity, as the ash is alkaline. Examples of this are **Olivet Bleu** and **Frinault**, both similar to Coulommiers, with a bluish mold. **Rocroi Cendré**, from the Ardennes, is made from skim milk as a half-fat cheese. **Carré de l'Est**, with a bloomy white rind, spread outwards from its native eastern France. It is manufactured in three sizes. **Petit Carré de l'Est** weighs 4 to 5½ ounces; Carré de l'Est, 9 to 10½ ounces; and **Grand Carré de l'Est**, 1¾ to 2½ pounds. All contain at least 40 percent FDB and 44 percent dry matter. Although this cheese usually has a white bloomy rind, in individual cases a flora dominated by reddish-brown *Linens* bacteria predominates. Examples of German white bloomy rind cheeses of this type are **Weisse Lady** as well as the firmer, trapezoidal **Tettnanger**. In the 1970s a new type of white-mold cheese, which, as a result of a change in manufacturing, ripened from the inside rather than from the outside inwards, as with Camembert, became increasingly widespread. Some of these cheeses have a higher fat content. They are oval in shape, with more or less rounded ends. Examples of such cheeses with a ripened-through interior, but unmistakable individuality, are **Caprice des Dieux, Champignon de Luxe, Crème des Prés, Géramont, Le Carré, Val des Moines** and newer types such as **Bresso**, which also has added ingredients, as well as **Ramee Royal** in the form of a torte, and **Cremeroll**. The Neufchâtel principle — the transition of the fresh cheese to a slightly ripened soft cheese — is found in several French types, such as **Boursault, Brillat Savarin, Butte de Doue, Explorateur**, and **Vignotte**, as well as in **Chaource**, and in Italian types such as **Formagella** and a number of Toma-style cheeses, including the smaller **Robiola** and **Tomino**. The variety has been produced and increased by new production processes that led to products with a compact but nonetheless fine, supple interior, for example, **Henry IV** or **Pavé d'Affinois**.

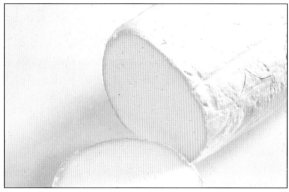

Cremeroll is a specialty soft cheese, whose cylindrical shape makes it ideal for cheese platters. Mild and creamy in taste, it is smooth and soft in consistency, containing 60% FDB.

Formagella is made in the foothills of the Alps around Bergamo and Brescia. With 45% and 20% FDB, it is a typical eating cheese, both fresh and, here, ripened with a bloomy white rind.

Tomino has a slight lactic tang when fresh (Tomino Fresco, left). When ripened with a delicate bloomy white rind (*stagionato*), it develops a delicate Camembert flavor.

Chaource has a bloomy white rind. Here, a brownish flora has developed around its edge during ripening. The fresh-cheese style body has a lactic-acid taste and aroma, and contains 50% FDB.

When cut into, this fresh Chaource shows how ripening begins at the edges under the skin with white and milk molds.

Formaggini means "little cheeses." In Italy this term is used to describe fresh table cheeses with a soft, supple consistency, like the cheese shown above. When absolutely fresh, they are considered to be **latticini**, a type of milk product. Sometimes they are ripened for several weeks, during which time their initially mild tart flavor develops into a delicate, full-bodied taste.

Robiola is the name given to greatly differing Italian cheeses, such as this creamy, gently tart fresh cheese, **Robiola Osella**, with 70% FDB, made in Piedmont. A number of Robiola types, mostly with 45% FDB, ripen with a reddish skin, like Robiola di Roccaverano and Robiola del Bec; some have a white surface mold. Smaller cheeses are called Robiolette or Robiolini.

Burgos is the best-known cheese in Spain next to Manchego. It is a fresh rennet cheese — that is, is made with rennet only, without lactic acid bacteria — from sheep's milk, which gives it its characteristic aroma. In addition, it may taste slightly salty. The milky-white, soft gel-like interior still gives off a bit of whey in the first few days after manufacture, a sign of freshness. Sold fresh daily, the cheese can be kept only for a few days.

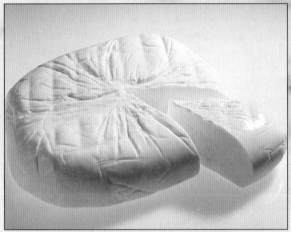

Flor de Oro from the Spanish province of Valencia, is a *queso fresco valenciano* (Puzol and Cervera are two similar cheeses). It is made from goat's, cow's, and sheep's milk, and contains 40% FDB . With its supple interior and mild flavor, it resembles Cuajada, which is also made in the Andes in Venezuela.

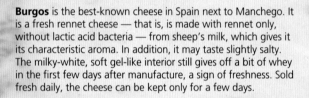

Fresh cheese is generally taken to mean freshly made, unripened products that are ready to eat immediately after manufacture and are intended for speedy consumption, such as cottage cheese and the similar *fromage blanc* or Quark. Cheeses like Ricotta, which are either consumed fresh or rendered less perishable by salting, smoking or drying, or those like Caciotta, which undergo a slight ripening, also belong to this group. The term is also applied in a broader sense to cheeses that are meant to undergo a relatively long ripening period but are also sold fresh or only slightly ripened, as is the case with a number of Pecorinos (*primo sale*), Cantals (*Tomme fraîche*) and Stiltons (white Stilton). Last but not least, products such as Kash, Zieger and curd cheese, intermediate products arising during manufacture, which are consumed fresh and plain, fall into this category. Of course, the terms "fresh" and "fresh cheese" have different meanings in different countries. Some types belonging to the fresh cheese group, like Mozzarella, are discussed elsewhere in this book. Several styles of fresh cheeses are recognized, depending on their structure: fresh cheeses with a delicate-firm structure (examples are Schichtkäse, Burgos, and Cambridge); soft curd cheeses (like cottage cheese); cheeses with a certain firmness and moldability (such as Suisse and cream cheese); cheeses with a paste-like structure (Quark and Ricotta); whipped fresh cheeses, and fresh cheese preparations.

Robiola is used as a generic term for very different round, mostly small cheeses. A number are reminiscent of Taleggio, others of Caciotta. The Spanish Burgos is a renneted fresh cheese made from sheep's milk, usually with over 50 percent FDB, which comes in the shape of a round loaf weighing 2 to 4 pounds. Similar is Villalón, weighing 1 to 5½ pounds, and also known as Pata de Mulo (mule's hoof) because of its shape. In the southern provinces of Spain, fresh cheeses made from sheep's and goat's milk, sometimes mixed with cow's milk, include Queso Fresco Valenciano, Flor de Oro, Puzol and Cervera, as well as Málaga and Cádiz from Andalusia. These cheeses vary in shape and size. There are similar white, soft, unripened Mexican style cheeses in California. Stracchino, similar to Crescenza, is an Italian fresh cheese from Lombardy. German Schichtkäse is manufactured in fat levels of between 10 and 60 percent FDB. Cream is added during manufacture to the varieties containing 40 to 60 percent FDB to produce Sahneschichtkäse (cream layer cheese). Cambridge and York are comparable cheeses made in Britain.

Fresh curd cheese describes the structure of the cheese: small, soft-supple curds. Three styles of fresh curd cheese are made in the United States: dry-curd

Stracchino is a fresh cheese with a delicate paste that nonetheless holds its shape, and a mild to delicately tart taste. It is eaten fresh, or after up to two weeks' ripening. Closely related to Crescenza, it is also sold as Stracchino-Crescenza. Originally made only north of Milan, today it is manufactured throughout all of Lombardy and in Piedmont.

Schichtkäse (layer cheese) owes its name to its layered texture, created by scooping the coagulum during manufacture. Aromatic-tasting with a lactic tang, the body is matte and delicately supple, and has only a few curd holes and round fermentation holes. Depending on fat content, it is milky white to creamy yellow.

The size of the individual soft curds in cottage cheese varies, from small (top photo) to large (above).

Cottage cheese is a widely available fresh curd cheese, originally developed in America. The picture shows creamed cottage cheese with 20% FDB: easily recognizable are the soft curds in the strainer, and the cream dressing in the bowl. It is also made with additions such as fruit, herbs, and spices.

Petit-Suisse is the name given to these little fresh-cheese cylinders, which come not from Switzerland, but from Normandy. The flavor is mild and the texture fine.

Cream cheese is a mild, aromatic fresh cheese with more than 70% FDB. Originally developed in America, it is compact yet creamy, and is also made whipped and with added ingredients.

Mascarpone originated in Italy. This whitish to straw-yellow, creamy, mild fresh cheese is compact, but supple and spreadable. It is an ideal basis for sweet desserts.

Whipped fresh cheeses, such as this **Bresso** with finely minced aromatic herbs, have an airy, creamy consistency that makes them melt on the tongue.

There is a huge variety of fresh cheeses available, especially in European markets. They go down well both plain and prepared with all sorts of seasoning ingredients, like Le Tartar with herbs, or Boursin with garlic or pepper. Whipped cheeses such as Bresso, Cantadou, Colette, and Mirée are also popular. In addition there are semi-firm, sliceable products, including Dania tortes with chives; Tolko rings with rum and pepper; Danslot with pineapple, nougat, and Madeira; and Gourmos in vine leaves with chopped olives and a hint of garlic.

cottage cheese, or **pot cheese**, is soft curd cheese made from skim milk, containing less than 0.5 percent butterfat; **low-fat cottage cheese**, which must have a fat content of less than 4 percent, and **cottage cheese**, which has a fat content of at least 4 percent. The latter is made by mixing dry-curd cottage cheese with a cream dressing, and therefore is also called **creamed cottage cheese**. A distinction is made between large and small curd in all three styles. **Farmers' cheese** is cottage cheese that has been pressed into a block.

The firmer fresh cheeses with a more compact structure have a very delicate curd that melts on the tongue. Among them is **Suisse**, a small roll-shaped cheese from Normandy. It is available as **Petit-suisse**, weighing about 2 ounces and with 60 percent FDB, as well as weighing 1 ounce and having 40 percent FDB. **Demi-sel** with 40 percent FDB is similar, but contains 2 percent salt. Similar cheeses were marketed with moderate success in mid-nineteenth century Paris, until a cheesemaker from Switzerland — or his wife — created a great upturn in demand by mixing cream in with the cheese. The cheese was sold successfully from then on as "Suisse"; in some countries it was introduced as a unique type under the name of the subsequent manufacturer, Gervais.

The fresh cheese manufactured and sold in the United States as **cream cheese** contains at least 33 percent fat, which is equivalent to over 70 percent FDB. The best-known cream cheese was developed at the end of the nineteenth century and is marketed as "Philadelphia," nicknamed "Philly." It is also available with chives and in a low-fat version. A softer variety of cream cheese is the American **Neufchatel** with 20 to 33 percent FDB, and more than 35 percent dry matter. German **Rahmfrischkäse** (fresh cream cheese) contains at least 50 percent FDB, while **Doppelrahmfrischkäse** (fresh double-cream cheese) has at least 60 percent. Both are characterized by a mildly lactic-acid aroma and a slightly salty taste. In Britain, **single cream cheese** has a minimum of 45 percent FDB and **double cream cheese** has at least 65 percent. The best-known high-fat fresh cheese of Italy is **Mascarpone**. During its manufacture, cream containing 30 percent butterfat is heated to 194°F and curdled by means of lemon juice, a citric acid solution, or another acid. The curd is then left to drain and cool. **Quark**, which is also called **Topfen** in Austria, is a fresh cheese with a paste-like consistency. It comes in many fat levels, but is popular mainly as a low-fat cheese. The 20 percent FDB Quark has about 5 percent actual fat, but nonetheless is a very smooth cheese with a fine consistency. A Danish smoked Quark with caraway is **Rygeost**. **Bakers' cheese**, is soft, sharp fresh cheese made in the United States, which is particularly popular for use in cheesecake. In

Finely chopped herbs give this fresh cheese roll a fine flavor through and through.

Low-fat Quark contains only 1–2% FDB. Since the protein content is very high in comparison with the fat (0.3%), the mixture is firm, crumbly, and dry rather than creamy.

Quark with 10% FDB is still slightly crumbly in consistency, but somewhat creamier and smoother than low-fat Quark. The actual (absolute) fat content is only about 2.5%.

Quark with 20% FDB is distinctly softer as well as creamier than the 10% version. Not only can you see the difference, you can feel it on the tongue. The absolute fat content is around 5%.

Quark with 40% FDB, as can clearly be seen in this photo, is very smooth and creamy; it has a correspondingly creamy taste. The actual fat content is approximately 11%.

Britain, similar fresh cheeses include **Lactic Cheese, Colwick Cheese**, and **Cottager's Cheese**, which has nothing to do with the curd cheese we call cottage cheese, but is a farmhouse-style preparation that sometimes is salted, and may also be made with cream, herbs, spices, onions, olives, or nuts. The French soft cheeses **Caillebotte** and **Jonchée** (also made from goat's milk) correspond to the Italian **Giuncata**. The French **Fromage Frais Battu Maigre** (whipped low-fat fresh cheese) contains less than 1 percent FDB and over 85 percent water.

The Italian **Ricotta** was originally made only from sheep's cheese whey (**Ricotta di Pecora**), and often named after the Pecorino areas, such as Ricotta Romana, Ricotta Canestrata, Ricotta Siciliana. A similar product is **Ricotta di Vacca** or **Ricotta Vaccina**, made from cow's-milk-cheese whey. To make it, the whey protein is separated from the whey by heating, with acidulated whey or acids sometimes also being added. It is normally produced as the unripened, unsalted **Ricotta Tipo Dolce**, but also salted as **Ricotta Salata**, as well as salted and ripened as **Ricotta Tipo Forte**. The very firm to hard **Ricotta Secca** can also be used as a grating cheese. The term Ricotta may also be used for Quark or curd cheese. **Cacioricotta** is a type of fresh rennet cheese made from milk. Sheep's milk Ricotta, thanks to the higher fat content of sheep's cheese whey, usually contains more fat than cow's-milk Ricotta. The Spanish **Requesón** and Portuguese **Requeijão** largely correspond to Italian sheep's milk Ricotta. In Brazil, the term **Requeijão** includes Quark-or curd-cheese-style products that have cream or butter and salt mixed into them and are processed. The term **Zieger** or **Ziger** is generally used in Switzerland for the fresh cheese precipitated when acidulated whey is heated. It is spreadable and crumbly soft, and may be white or creamy yellow in color. A distinction is made between **Molkezieger** (whey Zieger), **Milchzieger** (milk Zieger) and **Mischzieger** (mixed Zieger). Whey Ziegers are also known as **whey-protein** or **albumin cheeses**. Across the border, Ziegers are called **Sérac** or **Cérat** in Savoie in France, and **Seirass** in Piedmont, in Italy. Zieger is also used to make other cheese products such as **Glarner Schabziger** (Sapsago), **Urda** (Myzithra), and **Manouri**.

A very popular fresh cheese in Latin America is **Queso Blanco**, also called Queso del País. It is made by heating milk with acidulated whey, acidic fruit juices or acetic acid, then, in some cases, pressing, molding, and lightly salting the resultant cheese. Variants of this cheese are **Campesino, Queso de Hoja** (wrapped in a leaf), **Queso de Puna** (which when made with rennet and lactic acid bacteria may be known in the United States as Spanish cheese), and **Queso Fresco**.

Ricotta di Pecora (sheep's-milk Ricotta) is made from the whey obtained from the manufacture of sheep's milk cheese. Shown above molded, it has a whitish, fine, smooth curd.

Ricotta di Vacca, a cow's-milk whey-protein cheese molded in little baskets, is made primarily in the provinces of northern Italy.

In Italy, Ricotta Salata is sold daily in the markets, as are the typically shaped Pecorinos from Sicily.

Ricotta Piacentina is produced in the Po Valley. A cow's-milk Ricotta, it is sold in the cheesecloth it drains in during manufacture, and has a creamy, slightly crumbly structure.

Ricotta Salata is made mainly in the form of **Ricotta Tipo Moliterno** (here from sheep's-milk cheese whey), which is somewhat dry, owing to a long draining process.

Ricotta Salata made from cow's-milk-cheese whey has a compact–supple curd. In the background is a **Ricotta Salata Affumicata**, whose skin is tinged brown from the smoke.

Goat's-milk Zieger, produced in Switzerland, has a delicate, mild, aromatic curd. It is obtained by heating the milk to a high temperature and precipitating the protein with acid.

Cow's-milk Zieger, shown here molded, is eaten fresh or used in the manufacture of Sapsago.

Ricotta Salata al Forno is a salted Ricotta baked dry in an oven. It is quite often found on the menu in central and southern Italy.

Manouri is a dried goat cheese from Greece with a relatively high fat content and an especially fine curd. It is similar to the salted and dried products made from Ricotta.

Cheese is made every morning from Easter to All Saints' Day. By 7 a.m. at the latest, Farmer Merlot comes out of the goat barn with the fresh milk from his 30 goats, which is then mixed with the previous night's yield.

Goat cheeses make up quite a special cheese group, which includes a vast array of types and varieties. Goat's milk is not always used exclusively in the manufacture of these cheeses: cow's and sheep's milk are often added, a fact that should be clearly stated on the label. In France, for example, the word *chèvre*, which means "goat," is used for cheeses made exclusively from goat's milk; a cheese made of only 50 percent goat's milk is called *mi-chèvre*. There, cheeses that state on the label that they are made with goat's milk must contain at least 20 percent goat's milk (calculated as dry matter in the milk).

Either fresh raw or pasteurized milk may be used for these cheeses. Curd is also frozen and stored for use when sufficient fresh milk is unavailable, but its use is not allowed in all cheeses. Three basic types may be distinguished by their curd qualities and ripening behavior, and, dependent on these, sometimes also by their aroma and taste. In the first type, lactic acid is the dominant factor during coagulation, and the impact of the rennet is distinctly reduced. The characteristic fine-grained structure of the whitish, firm paste remains preserved after draining. An example of this type is Selles-sur-Cher. In the second basic type, the effect of the lactic acid and rennet are more evenly balanced, as in Camembert-style cheeses. As ripening progresses, the cheese changes from firm and sharp to soft and supple, particularly under the influence of a surface ripening bacteria. An example of this type is Bougon. In the third basic type, the effect of the rennet predominates slightly, as in Chevrotin.

The widely differing shapes of the cheeses also contribute to the great variety available. Four styles can be distinguished. The gel-like mass is ladled directly into the molds, as in the case of Selles-sur-Cher; or it is packed into sacks or cloths and is left to drain for several hours, as for crottin. For some cheeses, like Rocamadour, the coagulum is stirred until the curd is very fine. When it is as homogenous and paste-like as possible, it is packed into the molds. For other cheeses, such as Bougon or Chevrotin, the curd is prepared, worked, and shaped as usual.

There are goat cheeses without a covering; with a bare, or whitish, golden-yellow or brownish surface; with a whitish milk mold or with a whitish or bluish-gray mold; and with yeasts or red bacteria. In the case of *chèvre cendré*, the cheese is dusted with powdered charcoal. Often, some salt is mixed into the charcoal, so that the cheese is salted at the same time. Depending on the type of milk, the manufacturing process, and the ripening, the cheese can taste creamy and mild or distinctly strong. A special rennet with fat-ripening enzymes can enhance the *chèvre* character. Some types acquire a quite distinct flavor through ripening in *marc*; others are covered with

The fresh curds, seasoned with a few grains of salt and eaten with a chunk of bread, are a delicacy in their own right. The typical goat's milk taste, which is not to everyone's liking, cannot yet be detected in this completely fresh cheese. It is thus well suited for combining with fruit to make sweet desserts.

At daybreak, the herd is driven into the Bergwald, above Stampa. The black goats belong to the Frigia breed, native only to this valley in Switzerland. The milk yield of about 1½ gallons a day per goat is considerable; reason enough for the Swiss government to subsidize the raising of this breed. Incidentally, the "black sheep" in Farmer Merlot's herd is a white goat.

Fresh air is important during storage. Protected by a fly screen, Guiseppe Merlot's cheeses ripen on well-ventilated shelves. Marketing problems are unknown to him: his entire production is usually sold in advance. Customers can even specify how ripe they want their cheeses to be.

The traditional production method has stood the test of time. The milk is heated in a copper kettle over a wood fire. Farmer Merlot has the knack of controlling the heat with admirable precision. The curdling of the milk and the swinging out of the kettle are also a question of instinctive feel. The curd is ladled into tin cans with holes punched in them so that the whey can run out. After about an hour the cheeses are carefully turned out, rolled in salt, and placed on a board to ripen.

Goat cheese: a farmhouse product

The manufacture of goat cheese is still largely in the hands of small workshops and farms. In France particularly, farmhouse cheeses contribute to the legendary variety of cheeses available. From the quite fresh to gutsy well-ripened varieties, goat cheese is once again in demand. This is in part because the individually produced cheeses still offer some surprises where taste is concerned. These photographs were taken on the farm of Guiseppe Merlot in a valley in southern Switzerland.

Fresh goat cheese made in Italy, with 45% FDB, is creamy with a mild aroma, lightly salted and a slightly tart taste.

Chavroux, produced in France, is a fine gel-like fresh cheese with a very mild flavor.

Los Vazquez, a Spanish fresh cheese made from goat's and cow's milk, has a relatively firm curd and a strong taste.

Lingot Blanc, made in Poitou in France, is a goat cheese with a relatively mild flavor

Limburgse Geitekaas is a fresh cheese made in Holland with 50%–60% FDB. It is seasoned with herbs.

Zick de Zwiener, a German fresh cheese with 50% FDB, has a mild but nonetheless pronounced taste.

Cabri Doux, from Burgundy, it is supple and tastes distinctly of its chive coating.

Fresh goat cheeses with herbs and spices are made in various countries. They usually contain between 45 and 50% FDB.

herbs or spices, or wrapped in vine leaves; or are mixed directly with seasonings.

Like fresh cheeses in general, fresh goat cheeses are unripened products intended for immediate consumption. A number are still considered "fresh" after a few days. In Spain generally, there is **Fresco de Cabra** and **Fresco Valenciano**. In Andalusia, there is **Cádiz** and **Málaga** (sometimes stored in oil); and in the north, **Camerano (Logroño)**, **Soria**, and **Valdeteja**. In Italy, various **Caprini** are produced in the mountainous regions of Piedmont, Formagetta in Liguria, and soft and firm Caprini on Sardinia, as well as goat's Caciotta, Caciotella, and Cacioricotta. On Corsica, there is **Broccio** and **Canestrelli**, often made from mixtures containing sheep's milk. **Brousse** is made in Provence. Other French fresh cheeses are **Jonchée Niortaise**, **Aunis** (known as **Trois cornes** or **Sableau** when triangular in shape), and **Cremet**. **Limburgse Geitekaas** is a goat cheese from the Netherlands. In the Middle East, **Labneh** is produced by draining Laban, a yogurt-like cultured sour milk.

Goat cheese is produced in many countries, but in particularly large quantities in France, all with at least 45 percent FDB and the majority with at least 40 to 45 percent dry matter. One reason for the great variety of goat cheeses in France is that different names for the same or similar cheeses are used in different areas, while the same or similar names are often given to different cheeses. Large cheeses such as **Lingot** (meaning "ingot" or "bar") were developed for the cheese counters of delicatessens. This cheese is called **Lingot Blanc** when it has a bare surface, and **Lingot Cendré** when it has been given a dusting of charcoal. (Cheese of the same name is also made from cow's milk.) **Ligueil**, with 48 percent FDB, carries the imprint "Poitouraine" on its label as a reference to the area of production. Similar large cheeses are **Soignon**, **Bûche du Poitou**, and **Géant du Poitou**, the "giant of Poitou," with a mild to slightly spicy taste, and a white surface mold or, depending on the ripening climate, also with a red surface bacteria. Cheese made in the shape of a truncated pyramid is called, simply, **Pyramide**. Without a surface coating it is called Pyramide Blanche; with a dusting of charcoal, it becomes Pyramide Cendré. Other well-known types are **Valençay** and the very similar **Levroux**. After a minimum ripening period of one week, these cheeses taste mild to distinctly goaty. The white interior is firm, but melts delicately on the tongue. **Valençay de l'Indre** has a regional quality label from the Centre Val de Loire-Berry. A red label means that the cheese was manufactured in a dairy plant or on the premises of an *affineur*; a green label with the imprint *fermier* may be borne only by farmhouse cheeses made from milk processed without the addition of frozen curd.

Crottin de Chavignol is a small, firm goat cheese from France with at least 45% FDB. Like many other young, unripened goat cheeses, it is often stored with herbs in oil. The same is true for **Geisskäse** from Austria (in the preserving jar), with different spices being added to the oil as well as herbs. In the foreground are young Crottins.

For canapés, goat cheese can be coated with herbs or spices, whose aromas spread to the relatively mild-tasting, soft curd.

Bougon, made in Poitou in France, is a soft, piquant cheese.

Valençay, named after a town in the *département* of Indre, is mild but with a pronounced goat's milk aroma.

Pouligny-Saint-Pierre, nicknamed Eiffel Tower, because of its tall shape, tastes mild to fruity.

Pavé blésois has a light covering of white mold, milk mold, and charcoal. It is soft and mild tasting.

Graçay is produced in Berry in France. Under its very firm skin, this cheese has a soft, spicy interior.

Clochette, the bell-shaped cheese, has a full-bodied goaty flavor. The mold starts off whitish, then turns bluish.

Selles-sur-Cher is handmade. Its delicate interior, under a layer of mold and charcoal, tastes agreeably mild.

Coeur de Selles, a cheese in the style of a Selles-sur-Cher, has a legally protected name of origin. It is mild and aromatic.

Crottin de Chavignol is mild and creamy as a young cheese, but dry with a strong flavor when fully ripened.

Sancerre, like Crézancy and Santranges, is a variant of Crottin de Chavignol with a distinctive taste.

La-Mothe-Saint-Héray is a bloomy white cheese with a supple interior and an increasingly spicy flavor.

Chabichou, shown here with a coating of charcoal, is sold in the traditional *bonde* shape. It has a spicy flavor.

Chabichou, shown here with increasing mold growth, has a very strong taste when ripened.

Pavé Touraine has the typical Pavé shape (*pavé* means "cobblestone"). It is similar to Pavé Blésois, but is often drier, and hence firmer, with a full-bodied taste.

Sainte-Maure has a bluish surface when made on the farm, whitish when produced in a factory. The straw lends stability to the cheese, which has a fragile curd and a very mild taste.

Bûchette d'Anjou is similar to Saint-Maure. A whitish-gray mold increasingly covers the layer of charcoal. The flavor is mild, with a pronounced goat's-milk aroma.

Goat cheese roll from Holland, which resembles a Chèvre Long from the Touraine, has a white curd with a mild but distinctive flavor, and a downy white surface mold.

Pouligny-Saint-Pierre is an AOC cheese that may be made only in the west of the *département* of Indre. In the course of the two- to four-week ripening period aroma and taste alter from mild to distinctly typical. The body is white and firm but supple. **Selles-sur-Cher**, named after a village in the *département* of Indre, is also an AOC cheese. It is 3½ inches in diameter, about 1 inch high, weighs 5 ounces, and is dusted with charcoal. After a ripening period of about ten days, whitish mold develops, which becomes bluish. The interior is soft and melts on the tongue, and the flavor is mild, growing in piquancy. Connoisseurs do not shave off the skin of this cheese, which is popular as a dessert cheese.

Coeur de Selles, also known as **Coeur de Chèvre**, is popular on account of its shape. Further variants of Selles-sur-Cher are **Pavé Blésois**, which is made in the area around Blois on the Loire, and **Pavé Touraine**, whose origin is revealed by its name. **Graçay** is shaped like a truncated cone. **Montoire**, which is rather firm but otherwise similar, is named after a goat-rearing area north of Tours. **Clochette**, from Charentes-Poitou, is, as its name indicates, a bell-shaped cheese; it weighs about 8 ounces and has a relatively firm curd. **Sainte-Maure** is named after a village south of Tours, but is made in various regions, with or without charcoal and straw. The name **Sainte-Maure de Touraine** is protected; the cheeses bear the quality label of the Centre-Val de Loire-Berry region. Here, cheeses made in dairy plants carry a red label, and traditionally made farmhouse cheeses carry a green one. Farmhouse (*fermier*) cheese is rather bluish, dairy cheese is white. The flavor of this table cheese is typical and distinctive, the interior milky and delicate. Comparable cheeses are simply called **Chèvre Long**. Similar but smaller is **Bûchette d'Anjou**.

Chabichou, or **Chabi**, is produced in various regions of France. This description may be used only for cheeses in the traditional *bonde* form, a cylinder with a maximum diameter of 2½ inches and a height of 2 to 2¾ inches. The surface mold is whitish in the case of dairy cheeses, bluish-gray in the case of farmhouse cheeses, with a light red bacteria also developing sometimes. There are many varieties of Chabi, some of them dusted with powdered charcoal.

Small round cheeses such as **Rond-de-Lusignan** and **Saint-Loup**, as well as Petit Fromage de Bique and Sauzé, come from the area between Poitou and Cognac. According to Pierre Androuët, **Mothais** is the archetypal *fromage à la feuille* (leaf-wrapped cheese) of this region. It comes from the Loire, like **Bougon** and **La-Mothe-Saint-Héray**, a small cheese with 50 percent FDB. Variants contain seasonings such as garlic. Square cheeses ripening in plane-tree or chestnut leaves, and sometimes sold as Chèvre Feuille,

In this goat-cheese curing cellar, both temperature and atmospheric humidity are controlled to promote the desired mold growth and ensure that the cheese dries to the appropriate degree.

Bûchette Sarriette is decorated with a stalk of savory, from which it gets its name. It tastes mild and aromatic.

Cabécou de Rocamadour is one of the best known of these very small chèvres, with a delicate, golden-yellow skin and sometimes a light surface mold. It has a mild, aromatic flavor.

Pélardon des Cévennes, produced in Languedoc and closely related to Cabécou, comes in many varieties. It has a mild to aromatic taste.

Picodon de la Drôme, like many Picodon cheeses, is produced in the *département* of Drôme and enjoys AOC status. Its medium-firm curd is spicy tasting.

Picodon de l'Ardèche, also known as Picodon de la Drôme, is ripened with white and bluish surface molds or milk molds, and sometimes also with red flora.

are the piquant **Ruffec**, **Couhé-Vérac**, and **Saint-Maixent** with a bluish-gray, sometimes reddish skin. **Pigouille** is spicy and without surface mold.

Various small goat cheeses are sold under the name **crottin**, mostly in combination with the place of origin. The best-known is **Crottin de Chavignol**. Its name, which enjoys AOC status, comes from a village in the *département* of Cher. The little disks are about 2 inches in diameter and about 1½ inches high, and weigh 2 to 3 ounces. Their surface is bare, yellowish to brown, and increasingly colonized with a bluish-gray mold. The cheese is often dry, and firm. Similar cheeses from the same region are **Sancerrois**, **Sancerres**, the somewhat larger **Crézancy**, and **Santranges**. In northwest Burgundy small cheeses similar to crottins, such as Dornecy, Lormes, and Vermenton, come from the area around the village of Vézelay. **Gien** ripens on sweet-chestnut leaves with a bluish mold. **Bouton de Culotte** (trouser button) is a very small cheese weighing only 1½ to 2 ounces, and is eaten at all stages of ripeness. Around Mâcon it is called **Mâconnais**, **Cabrion de Mâcon**, and **Cabrion de Beaujolais** or **Chevroton du Mâconnais**. Similar cheeses are Baratte and the firm Bressan. **Charolais**, or Charolles, little cylindrical cheeses, and **Montrachet**, which has a bluish mold, are often piquant. **Mont-d'Or de Lyon** is strong tasting, like **Rigotte de Pelussin** and **Rigotte des Alpes**. **Brique de Forez**, or Brique de Saint-Etienne, Chevroton d'Ambert, the bluish Galette de la Chaise Dieu and Chevroton de Bourbonnais (Chevroton de Moulins) are usually rectangular cheeses, but are sometimes round, like the related, fruity to piquant **Tomme de Belley** or Chevret and Chevroton des Boutières. Two varieties of **Cabécou** (colloquial for "little kid") are famous: **Cabécou d'Entraygues**, which weighs 3 to 4½ ounces and has a white, sometimes bluish surface mold; and **Cabécou de Rocamadour**. During the production of Rocamadour the coagulum is stirred to make the curds as fine as possible, salt is mixed in, and the paste-like mass is pressed lightly into the molds. The skin of the resulting cheese is yellowish or pink, or covered with a mold that is first white, later turning bluish. Similar cheeses are **Gramat** and **Mayrinhac**. When well ripened, they are called Cuffi or Truffi. A relative of Cabécou in the Languedoc is **Cajassous**. **Picadou** is a preserved cheese (**Cabécou Confit**). From the Cevennes comes **Pélardon**, a small round cheese related to Cabécou, many varieties of which are available. The mountainous countryside west and east of the Rhône between Valence and Orange is the home of **Picodon**. **Picodon de l'Ardéche** and **Picodon de la Drôme** enjoy AOC status. The little disks weigh 3 to 3½ ounces. They are worked with wine, oil or spices, preserved in wine or *marc*, and ripened under

Poivre d'Ane (donkey's pepper), is similar to Banon. It is rolled in savory and rosemary, and is aromatic.

Banon, made in Provence, is traditionally wrapped in chestnut leaves, and is often covered with savory. It is mild to spicy.

Arômes au Gène de Marc is made from a mixture of mashed, ripe goat cheeses, and then continues to ripen in *marc*.

Roves des Garrigues, from Provence, has a firm curd and a very strong but pleasant aroma.

Meusnois is from Berry. It has a semi-firm curd and tastes slightly tart and aromatic.

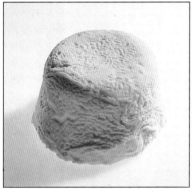

Pourly, from Burgundy, is esteemed when fresh and mild, or when ripened with a milk mold and a nutty taste.

Bouton de Culotte from Burgundy will be soft to hard, depending on age, and may become strong to piquant in taste.

Chèvreton de Mâcon, Mâconnais, a variant of Bouton de Culotte, may become firm and very sharp.

Brique de Forez or **Chèvreton d'Ambert** is strong, but when made partly with cow's milk is rather mild.

Brique de Livradois, or Briquette, is similar to Brique de Forez, but smaller, and mild to strong.

Persillé Bourguignon is dusted with charcoal and has two layers of charcoal inside. It is mild to slightly spicy.

Brin d'Amour, or Brindamour, also known as Fleur du Maquis, tastes of its coating of herbs.

Chèvre Feuille, from the Périgord, is wrapped in chestnut or plane-tree leaves. It is mild to strong.

Goat's-milk Camembert is made in various countries. Pictured above is a soft cheese from Austria with a delicate Camembert bouquet and a spicy goat's-milk taste.

Goat cheeses have a long tradition in Germany. The range of these mostly regional varieties, such as Altenburger goat cheeses from eastern Thuringia and Einetaler goat cheeses from the Unterharz, has expanded since the 1970s. In addition to fresh cheeses with or without seasoning ingredients, traditional goat cheeses such as **Inntaler Camembert** (above) continue to be produced alongside new products, such as Inntaler Ziegenrolle (goat-cheese roll) (top), which has a lactic acid–rennet curd and a Provençal-style herb coating.

Tomme de chèvre is made in the mountainous regions of Savoie up to the Provençal Alps, as well as on Corsica. The types are as varied as the geographical range: the surface of the cheeses may be bare, covered with a whitish or bluish mold or with red flora, the interior fresh or ripe, the taste mild to strong.

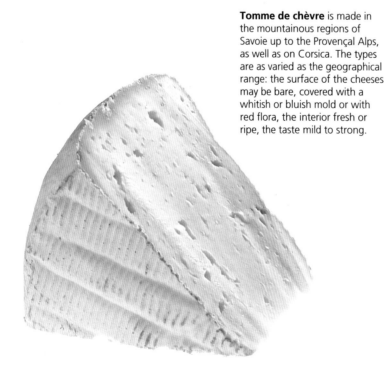

leaves. The aroma and taste become strongly pronounced as ripening progresses. Well-known varieties of this type are **Picodon de Dieulefit** and **Picodon de Valréas**, Tomme du Mont Ventoux, Cachat d'Entrechaux, Cachat de Gavoie, and Malaucène, and in the Cévennes, **Rogeret** and **Picodon des Cévennes**. In the Ardèche, fresh, white Picodons are also called **Pidances**. There, **Ardèchois** is a generic term for small cheeses. **Banon** is made from pure goat's milk, from mixtures of goat's and sheep's milk, or from cow's milk. It is sold fresh, with a bare surface or decorated with savory, or ripened and covered with a whitish or bluish mold, wrapped in chestnut leaves (Banon au Feuille), and sometimes dipped in *eau de vie* beforehand. Some of these cheeses are broken up, mixed with seasonings and ripened further to make *fromage fort*.

In the mountainous region of Nice, relatively firm cheeses are produced from goat's milk and mixtures of goat's and sheep's milk. Examples of this type include **Bairols** and **Annot**, as well as **Tomme d'Annot**, **Tomme de Val de Blore**, and **Sospel**. On Corsica, apart from **Sartène**, which is made in the south, firm cheeses from goat's or sheep's milk, or from mixtures, are produced mainly in the north, including the cube-shaped **Niolo, Ascot, Venaco** and **Calenzana**. All sorts of **Tommes de Chèvre**, of varying sizes and characteristics, are produced, in addition to cow's-milk and sheep's-milk Tommes. They are often sold under local place-names. Well-known ones are **Tomme de Drôme, Tomme de Crest, Tomme de Vercors, Tomme de Chabeuil** and **Tomme de Romans**, which are reminiscent of varieties of Saint-Marcellin.

In the mountains east of Annecy, Chambéry and Grenoble, **Chevrotin des Aravis, Chevrotin (Chevrette) des Bauges, Chevrotin de Haute-luce, Grataron d'Arèches, Tomme de Tarantaise (Praslin), Tomme de Courchevel, Tomme de Pralognans,** and **Tomme des Allues** are made like semi-hard and semi-soft cheeses with a supple consistency. They can also be labeled with the generic terms **Chevrotin des Alpes** and **Chevrotin de Montagne**. In other countries, too, a variety of cheeses are made according to ancient traditions: **Bündner Geisskäse** and **Frutigkäse** from Switzerland, **Altenburger Ziegenkäse** and **Einetaler Ziegenkäse** from Germany, **Geitekaas** from the Netherlands, **Getost** from Sweden, and **Hardanger** from Norway

Cheesemakers in the United States produce a range of goat cheeses: fresh or ripened, young or aged, spreadable or firm, plain, seasoned, or with vegetable ash. As well as cheeses in the style of Cabécou, Calistogan, and Chèvrefeuille, there are mild, creamy **Texas Chèvre, Carmel Valley Chèvre, Palin** and **Pepper Capri**, and a **Goat Monterey**.

Hardanger is a Norwegian semi-hard cheese made from 100% goat's milk and contains 45% FDB. It is compact yet supple and sliceable, the taste aromatic and slightly tangy. In Norway it is also called Rosendal.

Monte Caprino (top) is made in Switzerland from goat's and cow's milk, has 45% FDB, is covered with white mold, and has a spicy goat's-milk taste. **Ziegett** from Austria (above), made from 55% goat's milk and 45% cow's milk, has an agreeably mild flavor.

Goat's Gouda from Holland (top) is a semi-hard cheese with a very distinctive, pleasant flavor. The spicy Goat's Gouda from Germany (above) has a distinctly ripened interior beneath a firm rind.

Semi-hard goat cheeses from Spain come in many varieties, some from the islands, such as this firm Majorero from Fuerteventura in the Canaries. Often, they are made from mixtures of goat's and sheep's milk, or goat's and cow's milk. When well ripened, they have a strong, sometimes tart taste. **Queso Sierra Ibores** (top left), with a wax coating, has a firm curd and strong taste. **Queso del Casar** (top right) has a dark rind and a firm interior, and tastes strong and slightly tart. **El Risquillo** (on the platter) has a red flora covering; its supple interior tastes slightly salty.

Bauern-Handkäse has a golden-yellow surface, and, to its right, **Vienenburger Schimmelkäse** has a bloomy white skin. Both are mild to slightly spicy.

This Korbkäse with a light yellow flora is a mildly spicy to piquant breakfast cheese.

Harz cheese, shown here as a yellow cheese, is small but has a strong, full-bodied taste.

Hausmacher Bauern-Handkäse (above left), is speckled with caraway seeds, and **Korbkäse** (left), with a bloomy white skin, is sold primarily as a mild, aromatic breakfast cheese.

Gamalost, a well-known Norwegian mold-ripened cheese with a brown granular interior, is covered with the *mucor* mold. It is prized for its characteristic piquant taste.

Quargel is a yellow cheese, with a surface flora, a very firm curd, and a strong taste. It was first made in Olomouc in the Czech Republic, where it is known as Olomoucké tvarôzky. It is also made in Germany, where it is called Olmützer Quargel.

Sour-curd cheese is a term that refers to entirely different products in different countries, sometimes including even fresh cheeses. In Germany, Austria and the Czech and Slovak Republics, it is applied to cheeses that are made from sour-milk Quark. In Germany, two types are distinguished: Gelbkäse (yellow cheese) and Edelschimmelkäse (noble-mold cheese). **Harz Cheese** and **Mainz Cheese**, weighing 1 to 4 ounces, and **Olmützer Quargel**, a mere ½ ounce in weight, are "yellow cheeses," which are actually golden-yellow to reddish-brown in color, and piquant in taste. The noble-mold type is covered with the Camembert mold, and smells and tastes milder. Some cheeses exist as both yellow and noble-mold types: **Handkäse** (hand cheese, because it was originally shaped by hand), **Bauern-Handkäse** (farmer's hand cheese), **Korbkäse** (basket cheese), **Stangenkäse** (bar cheese), **Spitzkäse** (pointed cheese). Traditionally, sour-curd cheeses, which often contain caraway seeds, are low-fat cheeses; depending on their water content, they are either semi-soft or soft. During their manufacture, *metton* is first mixed with common salt and ripening salts, and after a couple of hours formed into small cheeses. These are ripened into yellow cheeses with the aid of yellow or red bacteria. To produce noble-mold cheeses, the freshly shaped cheeses are sprayed with Camembert mold. In the Alps, several types of low-fat sour-curd cheeses are made with or without mold or red bacteria. **Steirischer Graukäse** comes from the Steiermark. As with **Tiroler Graukäse**, from the Tyrol, its name reflects the color (*grau* means gray) imparted to it by the growth of the mold. **Sura-Käs**, a sour-curd cheese from Vorarlberg, is similar to Quargel. A Swiss sour-curd cheese with a long tradition is **Toggenburger Ploderkäse**. **Glarner Schabzieger**, also called **Sapsago**, is a well-known Swiss sour-curd cheese made from ripened Zieger mixed with salt and a plant known as honey lotus clover. It is sold in this form as a grating cheese, and, ground, as a condiment. A sour-curd cheese with a pungent note is **Gamalost**, or Gammelost, from Norway.

Products of an entirely different style are the Norwegian **Brunost** (brown cheese) and **Gudbransdal Gjetost**, which have 35 percent FDB. In addition, Norway produces a large number of regional Mysost types (from *myse*, meaning "whey"), which differ from one another mainly in the proportion of cow's to goat's milk whey and the amount of added cream, or which consist only of goat's milk whey with added cream, such as **Ekte Geitost** (genuine goat cheese), or of cow's milk whey only, such as **Fløtemysost**. **Prim** contains 20 percent FDB, and **Mager Mysost** (low-fat whey cheese), 10 percent FDB; both are spreadable. They are produced by evaporating the whey and,

Tiroler Graukäse has been produced since time immemorial in rural households and cheese dairies in the Tyrol. The sour-milk Quark, which is "scalded" at 140°F, is shaped and ripened for two to three weeks, both through natural mold development and through inoculation with Roquefort mold. The tart to strong cheese is enjoyed with vinegar, oil, and onions.

Steirischer Graukäse is produced in the traditional manner, from the spontaneous acidification of skim milk. The fresh cheeses are left to dry for a few days (in the past, often next to a warm oven or fire), and then, well-ripened for one month. They are enjoyed as a strong grating cheese on traditional round, flat bread or in a sandwich.

Zillertaler Zieger is a strong cooking and grating cheese made from raw milk, shaped by hand, dried, and ripened with blue-gray mold.

Gjetost, found in Norway and elsewhere mostly as Gudbrandsdal Gjetost (35% FDB), is produced from cow and goat-cheese whey through evaporation and the addition of cream. This very firm Brunost tastes sweet and like caramel, and is popular as a sandwich filling as well as for desserts, fruit salads, and in hot dishes.

Gjetost is particularly well suited to slicing or planing into thin slices.

A wide variety of processed cheeses

The variety of processed cheeses is extensive, their uses manifold. Whether plain or with seasonings, spreadable or sliceable, processed cheeses are not just a topping for bread but are also a versatile ingredient in cold and hot dishes, for party nibbles, soups, sauces, and casseroles. The creamy soft preparations containing cream, herbs, chives, pickles, peppers, salami, or ham, enjoy a particular popularity. Convenience products, such as the ever-popular cheese slices for toasting or broiling, ready-shredded and spiced processed cheese especially for pizzas, and even processed cheese pastes in plastic containers ("squeezable cheese") are common. Over half of all processed-cheese products are produced with 45% FDB; the rest are higher- and lower-fat types.

often, adding cream. The brownish hue is a result of the natural caramelization of the lactose during evaporation, which is why the cheeses taste slightly sweet and reminiscent of caramel.

From an early stage, cheese-exporting countries made great efforts to improve qualities that would prevent deterioration during shipment to distant parts, a trend that led eventually to the invention of processed cheese. The manufacture of **processed cheese** dates back to 1911, when, in Switzerland, Emmental was "melted" with citric acid salts, producing — in comparison with cheese that continued ripening — a much less perishable product. In 1916 the same result was achieved in the United States with Cheddar, which was treated with phosphoric acid salts. It now became possible to heat the broken-up cheese without the protein becoming rubbery and the fat separating out; with the new process, the protein could be distributed quite finely and fat and water could be emulsified by stirring. In the 1920s the process spread rapidly to other countries, and a varied range of processed-cheese products developed in just a few decades, each country determining its own composition and methods of manufacture. The quality of such products depends on carefully selecting cheeses according to quality and degree of ripeness, aroma, and taste. The cheeses are first broken up and milled or shredded, then mixed with approximately 2 to 3 percent emulsifying salts and other ingredients, including cream, butter, and whey powder as well as seasoning ingredients and, according to the desired firmness, with water. The ingredients are heated while being stirred, and produce a liquid to paste-like, fine curd, which is drawn off while still hot and then cooled. The varieties marketed in different countries vary according to local eating habits. In Switzerland, for example, products made from firm cheeses, such as Emmental, dominate; in the United States, it is products from Cheddar and related types, like Colby; and in other countries, softer varieties. Processed-cheese slices, which are particularly popular for melting or broiling, are now available just about everywhere, not least of all because of the spread of fast-food restaurants.

Cheese food and other pasteurized processed cheese products come in jars, cartons, tubes, and cans, and contain a smaller percentage of cheese than that in cheese slices. In imitation cheese the milk fat has been replaced by non-milk fat, while substitute cheese is made with vegetable oil and milk or soy protein. These foods may meet the requirements of people on various special diets. In addition, because both imitation and substitute cheeses have a long shelf life and require minimal refrigeration, they are useful in poor, hot countries.

Smoked cheeses are processed cheeses or processed-cheese preparations that, in addition, undergo a smoking process. The brownish-red skin contains a firm interior with a spicy smoked taste. The cheeses in the photo above have been carefully smoked: in many countries, including the United States, it is permissible to produce "smoked" products by using smoke flavoring.

Fjäll Brynt, from Sweden, is a delicate, creamy processed product with a slightly sweetish taste.

Processed cheese from blue-veined cheese is yet another addition to the already varied range of spreadable cheese products. The photo shows a spicy spread made with Roquefort that has a very delicate "melt." This is an indication of the versatility of such products, which can also be used in a multiplicity of ways in cooked dishes.

Kochkäse is a German cheese food produced by melting sour-milk Quark or rennet Quark and adding salt, caraway, sometimes a bit of emulsifying salt, and then adjusting the fat and dry matter content with cream, butter, butterfat, water or skim milk. The spicy paste is spreadable to a greater or lesser extent, depending on the fat level (10%-60% FDB).

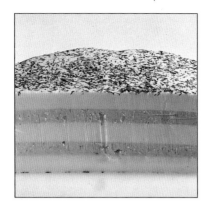

A colorful palette

There is a lot more to processed and prepared cheese than the familiar wedges and slices, as this selection shows. There are simple cheese loafs mixed and coated with a variety of nuts, fruits, or other seasonings. Imaginative compositions include fresh cheese with layers of smoked salmon pâté and toppings of herbs or spices, and Mascarpone layered with Gorgonzola. There are also cold-packed foods made by crushing together cheeses and seasonings without heat treatment or ripening. Asadero, produced in California, is a blend of semi-skim milk cheeses, which is often used for pizzas and nachos. A cheese of the same name is made as a *filata* cheese in Mexico, where it is also called Oaxaca. Other cheeses, known as *fromages forts* in France, are made from mixed fresh or ripe cheese blended with herbs and spices, then macerated in wine or spirits, shaped into balls, and then often ripened further. Entirely different again are cheese preparations incorporating smoked ham or mushrooms; and preparations such as dressed Liptauer, which used to be made from sheep's-milk, and now is made from Quark mixed with cream, butter, onions, and paprika, a product intended for immediate consumption.

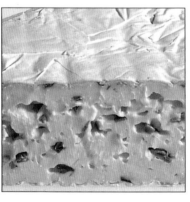

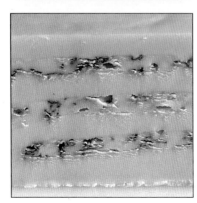

Larzac is a cheese preparation made from a blue cheese and Caillé, a fresh cheese similar to Quark.

Layered cheeses come in a wide variety. When prepared with fresh cheese, as here, they should be eaten fresh. Top: A composition made from sliceable cheese with Mascarpone and walnut pieces. Above: Torta Crema made from butterfat-rich Mascarpone, with layers of Gorgonzola.

Boules and Boulettes are popular shapes for cheese preparations in France. Top: Boule de Périgord is made from goat cheese and herbs. Centre: Boule des Moines, is a cheese mixture flavored with herbs. Above: Boulette d'Avesnes, broken-up cheese, mixed and colored with tarragon, pepper and parsley.

The Liptauer in the bowl is prepared from Quark, cream, butter, and paprika. Obatzter is the name of the preparation on the cheeseboard. It is traditionally eaten with beer in Germany and Austria. To make it, ripe Camembert is mixed with onions and paprika, and often pepper as well.

Cold-pack cheese food in the shape of logs or little balls, with sweet or spicy coatings, is popular.

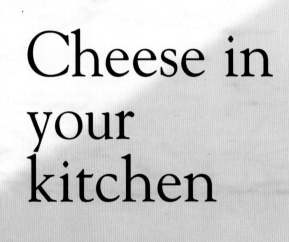

Cheese in your kitchen

Cheese fulfills two essential culinary functions: first, as a food that can be enjoyed plain, without further processing or refining; secondly, as a basic ingredient in many cold and hot dishes. But cheese is also a living, natural product, which is subject to constant changes, and reacts highly sensitively to the different influences to which it is exposed. Be sure to look closely when you are buying cheese, which is both a luxury item and a staple, paying particular attention to quality. Anyone who buys cheese in relatively large quantities should know how it must be handled during storage for it to continue to ripen optimally. Cutting and grating are fundamental steps when preparing cheese in the kitchen. Here, it is important to present cheese at its ideal degree of ripeness and as appetizingly as possible, keeping the loss from slicing to a minimum.

Buying and storing cheese

Buying cheese is a matter of trust. While this obviously also applies to the purchase of other foods, it is especially true for cheese, and this is equally important whether you are an individual buying your modest requirements at a local store, or a major consumer buying from a cheese wholesaler. In both cases, you should be able to rely on the expert, who, as a specialist in the field, knows and takes care of his or her stock, and stores it under ideal conditions. Of course there are several important criteria — for example, degree of ripeness, quality of the body, a pure aroma, and a well-care-for rind — that you could check for yourself. The truth is, however, that nowadays consumers are largely unable to carry out checks of this kind, at least at the cheese counters in large stores and supermarkets. This makes informed advice all the more important. You should be able to expect a good cheese seller to be capable of judging the constantly changing natural product that is cheese at each stage of ripeness.

Cheese is a natural product that continues to ripen from the day of its manufacture to the moment it is consumed. Temperature is important during storage: too much warmth and the cheese ripens too quickly, while severe cold can make it bitter — and for this reason cheese should be frozen

A specialist store where you can get advice: At Paxton & Whitfield's in London an excellent selection and good service go hand in hand. The focus in this store is on traditional English cheeses.

Packaged soft cheeses can be tested by thumb pressure. Younger cheeses feel firm, riper ones are more yielding.

The modern cheese counter in large stores or supermarkets guarantees a fresh, wide selection. The cheese connoisseur can happily buy here when in search of common cheeses or regional specialties. The advice you are likely to receive, however, seldom does justice to the wide variety of cheeses available. If in doubt, sampling the wares is the best decision-making aid.

Regional markets sell mainly locally produced cheeses. At this market in Palermo, Sicilian cheeses such as Pecorino, Ragusano, and Ricotta Salata naturally dominate, and they are available at all stages of ripeness. Parmesan is an obvious concession to changing demand.

only in exceptional circumstances. Temperatures of about 54°F for short-term storage and 39 to 42°F for longer storage are essential. A dark, cool, well-ventilated cellar or pantry is ideal; if you store cheese in the refrigerator, be sure to keep it in the specially designated section or in the vegetable compartment. It must be protected during storage so that it does not dry out, but at the same time is able to breathe. You can place hard cheeses that have been cut off a larger piece in a stoneware pot with some salt, and cover them with a cloth dipped in wine or salt water and wrung out; alternatively, wrap the pieces in perforated foil or plastic wrap. Protect semi-hard cheese similarly with foil, plastic wrap, or a damp cloth. Wrap cheeses that have an interior mold in aluminum foil. Wrap soft cheeses in parchment paper or a damp cloth, and store them in the refrigerator; refrigerate fresh and processed cheeses. It is important to check the cheese regularly during storage.

Keeping the temperature and humidity constant is important: about 41°F and 80–90% relative humidity are ideal.

A cheese storage area in a restaurant or shop requires great attention: the relative humidity and temperature must be just right. Every cheese that has already been cut must be individually wrapped, and it is important to know how to store different, unpackaged cheeses: huge Emmental wheels, for example, must never be stacked, while the smaller Gouda wheels can be placed on top of another.

Storing cut cheeses means protecting the cut surfaces from drying out by wrapping the cheese while at the same time letting it breathe. Damp cloths are a tried and true solution, but must be moistened at least once a day. Clear plastic wrap is probably the best modern alternative. Aluminum foil may also be used, but must be perforated at close intervals.

A cheese bell is suitable for short-term storage only. The glass bell should not create an airtight seal, since the cheese needs to breathe.

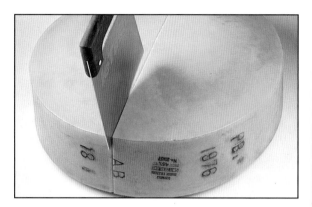

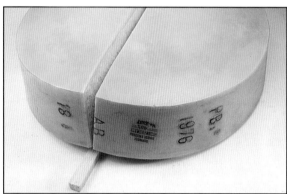

Splitting open extra-hard cheeses is a tradition. This is demonstrated in the photo using a Sbrinz: The wheel is cut into with a knife (here, a cheese spade) about ½–¾ inch deep all the way around. It is then placed with the cut on a strip of wood and both sides are pressed down. In this way, the cheese breaks in the desired place. In practice, however, "extra-hards" are also cut with modern implements, since smoothly cut surfaces can be more easily protected with foil or plastic wrap.

A typical Parmesan knife is used to carve into and then break even the large Grana drums.

Hard-cheese knives such as these are used to break off small pieces from extra-hard grating cheeses that are too hard to slice.

Grated, it becomes a condiment

Cheese lends a fine flavor to many dishes. The convenience of using packed grated or shredded cheese is at the expense of taste. The quality of the cheese cannot be checked, and shredded or grated cheese soon loses its flavor and aroma. For this reason, always buy cheese by the piece and freshly grate or shred it as needed. There are various devices available to help make this job easy. Simple hand graters (top of photo) perform well as long as they remain sharp, but are suitable only for small quantities. The wooden grater (center right) is ideal for grinding even fairly large amounts of extra-hard cheese. A cylinder finely grinds the cheese into granules, which are caught in a drawer below. Drum graters (far right) have different attachments, making it possible to produce both fine and more coarsely shredded cheese. It is important for the device to fit the hand comfortably.

Graters with jagged, star-shaped holes are well suited to grating low-fat hard cheeses such as Parmesan, yielding fine-grained granules.

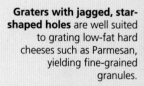
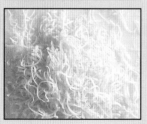

Small straight holes produce thin curls of cheese. This grater can also be used for softer cheeses.

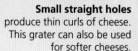

Large holes produce similarly large strips of cheese. This grater makes quick work of shredding semi-soft cheeses.

Semi-hard cheese wheels are cut into wedges of the desired size with a cheese spade.

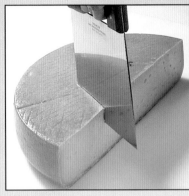

1 Cutting a cheese wheel. Halve the cheese with the wire and lightly score a trapezoid on the rind in the center.

Tilsit and other semi-hard loaf-shaped cheeses are cut into slices with a two-handled knife.

Maximum use and minimum waste is the watchword when dividing up cheeses, both in the store and in the professional kitchen.

Hard and semi-hard cheeses can be cut relatively easily with a wire. The rind is cut with a knife only at the edge, so that the wire can be placed in position easily.

2 Score a similar shaped piece at each end.

A wire slicer makes it possible to cut slices of even thickness from a piece of cheese.

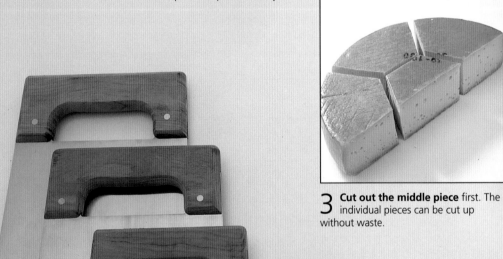

3 Cut out the middle piece first. The individual pieces can be cut up without waste.

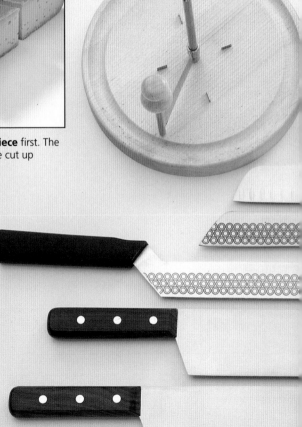

1 **Square semi-hard cheeses,** like this Steppe cheese, are best cut in half with a double-handled knife, but a wire is also a suitable tool.

1 **Smaller wheels,** with a maximum diameter of 12 inches, can be neatly halved with little physical effort using a double-handled knife.

2 **Continue to slice** the cheese halves into portions, for example into quarters, pieces or thick slices, using a single- or double-handled knife.

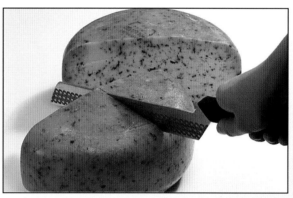

2 **The halved cheese wheel** can be cut into wedges with a single-handled knife, or divided up according to the waste-free method illustrated on page 118.

Loaf- and brick-shaped cheeses can be sliced one-handed without difficulty; however, a short double-handled knife makes the job easier and more precise.

Cutting with a system

All firmer cheese types can be cut up quite well using the illustrated cutting tools; however, quite specific tools have proved their worth in the case of particular sorts of cheese. In addition, there are traditional regional methods for cutting or breaking open cheeses, as is the case for the decorative breaking of Asiago and Montasio in northern Italy. Emmental and related cheeses in particular are divided up with the use of a cheese spade, although this tool does not allow one to slice smoothly through the entire wheel. A wire (left), which produces a clean, smooth cut surface when drawn through the cheese in one movement, is used for this. The *girolle* (far left) is a special cutting device for Tête de Moine: The cheese is placed on the metal rod attached to the wooden base; the blade is then place on top of the rod and drawn over the cheese in a circular motion, shaving off curls. The single-handled knife with depressions along the blade (top left) is suitable for the softer types of semi-soft cheese. The engraving on the two knives shown below it stops the cheese from sticking after the cut is made. Double-handled knives are used to cut firmer cheeses evenly into relatively thin slices.

1 **Cylindrical blue cheeses,** such as Blue Bayou, are cut into slices with a lyre-shaped wire.

1 **Using the wire,** cut the halved cheese in half horizontally. Lift it slightly, so that it is cut through completely.

With veined cheeses, nicking the surface mold with a knife before slicing makes the job easier.

2 **A lyre-shaped wire** does not cut the cheese all the way through. Roll the cylinder to separate the slice completely.

2 **Now, cut wedges** from the halved cheese.

Using a wire slicer, it is easy to cut blue-veined cheese into little cubes.

Large cylinders that must be divided without a guide should be cut through in a single stroke, otherwise the slices will be wavy.

This cutting device is the ideal aid. The guide for the wire creates an even cut. The slit in the marble base allows the cheese to be cut through completely.

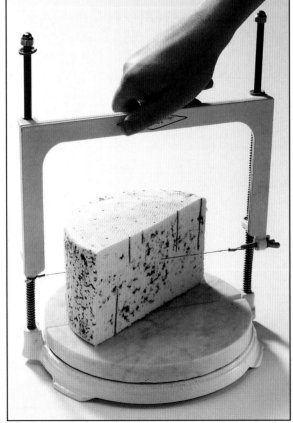

Slices and wedges can be cut effortlessly with this device. The taut wire and firm frame allow even thin slices to be cut.

Cutting blue-veined cheeses

The sliceability of cheeses with an interior mold varies greatly. It is almost impossible to cut thin slices from a Roquefort, with its rather flaky interior, while this is not a problem for smooth-textured blue-veined cheeses. The degree of ripeness also has a significant impact; the riper and softer the cheese, the more difficult it is to cut. Temperature is another important factor regardless of the type of cheese and its degree of ripeness. Cheeses stored at too warm a temperature become soft and smeary, and the pieces stick together after being cut with a wire. Cheeses can be sliced more easily when they are cool, so in stores and supermarkets they should be placed in as cool a spot as possible in the cheese display case. If you use a knife for cutting (preferably one meant specifically for soft cheese), dip it in hot water as often as possible, since the fat in the cheese will melt easily from the heat of the blade. The ideal tool, however, is the wire, although it is very difficult to cut exactly vertically through large cheeses unless the wire is attached to a stationary device. The cheese must be cut through in a single stroke, otherwise ridges are unavoidable.

Soft cheese can be temperamental

Depending on type and degree of ripeness, soft cheeses can range from firm to runny. Before cutting into a soft cheese press down with your thumb to check just how ripe it is; you can prevent fully ripe cheeses from running by laying a narrow strip of wood on the cut surface. It is also important to check the surface; a smeary mold should always be partially scraped off before the cheese is cut so that it is not transferred to the inside.

Special soft-cheese knives make expert cutting possible. The handle is higher than the blade, so the cheese can be cut through completely. Short blades are etched and have a very narrow blunt edge, so that the cheese does not stick to them. The blades are perforated or extremely narrow, and very sharp. Such knives cut through soft cheeses effortlessly, without the cheese sticking together again immediately. Wire is also a useful aid for dividing up soft cheeses.

At cheese counters there should always be several lyre-shaped cheese wires, or bows, and soft-cheese knives for the different types of cheese to prevent the unwanted transfer of flavors.

Brie is traditionally cut into wedges. A good soft-cheese knife is especially important when the cheese is nice and ripe.

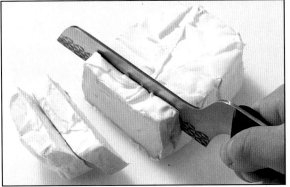

Oval soft cheeses are best divided into slices. The thickness of the slices depends on the cheese, but they should not be thinner than ½ inch.

Pyramid- or cone-shaped cheeses, like this goat cheese, are quartered with the wire and then, if need be, divided into triangular portions.

For Camembert, an extremely narrow knife sharpened into the shape of a wedge is an ideal cutting aid for both young and ripe cheeses.

The soft-cheese knife is also ideal for cutting cheese preparations, such as this mixture of processed and natural cheeses.

Loaf-shaped cheeses with a red surface bacteria can be cut into slices effortlessly with a soft-cheese knife or a wire.

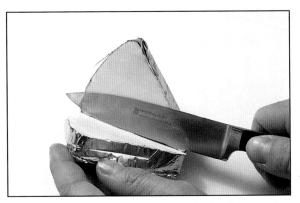

Cut through processed-cheese wedges in their foil wrapping, stopping short of the edge. For further storage, simply wrap the foil around the cheese again.

Cold
cheese
dishes

Good-quality cheese needs no enhancement, but a special occasion may require a special presentation, not only on visual, but also on practical grounds. At a stand-up reception, for example, it makes sense to offer around tidbits that people can eat without having to put down their glass. The composition and presentation of cheese platters must do justice to the occasion: cheese for breakfast, after a meal, or as a between-meal snack will be combined with different ingredients. Cheese should always be served in a manner that does not impair its quality, for example, by letting it dry out.

All recipes serve 4 unless otherwise indicated.

Greyerzer paprika hearts. The hearts are stamped out from ½-inch-thick slices of Greyerzer, and their top surfaces pressed in sweet paprika.

Cheddar and pickled chile peppers go well together. The cheese takes on the heat of the pickled pepper.

Saint-Paulin and pineapple are complementary tastes. Cheeses of this type are also highly compatible with all piquant, sharp ingredients.

Bergkäse with grapes. Similar types of cheese, such as Comté or Gruyère, are also ideally complemented by tart fruit.

Semi-hard herb cheese is even tastier with freshly chopped herbs. Pickled vegetables, such as cocktail onions, are a nice touch.

Tilsit and Roquefort, a highly harmonious combination. Place a ¼-inch-thick slice of Roquefort between two ¼-inch-thick slices of Tilsit, and cut the whole into small squares.

Cheddar and Fontina. Cut a ¼-inch-thick slice from each cheese, place one on top of the other, then cut into ¾-inch squares. The cubes can be decorated with piquant ingredients. Other highly recommended double acts: young Gouda with semi-hard goat cheese or Roquefort with Port-Salut or a similar, mild semi-soft cheese.

Medium-aged Gouda cubes can be rolled in sweet paprika. Kashkaval is also well-suited to this treatment.

Mycella cubes. The milder blue-veined cheeses combine well with fresh fruits such as grapes and kiwis.

Just a bite

The ever-popular cheese canapé should be just big enough to pop in the mouth all at once. With a good selection of cheeses, garnishes are actually superfluous, but sweet or savory decorations can yield some interesting taste combinations. The shapes of these cheese morsels should be kept simple, so that there is no waste when cutting them into portions. On the other hand, there is almost always a use for any leftovers in creams, sauces, and gratins.

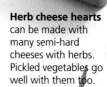

Emmental has a nutty flavor, so it also tastes particularly good with walnuts.

Herb cheese hearts can be made with many semi-hard cheeses with herbs. Pickled vegetables go well with them too.

Good English Cheddar tastes best plain when accompanied by a Martini. If you must garnish, then go for the classic olive.

Mild blue-veined cheeses, such as Gorgonzola Dolce and Montagnolo, are excellent with Italian *mostarda* and maraschino cherries.

German Blue with Cheddar. Press ¼-inch-thick slices of both cheeses together, and stamp out round portions.

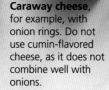

Caraway cheese, for example, with onion rings. Do not use cumin-flavored cheese, as it does not combine well with onions.

Smoked cheese with prosciutto, a very good, combination, but only if air-cured ham is used, as the smoky flavor would be too strong with a smoked ham.

Round Camembert and Brie should be served only in wedges. Cut oval-shaped Camembert into slices at least ½ inch thick. Your guests can cut off the rind themselves on their own plates.

Large pieces of cheese, such as Gouda, Gruyère, and Emmental, should be easy to slice on the cheese board, so cut off the rind or remove the wax coating beforehand. Cylindrical cheeses, such as the Cheddar at the back, can be cut either in thick slices or wedges.

Firm, cylindrical blue-veined cheeses are cut into wedges; bar- or loaf-shaped ones are cut into thick slices.

A selection of cheeses in chunks and slices

Whenever cheese is offered plain, whether as a cheese platter, cheese buffet, cheese board, or on a cheese cart in a restaurant, the question of how to serve it arises. Should it be in whole pieces, or in easy-to-eat slices or small cubes? As a matter of principle, it should be served so that as little quality as possible is sacrificed. If cheese that has been prepared has to be left out unprotected for any length of time, the pieces should be as large as possible, so that they do not dry out so quickly. In addition, the cheese should remain covered with plastic wrap for as long as possible.

Cheese should be served cut into slices only when your guests are to help themselves. Cheese that is laid out already sliced stays fresh for several hours if the slices are arranged overlapping on a platter, and protected by plastic wrap for as long as possible.

Keeping slices or pieces of cut cheeses as fresh as possible is not all that easy, as the cut surfaces dry out rather quickly. The only solution is to cover the cheese with a slightly damp cloth or with plastic wrap. A damp cloth has the drawback of often leaving marks on the cut surfaces, and it is not very attractive. Plastic wrap, on the other hand, protects carefully arranged and decorated platters when it is placed loosely over the top. For an airtight seal, however, it must be pressed firmly under the edges of the platter.

Foil-ripened cheeses, such as Esrom and Tilsit, have no rind, and, apart from peeling off the foil, require no preparation. **Goat cheeses,** such as this Saint-Maure and Chabichou, should be cut into thick slices. **Extra-hard cheeses** crumble into little chunks when sliced, and are eaten like that.

Arrange rustic cheese buffets with cheese in pieces as large as possible (as above). The proper cutting tools are essential for this.

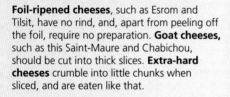

A selection of larger pieces is also a good choice for buffets since they do not dry out so quickly. Arrange the cheese on a platter, decorate with savory garnishes, and cover with plastic wrap until serving. Remember to put out the appropriate cheese knives.

Mild cheeses offer a great variety. Such different-tasting cheeses as Saint-Paulin, Emmental, Gorgonzola Dolce, fresh goat cheese, mild Brie, and young Bergkäse go very well with fruit and nuts, a combination suitable for any meal of the day.

Filled with fresh cheese

Fresh cheese tastes refreshing and goes superbly
with other ingredients. When it is combined with
pastry, it should be eaten as soon as possible after it
is made, because its high moisture content quickly
softens crisp choux or puff-pastry shells. Fresh-
cheese canapés should therefore always be
assembled at the last moment, although the pastry
and filling can easily be prepared in advance and
kept separate. Here is the basic recipe:

FRESH-CHEESE CREAM

Makes about 1½ lb
1¼ lb fresh cream cheese, ¼ cup heavy cream
½ teaspoon salt, freshly ground pepper

Using a whisk or hand-held mixer, blend the
ingredients until frothy. Add more cream if
necessary to make the mixture of piping consistency.

FILLED CHOUX PASTRY RINGS

Makes 30
30 choux pastry rings (see page 224)
3 tablespoons fresh chopped herbs (parsley, chives, and dill, plus lovage if available)
½ garlic clove, crushed

Prepare a fresh-cheese cream according to the basic
recipe. Set aside half of the mixture, stirring the herbs
and garlic into the remainder. Halve the choux pastry
rings widthwise with a sharp knife. Spoon each of the
creams into a pastry bag, pipe them onto the bottom
half of the rings, and top with the other half.

COLORFUL CHEESE SLICES

Makes 24
12 oz fresh cream cheese, 7 tablespoons butter, ¼ cup cream
¾ teaspoon salt, freshly ground pepper
3 heaping tablespoons fresh chopped herbs
a pinch of garlic powder
1 tablespoon tomato paste, 1 teaspoon sweet paprika
12 slices German black bread or pumpernickel

Work the fresh cheese, butter, cream, ½ teaspoon
salt, and pepper into a cream, and divide into three.
Stir the herbs and garlic powder into one-third of the
mixture, and the tomato paste, paprika, remaining
salt, and pepper into another third. Spread three
slices of bread each with a different cheese cream,
stack one on top of the other, and top with a fourth
slice. Repeat with the remaining slices of bread.
Weigh the sandwiches down with a chopping board
and chill in the refrigerator until firm. Cut each into
8 pieces.

Crackers. Season the fresh-cheese cream with a little crushed garlic, then pipe onto crackers. Sift some sweet paprika onto half of the crackers and top with small squares of blue cheese. Garnish the remaining crackers with chopped green peppercorns and rosettes cut from Edam slices.

Stuffed dates. Halve fresh or dried dates lengthwise, remove the pits, and spread open for ease of filling. Season the fresh-cheese cream with cayenne pepper, spoon into a pastry bag with a star-shaped tip, and pipe the mixture between the date halves. Garnish with chopped walnuts.

Filled puff-pastry pillows. Cut the puff pastry into rectangles, brush with egg yolk, and sprinkle alternately with poppyseeds, white sesame seeds, and black sesame seeds, then bake. Allow the puff pastry to cool, then cut off lids, pipe the fresh-cheese cream onto the bottom half and top with the lids.

Cheese canapés with fruit. Cut Gruyère or Comté into slices about ¼ inch thick, and stamp or cut out into shapes of your choice. Pipe a rosette of fresh-cheese cream onto each shape and garnish with fresh fruit. Both exotic and local fruits combine well with the cheese.

PUFF-PASTRY CONES. Preheat the oven to 400°F. Roll out puff pastry about ¹⁄₁₆ inch thick and cut into strips ¾ x 12 inches. Brush with egg yolk, taking care not to let it run over the cut edges, and wrap around the cone shapes. Sprinkle with caraway seeds and coarse salt and bake for 15 minutes until golden brown.

Stuffed tomatoes. Slice a tiny lid from yellow and red cherry tomatoes and partially hollow them out. Place a dab of Dijon mustard in each, and pipe a rosette of fresh-cheese cream on the top. Garnish the tomatoes with pieces of olive and chopped green peppercorns.

Cheese-cream horns. Make puff-pastry cones as described to the right. Place 1 teaspoon chopped pickled peppers inside each cone. Spoon the fresh-cheese cream into a pastry bag with a small round tip and pipe into the puff-pastry cones. Garnish with diamond-shaped pieces of pepper.

HERBED ROQUEFORT CREAM

5 oz each Roquefort and Camembert (rind removed)

5 tablespoons softened butter, 1 egg yolk

salt and freshly ground pepper

1 tablespoon finely chopped onion

½ garlic clove, crushed

2 tablespoons fresh chopped herbs (parsley, thyme, basil, dill)

⅓ cup heavy cream

Press the Roquefort and Camembert through a strainer and beat with the butter, egg yolk, and seasonings until light. Mix in the herbs and cream. This cheese cream goes nicely with white bread, puff pastry, and savory shortcrust creations.

GORGONZOLA CREAM

4 oz Gorgonzola (dolcelatte)

¼ cup low-fat Quark or Ricotta

½ cup grated Grana Padano or Parmigiano Reggiano

½ garlic clove, crushed

salt, 1 teaspoon chopped green peppercorns

¼ cup heavy cream, stiffly whipped

Mix the Gorgonzola with the Quark, mashing with a fork rather than stirring until creamy. Stir in the Grana Padano, the seasonings, and the cream. This cheese cream tastes especially good spread on toasted white bread, or as a filling for puff or choux pastry.

Cheese creams

Delicate combinations can be dreamt up with leftover bits of cheese, as the recipes on these two pages show. Not only can the cheese creams be used as a spread for bread, they are also a wonderful filling for eclairs or little cream puffs, for puff-pastry bouchées, and shortcrust pastries such as little boats or tartlets.

HORSERADISH CREAM

4 oz fresh cream cheese
¾ cup each grated Greyerzer and Sbrinz,
or Gruyère and Emmental
salt, pepper, nutmeg, ½ clove crushed garlic
1 tablespoon freshly grated horseradish
½ cup heavy cream, stiffly whipped
2 teaspoons sweet paprika

Beat the fresh cheese until fluffy. Mix in the grated Greyerzer and Sbrinz, the seasonings, and the horseradish, grated as fine as possible. Fold in the cream. This cheese cream should be airy and light. It can be combined both with hearty black bread and with delicate choux or puff pastry. The paprika rounds out the taste.

SAPSAGO CREAM

4 oz Sapsago
½ cup drained low-fat Quark or Ricotta
a pinch of salt, freshly ground pepper
½ cup mayonnaise
2 tablespoon freshly snipped chives

Finely grate the Sapsago and mix with the Quark and seasonings until smooth. Stir in the mayonnaise, followed by the chives. This cream is ideal spread on dark rye bread, as well as used as a filling for little cream puffs.

FROMAGE ROYAL, a spicy cream made from three different cheeses, is highly versatile, ideal spread on bread as well as used as a delicate filling for puff, shortcrust, and choux pastries. Stir together 7 oz Bleu de Bresse or Cambozola, 4 oz fresh cream cheese, 7 oz grated Gruyère, and 1 egg yolk until creamy. Season to taste with salt and pepper, then fold in ¼ cup heavy cream and 1 tablespoon chopped parsley. If wished, the cream can be made spicier with chopped chile peppers or cayenne pepper.

Petit fours and canapés

Little hors d'oeuvre with cheese for the demanding palate can make an unforgettable cold platter. These canapés should, of course, be attractive to look at, but you must also be careful that all the ingredients harmonize in terms of taste.

PETITS FOURS

These lend themselves to especially interesting and delicate fillings. The shortcrust pastry shells are baked blind, and are therefore ideally suited to being made in advance, to be filled with the cheese creams of your choice. To make the "daisies," fill a parchment-paper pastry bag with choux dough, pipe decorative flowers onto a lightly greased and floured baking sheet, then bake.

For the shortcrust pastry:
2 cups all-purpose flour
½ cup butter, cut into large cubes
1 egg yolk
a pinch of salt, 1–2 tablespoons water

Prepare shortcrust pastry according to the basic recipe on page 213, chill, and roll out. Stamp out little shapes and bake blind.

For the strong cheese filling:
4 oz each Stilton and ripe Camembert
¼ cup low-fat Quark or Ricotta and 2 oz Cheddar
2 oz prosciutto, 1 tablespoon finely chopped onion
½ clove garlic, crushed
½ teaspoon Dijon-type mustard
salt and pepper
1 tablespoon fresh chopped herbs (parsley, basil, thyme, and sage, plus lovage if available)
For the fresh cheese filling:
7 oz fresh cream cheese
1 teaspoon lemon juice, 1 tablespoon sour cream
salt, pepper, sugar

Petits fours with various fillings (from top to bottom):
Pipe the fresh-cheese cream into pastry boats, dust with paprika and garnish with cocktail onions.
Put a bit of anchovy and a piece of pepper in the tartlets, then top with the strong cheese filling. Garnish with a choux-pastry daisy, fresh-cheese cream and a piece of red pepper.
Sift some curry powder onto the strong cheese filling and garnish with a slice of olive.
Fill pastry boats with pieces of smoked salmon and capers, and pipe fresh-cheese cream on top. Garnish with a choux-pastry daisy and pieces of olive.
Sprinkle chopped herbs over the strong cheese filling and garnish with pickled chile peppers.
Fill tartlets with the fresh-cheese cream and garnish with choux pastry decorations and caviar.
Fill the square tartlets with the strong cheese filling and top with olives.

To make the strong cheese filling, cut the rind from the Camembert, and beat with the Stilton and the Quark until fluffy. Cut the Cheddar and the prosciutto into small cubes and stir into the cheese mixture with the onion. Next, stir in all of the seasonings and herbs. Chill the cheese filling thoroughly before using to fill the prebaked shortcrust pastry shells. To make the fresh cheese filling, stir together all the ingredients and season. The text to the left describes how to fill the petits fours with the two cheese creams. You can add different ingredients to alter the appearance and taste.

Havarti with sprats and scrambled egg. Thinly butter slices of white bread, sprinkle with freshly ground pepper, and top each with a lettuce leaf. Place a slice of Havarti or Tilsit on top, then a smoked sprat and a spoonful of scrambled egg. Sprinkle with snipped chives.

Goat cheese and fruit. Butter slices of bread, top with some frisée and drizzle over a dressing made of oil, lemon juice, salt, and a bit of sugar. Top with a slice of fresh goat cheese, Valençay for example, and decorate with fresh fruit such as kiwi, chunks of mango, and a raspberry.

French bread (a baguette) is the ideal size for small canapés, but other, heartier types of bread, such as coarse whole-wheat bread, can also be used, provided that they harmonize with the topping. Cut them to an appropriate size and shape before using. The bread can always be toasted beforehand, so it will stay crunchy longer.

Sheep's-milk cheese with herbs on tomatoes. Marinate tomato slices in olive oil, salt, and pepper for 30 minutes. Crumble the cheese, season with salt, and mix with chopped herbs (parsley, thyme, basil) and diced pepper. Drizzle over some olive oil and a dash of Cognac. Serve with the tomato and basil on buttered slices of bread.

Cheddar and roast beef. Toast slices of bread on one side and spread with creamed horseradish. Top with lettuce leaves and drizzle over some vinaigrette. Top with a slice of Cheddar. Spread the roast beef slices thinly with creamed horseradish, roll up and place on top of the cheese with a spoonful of cranberry dressing.

Sautéed shrimps on Steppe cheese. Mix together some butter and a little sweet paprika, and spread on slices of bread. Top with a leaf of iceberg lettuce and a slice of Steppe cheese. Sauté the shelled shrimp briefly in butter, and place on top of the canapés with a rosette of stirred fresh cheese. Garnish with black olives and a sprig of dill.

Prosciutto, Stilton, and melon. Grind some pepper over lightly buttered slices of bread and top with a thick slice of Stilton. Fold thin slices of prosciutto and place over the cheese. With a melon baller, cut balls or olive shapes from the melon, marinate briefly in vinaigrette, and place on top of the canapés. Garnish with lemon balm.

ROQUEFORT BALLS

Makes about 20

7 tablespoons butter, 7 oz Roquefort

a pinch each of salt and pepper

1 teaspoon chopped capers

4 oz Fontina

2–3 slices of German black bread, grated to make crumbs

4 tablespoons chopped parsley

Mash the butter and the Roquefort with a fork. Add the salt, pepper, and capers. Cut the Fontina into 20 pieces as close to the same size as possible, and coat each with the Roquefort cream. Roll one half of the cheese balls in the bread crumbs, the other half in the parsley. Refrigerate until firm. Makes about 20 balls.

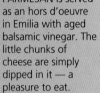

PARMESAN is served as an hors d'oeuvre in Emilia with aged balsamic vinegar. The little chunks of cheese are simply dipped in it — a pleasure to eat.

PIQUANT PISTACHIO BALLS

Makes 30–35

¼ cup butter, 1 cup grated medium-aged Gouda,

5½ oz mild blue-veined cheese

½ garlic clove, crushed; salt and pepper

4 oz prosciutto, in small dice; ⅔ cup chopped pistachios

Beat the butter with the Gouda, the blue-veined cheese, and the seasonings until fluffy, then stir in the prosciutto. Form the mixture into 30–35 balls and roll

Stilton is one of England's most important contributions to fine food. Today, genuine Stilton still comes exclusively from Leicestershire, where its rise to national fame began as far back as 1730. According to the experts, it is only there that the cows can graze on the special grass that imparts the unmistakable taste to their milk. Stilton ripens from the inside outwards, which gives it its characteristic gray, wrinkled rind. The cheeses are ripened in cool, moist cellars for at least six months. The spicy, sharp blue-veined cheese can be eaten in different ways. Traditionalists cling to the notion that Stilton should be eaten plain, as a dessert with port. Less purist cheese-lovers soak Stilton in port, sherry, or Madeira (as in the photo above), and leave the cheese to rest for a month. To do this, they cut off the upper third or quarter of the cheese, and cut out a cylinder 2–3-inches deep from the lower portion. They pour the wine into this well and replace the cut-off portion as a lid. The cheese is then covered with a cloth or plastic wrap, and left to rest. The softened Stilton is eaten with a spoon.

Little cheese platters

For a small platter to serve two to four people, offer as wide a variety
as possible, such as Swiss Gruyère, mild butter cheese, Gorgonzola Piccante,
Camembert and pistachio balls (above); or a more piquant selection with a ripe
Tilsit, various goat cheeses, Roquefort and smoked semi-hard cheese (below).

PERE RIPIENE (Gorgonzola-stuffed pears).
To make this typical Italian cheese
dessert, halve 4 small, ripe pears
lengthwise; core them, being careful not
to remove the stems; and drizzle the cut
surfaces with lemon juice. Beat together
2 tablespoons butter, 4 tablespoons
heavy cream and 2 oz Gorgonzola
Piccante until fluffy, season to taste with
pepper and, if necessary, salt. Spoon the
cream onto the pear halves, or pipe on
using a pastry bag with a star tip. Finally,
sprinkle with 2 tablespoons chopped
walnuts. For a delicate variation, poach
the pear halves in Barolo. This deep red
wine from Piedmont not only tints the
pears beautifully, but also imparts its
own flavor.

Salads

The word "salad" tends to make us think first of something green, rather than immediately conjuring up visions of cheese. On closer consideration, though, cheese is almost indispensable in modern salad-making. Almost all types of cheese can be used in salads, as a primary ingredient or part of a mixture, as a hearty counterpoint in a combination of fresh salad leaves or as a harmonious rounding out of a filling salad meal. Cheese is a main ingredient or seasoning in many salad dressings, often in combination with cream or yogurt, and in small amounts grating cheeses can be a welcome condiment. The photo below gives a good example of modern salad-making: crunchy fresh salad leaves, with julienned Gruyère and cubes of Roquefort, dressed in a piquant vinaigrette. Such salads can be served as an hors d'oeuvre or, in more generous portions and with fresh bread, as a complete light lunch or supper.

All recipes serve 4 unless otherwise indicated.

Salad dressings with and without cheese

Cheese can be used in a great variety of ways in salad dressings, as a primary ingredient or a subtle seasoning. In particular, the various fresh and blue-veined cheeses not only give the dressing taste and tang, but also a certain creaminess, serving simultaneously as a basis and a binding ingredient. Salad dressings with cheese are equally well suited for use on green, vegetable, potato, and meat or sausage salads, provided that all the ingredients harmonize with one another. Grated cheese, especially extra-hard ones such as Sbrinz, Manchego, and Pecorino, is a welcome condiment in many salad dressings. Grated Greek Kefalotiri, for example, lends quite a distinctive note to a vinaigrette. To make this vinaigrette, whisk together 1 tablespoon finely minced shallots with 2 tablespoons wine vinegar, a bit of salt, pepper and 5 tablespoons best-quality vegetable oil and season with 2 tablespoons grated Greek sheep's cheese. Herbs may also be added.

Cheese can be cut into a variety of shapes. The firmer the cheese, the thinner and finer it can be cut. The softer types should be cut into cubes, the extra-hard types crumbled.

MASCARPONE SALAD DRESSING WITH HERBS

¼ cup + 2 tablespoons Mascarpone
2 tablespoons low-fat yogurt
3 tablespoons chopped herbs (marjoram, parsley, chervil, and chives), ½ garlic clove, crushed
salt, white pepper, ¼ teaspoon Dijon-type mustard
2–3 tablespoons herb vinegar

Place the Mascarpone in a blender with the yogurt, herbs, and garlic, and blend until you have a pale green sauce. Season to taste with salt, pepper, mustard, and the herb vinegar. Add a little more yogurt if the sauce is too thick. This dressing goes well with all salads that are improved by the addition of herbs.

ROQUEFORT SALAD DRESSING

2 oz Roquefort
2 tablespoons yogurt, 1–2 tablespoons heavy cream
1–2 tablespoons lemon juice
2–3 tablespoons hazelnut oil
salt and freshly ground pepper

Press the Roquefort through a fine-mesh strainer and stir together with the yogurt, cream, and lemon juice until smooth. Work in the oil gradually, and season to taste with salt and pepper if necessary. Roquefort dressing is delicious with many green salads.

YOGURT DRESSING
WITH COTTAGE CHEESE

⅔ cup plain yogurt

2 tablespoons lemon juice

salt, freshly ground white pepper

a pinch of sugar

⅓ cup cottage cheese, drained

Season the yogurt to taste with lemon juice, salt, pepper, and sugar, then fold in the cottage cheese. This dressing is especially suited to salads made with fruits, or salads combining fruit with cheese, poultry, or shellfish.

SALAD DRESSING
WITH GOAT CHEESE

2½ oz fresh goat cheese, 3 tablespoons yogurt

1½ tablespoons sherry vinegar, 3–4 tablespoons olive oil

salt and freshly ground pepper

1 tablespoon fresh chopped thyme

Press the cheese through a strainer and stir with the yogurt until smooth. Add the vinegar, then gradually stir in the oil. Season to taste with salt and pepper, and mix in the thyme. Use this dressing for crunchy salad leaves, such as iceberg or romaine, or for lamb's lettuce (mâche).

MAYONNAISE

Mayonnaise remains a favorite dressing for many salads and other recipes.

2 egg yolks

¼ teaspoon salt

1 teaspoon Dijon-type mustard

a little freshly ground white pepper

2 teaspoons lemon juice or vinegar

1 cup vegetable oil

Make the mayonnaise as described in the step-by-step picture sequence below.

QUICK MAYONNAISE Here, too, the ingredients must be at room temperature. Unlike mayonnaise made by hand, blender mayonnaise can be made successfully using whole eggs. Place 2 eggs, 1 teaspoon salt, ½ teaspoon freshly ground white pepper, and 1 teaspoon wine vinegar or lemon juice in a blender. Switch the blender to its lowest setting and pour 1¼ cups of oil through the opening in the lid. This mayonnaise is ready in seconds!

SALAD DRESSING
WITH GRATED CHEESE

3 tablespoons crème fraîche or sour cream

5 tablespoons low-fat yogurt

½ cup grated cheese (Parmesan, Pecorino, or Sbrinz)

2–3 anchovy fillets, finely chopped

1 small garlic clove, crushed

2–3 tablespoons red or white wine vinegar

salt and freshly ground pepper (optional)

Stir the crème fraîche with the yogurt and the grated cheese until smooth. Mix the anchovy fillets and garlic into the dressing and add vinegar to taste. Salt and pepper are seldom required, since the cheese and the anchovy fillets usually contribute sufficient saltiness and sharpness.

SAPSAGO SALAD DRESSING

2 oz Sapsago, ¼ cup Mascarpone

1–2 tablespoons herb vinegar

3 tablespoons soy-bean oil or other neutral vegetable oil

salt and freshly ground pepper

½ tablespoon chopped fresh watercress or chives

Pass the Sapsago through a strainer and work in the Mascarpone in a food processor or with a hand-held blender. Gradually blend in the vinegar and oil. Season to taste with salt and pepper, and add the watercress or chives. This dressing is well suited to salads containing potatoes or tomatoes.

Mix the egg yolks with the salt and mustard, and season with pepper and lemon juice.

Add the oil drop by drop, whisking all the while. All ingredients must be at the same room temperature to combine smoothly.

After about a third of the oil has been whisked in, add the rest in a thin stream, still whisking constantly.

The finished mayonnaise should have a semi-firm consistency. It can be seasoned as wished, and blended with cream or yogurt.

PASTA SALAD

This basic recipe is an example of a filling dish that can be varied almost endlessly, especially since cheese and pasta harmonize so well. It is mainly the heartier types of cheese that combine well with meat, sausage, or salami, and vegetables. You can lighten these dishes by adding salad leaves, and you can also vary the result by choosing different dressings.

8 oz penne
2½ cups broccoli florets
1 bunch radishes, 2 tomatoes
4 oz boiled ham
8 oz Bergkäse or Swiss Gruyére
½ cup frozen peas, thawed
For the salad dressing:
3 tablespoons good wine vinegar
1 tablespoon chopped onion
1 garlic clove, crushed; salt and pepper
5–6 tablespoons salad oil

Cook the pasta in boiling salted water until *al dente*, drain, and rinse in cold water. Boil the broccoli florets in a little salted water until tender, plunge into cold water to cool, then drain. Slice the radishes. Blanch, peel, halve, and core the tomatoes, and cut the flesh into slices. Cube the ham and slice the cheese into strips. Mix all the ingredients together with the peas in a large bowl. To make the dressing, stir together all the ingredients, pour over the salad, and toss.

CHEESE-AND-SAUSAGE SALAD

This recipe too is only a suggestion, since there are so many possible combinations of cheese and sausage.

8 oz each Emmental cheese and smoked sausage
1½ cups mushrooms; 1 red pepper
2 hard-boiled eggs, cut into wedges
For the salad dressing:
2 tablespoons red wine vinegar
3 scallions
salt, pepper, 1 teaspoon Dijon-type mustard
5 tablespoons vegetable oil
2 tablespoons chopped herbs (parsley, chives, dill, basil, and pimpernel if available)

Slice the cheese and sausage. Cut the mushrooms into wafer-thin slices, and the red pepper into thin strips. Mix these ingredients in a large bowl. To make the dressing, slice the scallions into thin rounds and mix with the vinegar, seasonings, mustard, and oil. Dress the salad, leave for 30 minutes to allow the flavors to permeate and arrange on 4 plates. Garnish with the eggs and scatter the herbs on top.

Salad meals

Almost any type of cheese can be used in main-course salads. For the creative cook, the possible combinations are endless. Team cheese with meat, salami or sausage, vegetables, pasta, and even fish, to satisfy every salad craving. As well as hearty salad meals you can prepare light creations with vegetables or salad leaves. Quantity plays a role too. The same ingredients, arranged attractively on plates in appropriately reduced quantities, are perfect as an accompaniment or an hors d'oeuvre.

TÊTE DE MOINE WITH FIG SALAD

4 medium-sized fresh figs
salt, pepper
1 tablespoon red wine vinegar, 2–3 teaspoons red port
12 Tête de Moine curls or thin slices
12 walnut kernels
a little frisée or dandelion greens

Wash the figs and cut into slices, then lightly salt and pepper. Mix the vinegar with the port and marinate the figs in this mixture for about 10 minutes. Drain the figs on paper towels, then arrange the cheese on plates and garnish with the figs, walnut kernels, and salad leaves, drizzling over a little of the marinade.

PAPAYAS FILLED WITH COTTAGE CHEESE

1¾ cups cottage cheese
1 tomato, peeled
3 tablespoons small leaves from radish greens
or watercress
½ teaspoons freshly grated horseradish
salt and freshly ground white pepper
3 papayas

Drain the cottage cheese in a strainer. Quarter and core the tomato and cut into small cubes. Mix into the cheese with the radish greens or watercress and the horseradish, and season to taste with salt and pepper. Halve the papayas lengthwise and remove the seeds. Peel one of the papayas, cut the flesh into cubes, and stir into the cheese mixture; use to fill the remaining papaya halves.

MELON FILLED WITH CHEDDAR AND CHICKEN SALAD

2 Galia or other melons (weighing 1 lb each)
5 oz Cheddar, 5 oz roast chicken or turkey
2 kiwi fruits, 2 pineapple rings
salt and pepper
1 chile pepper, diced
2 teaspoons lemon juice, 1 tablespoon pineapple juice
For the dressing:
1 tablespoon mayonnaise, 2 tablespoons yogurt
salt and pepper

Cut off one-third of each melon in a zigzag pattern, remove the seeds, and scoop out the flesh using a melon baller. Slice the cheese and the chicken or turkey into strips. Peel and slice the kiwis. Cut the pineapple into chunks. Make a marinade by combining the salt, pepper, chile pepper, and lemon and pineapple juices, and marinate all the ingredients in it for 1 hour. Fill the melons with the chilled mixture and pour the dressing on top.

Tête de Moine is especially well suited to making these cheese curls, which can be arranged to resemble carnations. They are scraped from the cheese — a somewhat laborious job with a knife, but a cinch with the *girolle*, as shown on page 65.

Pecorino Marinato, so delicate in its very simplicity. The cheese is sliced thinly, marinated in extra virgin olive oil, and seasoned with salt and plenty of freshly ground pepper. Crunchy celery sticks are a good taste contrast.

Simply brilliant

The dishes on these pages are based on simple combinations of cheese and salad ingredients that have become traditional favorites in many countries. Variations on these recipes are to be found everywhere. In the Mediterranean countries, cheese is usually marinated only in olive oil, while in Central Europe acidic dressings are favored, mainly for low-fat sour-curd cheeses, which are ideally suited to a marinade of vinegar and oil. Hard cheeses, such as Emmental, also taste superb in a vinaigrette dressing, especially when served with draft beer. Hard cheeses made from cow's or sheep's milk, such as Parmesan, Pecorino, Manchego, or Kefalotiri, really need only a fine olive oil as a dressing. If they do need some acidity, add a drop of lemon juice or some aged balsamic vinegar, which becomes milder and sweeter as it matures, and then harmonizes particularly well with Parmesan or Pecorino.

MOZZARELLA AND TOMATOES

A favorite pairing in southern Italy is Mozzarella and tomatoes, a really simple and delicate combination. The cheese must be fresh. Buffalo milk Mozzarella is usually yellower than cow's milk Mozzarella, and heartier in taste. The following combination of ingredients can be viewed as a basic recipe, from which more sophisticated recipes may be evolved.

1¼ lb tomatoes
2 Mozzarella di bufala (about 5 oz each)
small bunch basil, salt and pepper
extra virgin olive oil
16 black olives
1 tablespoon salted capers, rinsed and dried

Wash, dry, and slice the tomatoes, which should be fully ripened. Cut the cheese into slices of even thickness. Arrange on a platter or plates. Strip the basil leaves from their stalks and tear them into ribbons. Season with salt and plenty of freshly ground pepper. Dress with first-class olive oil, the amount being left entirely to your discretion. Add the black olives and salted capers (the vinegary taste of pickled capers would jar). The last two ingredients are not called for in the original recipe, but they add a delicious note.

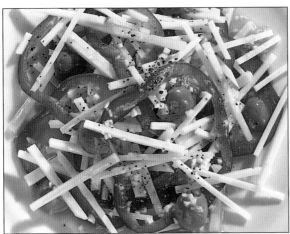

FETA IN HERB MARINADE

14 oz Greek sheep's milk Feta
2 garlic cloves
1 red chile pepper
salt and coarsely ground pepper
1 tablespoon capers, rinsed and dried
2 tablespoons coarsely chopped herbs (basil, parsley, rosemary, thyme, and mint)
½ cup extra virgin olive oil

Cut the Feta into cubes no bigger than ½ inch. Finely mince the garlic. Remove the stalk and seeds from the chile pepper and cut the flesh into wafer-thin slices. Mix the garlic and chile pepper with the salt, pepper, capers, and herbs, and lastly with the olive oil. Pour over the cheese and leave to marinate overnight.

KEFALOTIRI AND RED PEPPERS

14 oz Kefalotiri, 2 sweet red peppers
2 garlic cloves, 4 tablespoons extra virgin olive oil
juice of half a lemon, salt and pepper
12 green olives, pitted and halved

Cut the cheese into thin slices, then strips. Remove the stalks and seeds from the peppers and slice the flesh into thin rings. Chop the garlic finely, mix with the olive oil and lemon juice, and pour over the cheese and peppers. Season with salt and plenty of freshly ground pepper. Marinate for at least 1 hour and serve garnished with the olives (top photo).

MARINATED GOAT CHEESE

2 goat cheeses, 4 to 6 oz each (such as Selles-sur-Cher)
4 scallions, 1 garlic clove
1 teaspoon green peppercorns, 1 tablespoon good red wine
4 tablespoons extra virgin olive oil; salt and pepper
1 teaspoon snipped chives

Cut the goat cheese into ¼-inch-thick slices and arrange on a platter. Cut the scallions into thin circles, crush the garlic clove, and coarsely chop the peppercorns. Mix with the red wine and olive oil, and season with salt, pepper, and chives. Sprinkle over the cheese and allow the flavors to permeate (above).

Cheese and onions is a favorite combination in Germany. A gutsy cheese, such as one of the Handkäses or Graukäse, is served with onion rings, plenty of caraway seeds, and a dressing of vinegar and oil.

Soups

Delicate or gutsy, light or sumptuous, as an appetizing prelude to a fine meal, or an hors d'oeuvre before a hearty roast, as a modest entrée or a filling main meal — soups have earned a permanent place on the menu. If you sample the soups of the classic cheesemaking countries, you will quickly identify one of the most popular seasoning ingredients: cheese. This is because cheese harmonizes superbly with all of the ingredients normally used in soups: bread, rice, noodles, and eggs, but especially with fresh vegetables. Many Italian soups, such as minestrone (pictured here), the classic Italian vegetable soup, are sprinkled with a little grated hard cheese and thus rounded out perfectly. In France the hearty onion soup of the Parisian market district is always crowned with a golden-brown crust of cheese. Other soups, too, are lent a delicate melting quality by the generous use of cheese as a main ingredient.

Cheese also introduces even greater variety in an area of already seemingly limitless variation: soup garnishes and accompaniments. These make it possible to find new ways to dress up plain consommés or delicate cream soups. Grated cheese imparts a special spicy note to savory custard garnishes, crepes, and crackers, and it even forms the basis of recipes for dumplings.

All recipes serve 4 unless otherwise indicated.

MILLE FANTI is a famous Italian bread soup. Beat together 2 eggs with ¼ cup grated Parmesan and ½ cup fresh white bread crumbs, add to 4 cups seasoned beef broth, stirring, and bring to a boil.

ZUPPA PAVESE

4½ cups rich broth
Salt and freshly ground pepper
12 slices Italian bread
4 eggs
¼ cup freshly grated Parmesan

Preheat the broiler. Bring the broth to a boil and season to taste with the salt and pepper. Toast the bread and place in warmed, heatproof soup plates or cups. Carefully break an egg into each soup plate, making sure that the yolk stays whole. Ladle on the boiling broth, sprinkle the Parmesan on top, and brown under the hot broiler. Serve the *zuppa pavese* at once, before the bread softens too much and the egg becomes too hard. As a variation, fry the slices of bread and the eggs in butter instead of cooking them in the broth.

BUSECCA

⅓ cup pinto beans
½ cup each shredded white cabbage and leeks
¼ carrot, julienned
1 stalk celery, julienned
5 oz boiled tripe
5 tablespoons butter, 4½ cups broth
salt, freshly ground black pepper
1 oz pancetta or bacon
For the pesto:
1 garlic clove, 2 leaves each fresh sage and basil
2 slices white bread, 2 oz Parmesan, freshly grated

Soak the beans overnight in plenty of water. The next day, prepare all the vegetables, and cut the tripe into fine strips. Melt 2 tablespoons of the butter in a large pot, and sweat the vegetables and tripe in it. Drain the beans, add to the pot with the broth, and season with salt and pepper. Simmer until the beans are soft (1½–2 hours). Heat the oven to 400°F. Finely chop the pancetta or bacon, the garlic, and the herbs, and pound in a mortar. Cube the bread and sauté in a pan in the remaining butter until golden brown. Mix the bacon–herb paste into the cooked soup, heat, and season to taste. Divide among the soup plates, scatter the croutons on top, and sprinkle with Parmesan. Brown in the oven for about 3 minutes.

PARISIAN ONION SOUP

14 oz onions
3 tablespoons butter
½ cup dry white wine
3½ cups rich broth
salt, freshly ground black pepper
1 garlic clove
1 tablespoon olive oil
8 slices from a baguette
½ cup grated Beaufort or Laguiole

Peel the onions and slice into thin strips, then
sweat them in a pot in the butter until they are soft.
Add the wine and broth, and bring to a boil; season
with salt and pepper and cook for about 30 minutes.
Preheat the broiler. Peel and crush the garlic clove
and stir into the oil. Spread this mixture over the
slices of bread and toast under the broiler. Ladle the
soup into bowls, place the slices of bread on top,
sprinkle with cheese, and brown under the broiler.
As a variation, thicken the soup with a *beurre manié*
(see page 165) and serve with toasted slices of
bread. Pass the grated cheese around for everyone
to help themselves.

SAVOIE VEGETABLE SOUP

1½ oz smoked bacon
1 cup each diced celery, leeks, and onions
⅔ cup each diced turnips and potatoes
3½ cups meat broth
salt, freshly ground black pepper
freshly grated nutmeg
⅞ cup milk or heavy cream
2 tablespoons butter
8 slices from a baguette
1½ oz Tomme de Savoie or Beaufort

Dice the bacon and fry in a pot until brown. Add
all the vegetables and sweat together. Pour in the
broth, season, bring to a boil, and simmer over
gentle heat for 25–30 minutes. Preheat the broiler.
Scald the milk or cream, strain into the soup, and
stir in the butter. Season generously to taste, divide
among soup plates, and place the slices of bread on
top. Cut the cheese into small cubes and scatter on
top, and place under the hot broiler until golden.

SOUPE AU PISTOU

9 oz potatoes, 7 oz carrots
9 oz ripe tomatoes, 5 oz leeks
9 oz zucchini, 7 oz green beans
½ cup macaroni
6 cups cooked white beans, salt
For the pistou:
3 garlic cloves
salt, freshly ground black pepper
12–15 fresh basil leaves
½ cup grated Parmesan, ⅓ cup olive oil

Peel and dice the potatoes. Trim and clean the carrots, and slice them into rounds. Plunge the tomatoes in boiling water, then peel, core, and cut into cubes. Trim and wash the leeks and cut into rings. Trim and dice the zucchini. Trim and wash the green beans and break into long sections. Bring 6½ cups lightly salted water to a boil. Add the potatoes, carrots, and green beans. Simmer for 20 minutes, then add the leeks, zucchini, and macaroni. Simmer for another 10 minutes, then add the white beans and tomatoes, and simmer for 5 minutes. Add more water if the soup becomes too thick. Meanwhile, prepare the pistou. In a mortar, pound the garlic cloves, salt, pepper, and basil leaves to a coarse paste. Mix in a little Parmesan and work to a smooth paste, adding a little olive oil. Continue to add the cheese and oil alternately until both are used up. Serve the soup and hand round the pistou to stir into it.

VEGETABLE SOUP WITH HERBS

2 tablespoons butter
3 cups mixed vegetables (equal parts diced onion, leek, carrot, turnip, and celery)
1 tablespoon whole-wheat flour
4½ cups beef broth
1 garlic clove, crushed; ¼ bay leaf
½ cup heavy cream, 1 cup grated Pecorino
salt, freshly ground white pepper
freshly grated nutmeg
3 tablespoons chopped herbs (basil, tarragon, chervil, watercress, chives, and thyme)

Melt the butter in a pot, add the vegetables, and sweat them for a few minutes. Sprinkle on the flour and stir well. Add the broth, stirring constantly, and bring to a boil. Add the garlic and bay leaf. Simmer on low heat for about 25 minutes, then remove the bay leaf. Pour in the cream and bring the soup to a boil again. Blend or process with a generous half of the Pecorino, and season to taste with salt, pepper, and nutmeg. Add salt sparingly, as the cheese is salty. Stir in the herbs, serve the soup, and sprinkle with the remaining Pecorino.

Pesto is an Italian herb paste made from fresh basil, plenty of garlic, olive oil, Parmesan, and pine nuts. It lends a particular flavor to many soups, as well as being served with spaghetti and other pasta dishes. A French variation is *pistou*, which is made without the pine nuts.

Vegetable soups with cheese

Spicy specialties: from top to bottom, Tomato soup with Mascarpone, Soupe au Pistou from Provence, Spinach soup with goat cheese, Vegetable soup with herbs.

TOMATO SOUP WITH MASCARPONE

2 tablespoons butter
½ cup diced onion
¼ cup diced carrot
2 fully ripe plum tomatoes (about 5 oz)
⅔ cup tomato paste
1 tablespoon flour
4½ cups meat broth
a bouquet garni (leek, garlic, celery, bay leaf, and thyme)
salt, freshly ground white pepper
sugar
½ cup Mascarpone
⅔ cup grated Provolone Piccante

Melt the butter in a saucepan, and sweat the onion and carrot without letting them color. Slice the tomatoes finely and stir in with the tomato paste. Sprinkle on the flour and stir well. Add the broth and stir until smooth. Bring to a boil, add the bouquet garni, and simmer on a low heat for 20–25 minutes. Season to taste with salt, pepper, and sugar, stir in the Mascarpone, and strain the soup. Serve the grated Provolone on the side. Quark dumplings (see page 151), cubed tomatoes, or little ravioli stuffed with cheese taste good in the soup.

SPINACH SOUP WITH GOAT CHEESE

3 tablespoons butter
¼ cup diced onion
1⅛ cup diced potato
4½ cups goat's or cow's milk (or half milk, half broth)
¼ cup arborio rice
2 pinches saffron threads
½ lb leaf spinach
1 cup grated Valençay
salt
freshly ground white pepper
1 small clove garlic, crushed
⅓ cup grated Ragusano or Provolone Piccante

Melt 2 tablespoons of butter in a saucepan; add the onion, and sweat until transparent. Add the potato and sweat with the onion. Add the milk. Bring to a boil, stir in the rice and saffron, and simmer over a low heat until the potatoes and rice are cooked. Meanwhile, sort through the spinach, wash and drain well, and slice into ribbons. Cook the spinach in the remaining butter until it collapses. Stir the Valençay into the soup and allow to melt, then mix in the spinach. Reheat the soup, season to taste with salt, pepper, and garlic, sprinkle with the Ragusano, and serve at once.

Soup garnishes

CHEESE CRACKERS

Serves 8
2 eggs, separated
¼ teaspoons salt; a little nutmeg
4½ teaspoons flour
⅓ cup grated Emmental or Sbrinz
1 tablespoon butter

Preheat the oven to 400°F. Prepare a cracker mixture from the ingredients above as described in the picture sequence. Spread onto a baking sheet and bake for 8–10 minutes, but test for doneness before this, since this sort of thin pastry cooks and burns very quickly, and oven temperatures are notoriously variable.

CHEESE CUSTARD SHAPES

⅓ cup milk; 1 egg
salt, freshly ground white pepper
freshly grated nutmeg
⅓ cup grated Gruyère
butter for greasing

Preheat the oven to 250°F. Heat the milk. Whisk the egg, stir in the milk, and season with salt, pepper, and nutmeg. Pour through a fine strainer and mix in the grated cheese. Butter a small ovenproof dish and pour in the custard. It should be about ½ inch deep. Bake in a *bain-marie*, or water-bath, for 45–50 minutes, until set. Leave the custard to cool, turn out, and cut or stamp out attractive shapes. Serve in hot broth or tomato soup.

CHEESE TOAST makes a crunchy addition to broth and to onion and tomato soups. To make it, preheat the oven to 480°F. Stir together ½ cup grated Gruyère, 1 egg yolk and 1 teaspoon white wine or beer; season with mild paprika, and spread onto two thin slices of toast. Bake until golden, then cut into diamond shapes.

Whisk the egg yolks vigorously, and season. Whip the egg whites to stiff peaks.

Add the whipped egg whites to the yolks, partially fold in, then trickle in the flour mixed with the cheese as you carefully continue to fold.

Melt the butter. When it is lukewarm, stir it in. Do not overmix.

Put the cracker mixture onto a baking sheet lined with parchment paper, and spread to a thickness of ½ inch. Bake at once.

Turn the rectangle of baked pastry onto a work surface and leave to cool slightly. Peel off the parchment paper and cut into small squares.

RICOTTA DUMPLINGS

1 tablespoon butter, 1 egg yolk
½ cup Ricotta
salt, freshly grated nutmeg
chopped basil or tarragon
1 slice white bread

Melt the butter. Stir the egg yolk until creamy and mix with the butter. Add the Ricotta, season with the salt, nutmeg, and herbs, and stir until smooth. Grate or crumble the bread, stir into the cheese mixture and leave to soak for 30 minutes. Cook as shown below.

The best way to achieve uniform dumplings is to hold the dough in the palm of your hand and scoop out small portions with a teaspoon.

All the dumplings will be exactly the same size if you scrape along your palm with the bowl of the spoon.

Now use your index finger to push the dough as smoothly as possible from the spoon into boiling salted water. Cook for 4–5 minutes, until done.

The taste of soup garnishes with cheese is usually set off best in a clear broth, but these also harmonize with cream soups. It is important, though, that they be added to the soup only just before serving (this is especially true for baked garnishes).

ROQUEFORT BALLS

(not illustrated)
½ cup water, 2 tablespoons butter
pinch of salt
1 cup all-purpose flour, 2 eggs
2 oz Roquefort

Preheat the oven to 425°F. Bring the water, butter, and salt to a boil in a large saucepan. Add the flour all at once and stir until the mixture comes together in a ball. Place the dough in a bowl and stir in the eggs one at a time. Mash the cheese with a fork and mix into this choux pastry until completely blended. Use a pastry bag with a round tip to pipe small balls onto a baking sheet, and bake until golden brown.

CREPES WITH CHEESE

½ cup all-purpose flour
½ cup milk, 1 egg
salt, freshly ground white pepper
½ tablespoon melted butter
½ cup grated Parmesan
1 tablespoon snipped chives
butter for greasing

Prepare the crepes as described below.

Whisk the flour and milk together until smooth, then add the egg, seasonings, melted butter, grated cheese, and chives. Leave the batter to rest for at least 30 minutes.

Heat only enough butter to moisten the base of a pan. Pour in the batter and tilt the pan so that just a thin layer of batter covers the base.

As soon as the crepe is golden brown on one side, carefully flip and cook until golden brown on the other side. Use up the rest of the batter in this way.

Let the crepes cool completely, spread out in a single layer, so that they do not become soft, and so they dry out a bit before going into the soup. To cut, stack them and slice into strips ¼ inch wide.

Eggs, toast, and casseroles

Eggs and cheese: a versatile combination. These two staple products nearly always go well together. Eggs can be combined with almost any type of cheese, sharp or mild; it is just the quantities that need to be adjusted.

All recipes serve 4 unless otherwise indicated.

CREPES WITH ROQUEFORT FILLING.

Prepare a crepe batter according to the basic recipe (see page 163). Make 8 crepes and leave to cool. For the filling, press 4 oz each of Ricotta and Roquefort through a strainer, add 2 eggs, and stir until smooth. Mix in ⅔ cup grated Parmesan, ½ cup toasted oat or rye flakes, and 1 tablespoon each fresh chopped basil, parsley, and chives. If necessary, season the filling to taste with salt, pepper, and nutmeg, and leave it to rest for at least 1 hour. Divide the filling among the 8 crepes and roll them up. Preheat the oven to 425°F. Use about 2 tablespoons of soft butter to grease a casserole and to butter the tops of the rolled crepes. Place the crepes in the casserole and bake in the center of the oven for 10 minutes. Raise the oven temperature to 485°F. Sprinkle the crepes with ⅔ cup grated medium-aged Gouda and 4 teaspoons grated Parmesan, and brown in the center of the oven for 2–3 minutes. Peel, halve, core, and dice 2 tomatoes. Season with salt, pepper, and sugar, and turn in a saucepan in 2 tablespoons hot melted butter. Sprinkle with 1 tablespoon herbs (parsley, basil, and chives) and pour over the crepes.

Toast, fresh from the oven. This popular entrée and quick dish is ideal for testing which cheese is preferable for melting in slices. It should be types that do not run too much, otherwise the result is more cheese beside the toast than actually on it. Cheddar, Gouda types (as in the photo above), Trappist, and Steppe cheeses are particularly well suited. If you are willing to use a non-natural cheese, processed cheese slices especially developed for melting are available.

The different cheeses were all tested under the same conditions and at the same temperature: 400°F radiant heat from above.

Every cheese melts differently

Which cheese one uses for a specific au gratin dish is determined by a number of factors. In general, the cheese's ability to harmonize with the other ingredients has absolute priority. The next issue is how the cheese behaves when melting — does it keep its shape or become very runny? — and what consistency it has in a warm, melted state. There are cheeses that become very stringy, and others that remain "tight" and almost brittle. The most crucial factor in melting behavior is the ratio of water content to dry matter. Soft cheese containing a large proportion of moisture melts more quickly than extra-hard cheese, which has a small proportion of moisture. Age and fat content also play significant roles. Generally, younger cheese reacts more quickly to heat than well-ripened cheese. However, well-aged cheeses, which would be preferred because of their often very distinctive, piquant flavor, are for the most part not suitable for au gratin dishes, as they become runny when heated. The ideal cheese in most cases is a ripe cheese, neither too young nor too old. The melting behavior of some types is illustrated on the opposite page. Different dishes require the cheese to behave in different ways, so you should always take the time to melt a little piece of cheese as a test. In this way you can find out for certain whether the cheese is the right one for the desired purpose.

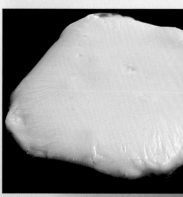

A low fat content, as in this Gouda with 30% FDB, was not a good qualification for melting. Although the cheese hardly ran, the consistency was rubbery.

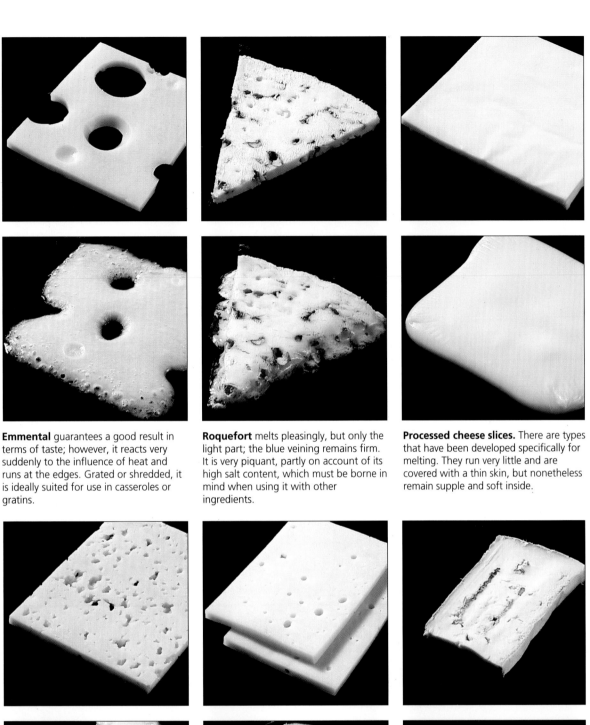

Emmental guarantees a good result in terms of taste; however, it reacts very suddenly to the influence of heat and runs at the edges. Grated or shredded, it is ideally suited for use in casseroles or gratins.

Roquefort melts pleasingly, but only the light part; the blue veining remains firm. It is very piquant, partly on account of its high salt content, which must be borne in mind when using it with other ingredients.

Processed cheese slices. There are types that have been developed specifically for melting. They run very little and are covered with a thin skin, but nonetheless remain supple and soft inside.

Trappist cheese. This entire cheese family has good melting qualities. The cheese hardly changes shape, but becomes soft and very supple through and through. It is ideal for toast and pizzas, as well as for gratins.

Fontina. This category also includes the related Fontal. These cheeses melt especially easily, but are also prone to excessive running, and hence ideal where the cheese is meant to combine well with the dish it tops.

Soft cheese with a moldy rind. Its fatty, soft interior melts quickly, but the rind and blue interior veining stay firm. The rind often tastes unpleasantly bitter, and so should be removed after the cheese is melted.

Ramequin, a traditional cheese dish from western Switzerland, is a good example of melted cheese in slices. The readily melting Emmental used in it is ideal, as it combines perfectly with the slices of bread.

WELSH RABBIT, OR RAREBIT: mature Cheddar melted in beer. For this traditional British dish, melt some butter in a saucepan, then add beer. Season with salt and pepper. Add several handfuls of shredded Cheddar to the beer, and melt over moderate heat. Round off the taste with mustard and Worcestershire sauce. Pour the creamy mixture over a buttered piece of toast, and broil or bake in a preheated oven until the surface is light brown.

MEDALLIONS OF LAMB ON TOAST

Preheat the oven to 485°F. Slice 8 oz lamb tenderloin into 8 medallions of equal weight, beat flat with a meat mallet, and season with pepper. Wash 1 zucchini, slice in rounds, and season with pepper. Clean and slice 8 oz fresh mushrooms. Toast 4 slices of bread. Fry the lamb and zucchini in 2 tablespoons of butter, and cook the mushrooms in 1½ teaspoons of butter. Arrange the ingredients on the toast and sprinkle with ½ teaspoon chopped thyme. Cut 4 oz of hard sheep's-milk cheese (such as Manchego) into thin strips and divide among the toasts. Place on the top rack of the oven until brown.

TUNA AND MOZZARELLA ON TOAST

Preheat the oven to 485°F. Halve and slice 2 onions and sweat in 2 tablespoons butter. Drain the contents of a 6-oz can of tuna fish. Remove core and seeds from 1 chile pepper and cut into thin rings. Halve and pit 12 green and 12 black olives. Toast 4 slices of bread. Cut 5-oz fresh Mozzarella into 8 slices. Divide the onions among the slices of bread and cover with the tuna, chile, and olives. Top each toast with 1 tablespoon chopped herbs, then 2 slices Mozzarella, and, finally, 3 tablespoons Parmesan. Place on the top rack of the oven until brown.

CHEDDAR TOAST
WITH LIVER AND CALVADOS APPLES

Preheat the oven to 485°F. Peel, halve, and core 2 apples, and slice into segments. Sprinkle with ¼ cup Calvados and ½ teaspoon sugar. Bring to a boil with ½ cup heavy cream and simmer for 3–4 minutes. Finely slice ½ red onion and sweat in a little butter until soft. Toast 4 slices of bread. Cut 7 oz calves' liver into 4 equal slices, season with salt and pepper, and fry in 2 tablespoons butter for about 3 minutes. Place a piece of liver and 4 apple segments on each slice of bread. Scatter the onions and some green peppercorns on top, and cover with 1 slice Cheddar. Cook on the top rack of the oven until golden brown.

TOAST WITH STILTON
AND PORT-WINE PEARS

Preheat the oven to 485°F. Peel, halve, and core 2 pears, and poach for 15–20 minutes in 1 cup red port; leave to cool. Drain the pear halves on paper towels and cut partway through them to form ¼-inch slices, fanning them out. Toast 4 slices of whole-wheat bread and spread thinly with butter while still warm, so that the butter can soak into the bread. Put a pear half on each slice of toast, top with 2 slices Stilton, and place on the top rack of the oven; check frequently, as Stilton melts quickly. Garnish each toast with a sprig of lemon balm, if available, and fresh green peppercorns.

Fresh from the oven

That is how these cheese toasts taste best, and it is easy to get them from the oven to the table at just the right time. Almost all these toasts can be prepared in advance up to the point where they need to go in the oven.

CROSTINI WITH PECORINO AND ANCHOVIES

2 oz Ricotta, 1½ cups grated Pecorino Romano
1 egg, 1 egg yolk, 2 tablespoons white wine
8 anchovy fillets
1 teaspoon chopped herbs (thyme and parsley)
2 garlic cloves, crushed; salt and pepper
4 slices white bread

Preheat the oven to 485°F. Press the Ricotta through a strainer and mix with the Pecorino, the egg, the egg yolk, and the white wine. Chop 4 anchovy fillets and add to the cheese mixture with the herbs and the garlic. Season to taste with salt and pepper. Toast the bread, spread with the cheese mixture, and place on the top rack of the oven until golden brown. Garnish each toast with an anchovy filet and serve at once.

SPANISH CROSTADA

10 oz sheep's-milk cheese (young Manchego)
½ cup white wine
salt, pepper, 1 teaspoon fresh oregano
3 garlic cloves, crushed
4 slices crusty bread
2 tablespoons olive oil, 1 egg
1 tablespoon finely chopped parsley

Preheat the oven to 485°F. Press the cheese through a coarse strainer or crumble finely. Work to a smooth mass with the white wine. Season to taste with salt and pepper, and add the oregano and garlic. Drizzle the bread with the olive oil and spread with the cheese mixture. Whisk the egg and spread the surface of the crostadas with it. Place on the top rack of the oven for about 3 minutes. Sprinkle with parsley and serve.

Delicate and luxurious — a combination that really should be tasted. Remove the rind and melt slices of ripe Brie de Meaux on toasted white bread and crown with plenty of caviar.

BAKED CAMEMBERT. Cut 4 oz Camembert into 8 wedges. Whisk together 1 egg and 1 tablespoon oil. Combine ½ cup white bread crumbs with ¼ cup ground walnuts. Dredge the cheese wedges in flour and dip in the beaten egg, then turn in the breadcrumb-nut mixture, pressing this on firmly. Deep-fry the Camembert wedges in hot oil until golden brown.

APPENZELL CUBES

¾ cup all-purpose flour
½ cup white wine, 1 egg
pinch salt, ½ teaspoon sugar
10 oz Appenzell
flour for dredging, oil for deep frying

Sift the flour into a bowl, add the white wine, and stir until smooth. Separate the egg and stir the yolk into the batter. Salt the batter and leave to rest for 20–30 minutes. Cut the Appenzell into ¾-inch cubes. Whip the egg white to stiff peaks while slowly adding the sugar, and fold into the batter. Heat the oil to 360°F Dredge the cheese cubes in flour, dip them in the batter, and deep-fry them for about 2 minutes, until golden brown. Drain on paper towels.

CHEESE AND BACON FRITTERS

(not illustrated)
14 oz medium-aged Gouda
4 oz thinly sliced smoked bacon
flour, 1 egg, beaten
3 cups bread crumbs, oil for frying
toothpicks

Cut the cheese into 1-inch cubes and the bacon slices in half. Wrap half a slice of bacon around each cheese cube and hold together with a toothpick. Dredge in flour, dip in the egg, and coat twice with the bread crumbs. Heat the oil to 360°F. Deep-fry and drain on paper towels.

GRUYÈRE CROQUETTES

2 tablespoons butter
4½ teaspoons flour
1 cup milk, 2 egg yolks
½ cup grated Gruyère
3 tablespoons grated Pecorino
a pinch of nutmeg, salt if needed
a sprig of thyme
flour, 1 egg, beaten
3 cups bread crumbs, oil for frying

Melt the butter in a saucepan, add the flour, and stir until smooth, taking care not to let it color. Pour in the milk, stir until smooth, and cook for 20 minutes, stirring constantly so that this béchamel does not stick. Remove the pot from the heat and stir the yolks into the sauce one at a time. Bring just to a boil and pass through a fine strainer. Add the Gruyère and Pecorino, the nutmeg, the salt (if needed), and the thyme leaves, stripped from their stalks. Spread the mixture onto a piece of buttered foil, making a 5 x 6-inch rectangle. Cover with foil and cool for 1–1½ hours. Now cut the rectangle lengthwise into three equal pieces and crosswise into strips about ½ inch wide. Dip the croquettes in the egg and coat twice in bread crumbs. Heat the oil to 360°F. Deep-fry for 2–3 minutes. Drain on paper towels.

CHEESE PATTIES

1½ oz blue-veined cheese, 4 oz Ricotta
1 egg, 2 tablespoons butter, 2 tablespoons grated Sbrinz
1 cup fresh white bread crumbs
1 bunch chives; pepper, salt, nutmeg
oil for frying

Press the blue cheese and the Ricotta through a strainer and mix together. Beat the egg in another bowl and add to the cheese mixture with the melted butter. Stir in the Sbrinz, bread crumbs, seasonings, and chopped chives. Leave to swell for 2–3 hours. With oiled hands, form the mixture into 8 flat patties of equal size. Shallow-fry in hot oil for 3–4 minutes, turning frequently.

GOAT CHEESE CRISPS

(not illustrated)
14 oz semi-hard goat cheese (such as goat-milk Gouda)
1 tablespoon sweet paprika, 2 tablespoons flour
1 egg, beaten; 3 cups bread crumbs
oil for frying

Remove the rind from the cheese and slice into bars ½-inch wide and 2 inches long. Mix the paprika with the flour. Dredge the cheese bars in the seasoned flour, dip in the egg, and coat twice with the bread crumbs, pressing them in firmly. Heat the oil to 360°F. Deep-fry until light brown. Drain on paper towels.

QUESO FRITO

9 oz sheep's-milk cheese (for example, young Manchego)
salt, black pepper
3 tablespoons chopped herbs (parsley and thyme)
4 garlic cloves, crushed
flour, 1 egg and 1 egg yolk, beaten together
oil for frying

Cut the cheese into 8 slices of equal thickness and season with salt and pepper. Mix the garlic with the herbs and spread the mixture on both sides of the cheese slices. Heat the oil to 360°F. Dredge the cheese slices in flour and dip in the egg. Take care that the flour is well soaked with the egg mixture. Deep-fry for 2–3 minutes. Drain on paper towels.

Preparing Mozzarella in carrozza:

Using a suitable knife, cut each of the well-drained Mozzarella balls into 6 slices.

Beat the eggs in a bowl. Add the milk, whisking until combined.

Using a fork, turn and soak the bread slices in the egg-milk mixture.

Place each slice of Mozzarella on a slice of bread, sprinkle on the anchovies, and season generously. Lay the remaining slices of bread on top, pressing firmly together.

Pour the fine bread crumbs onto a plate and coat the sandwiches in them.

Press the crumbs in with your hands, so that they stick to the bread.

Heat the clarified butter in a frying pan and put in the breaded sandwiches.

Fry the sandwiches on both sides until golden brown, turning as necessary.

GORGONZOLA SANDWICHES. Remove the crusts from 8 slices of bread. Cut 10 oz of Gorgonzola into slices ½ inch shorter than the slices of bread. Finely dice 1 oz prosciutto. Whisk 1 egg with ⅓ cup heavy cream and dip the slices of bread in this mixture. Cover half of the slices with the Gorgonzola and prosciutto, place the remaining slices on top, and press together tightly. Dredge the sandwiches in fine bread crumbs and fry until golden brown in 6 tablespoons of hot clarified butter.

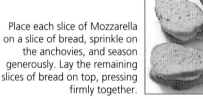

Fried between slices of bread

This traditional Italian recipe is an excellent example of just how good melted cheese between two slices of bread, surrounded by a crunchy shell can taste. Mozzarella is ideally suited for this dish, but other types of cheese can also be prepared in the same manner, like the Gorgonzola sandwiches shown at the left. A really delicate variation can be made with Tomme de Savoie: slices of white bread are dipped in an egg-milk mixture, and half of the slices are spread with Dijon mustard. On top of these is placed a ¼-inch-thick, rindless slice of Tomme de Savoie. Continue as described in the adjacent picture sequence.

MOZZARELLA IN CARROZZA

2 small fresh Mozzarellas (5 oz each)
2 eggs, ⅔ cup milk
24 thin slices baguette or Italian bread
4 anchovy fillets, chopped
salt, black pepper
fine bread crumbs
¾ cup clarified butter

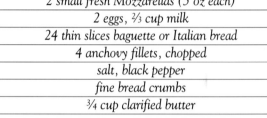

Prepare the Mozzarella sandwiches as described in the adjacent picture sequence. Place 2 of the finished sandwiches on each plate and serve with salad.

POACHED EGG
WITH SAUCE MORNAY

For the sauce:
2 tablespoons butter, 4½ teaspoons flour, 2¼ cups milk
salt, pepper, nutmeg
1 egg yolk, ½ cup heavy cream
3 tablespoons grated Parmesan
1–2 tablespoons whipped cream
For the spinach:
10 oz spinach leaves, 2 tablespoons butter
salt, pepper, nutmeg
For the eggs:
4 poached eggs (see recipe right)

Preheat the oven to 485°F. Prepare a sauce Mornay as described below. Wilt the spinach in the hot butter and season to taste with salt, pepper, and nutmeg. Poach the eggs, arrange on top of the spinach, and coat with the sauce Mornay. Place in the oven for 2–3 minutes.

Sauce Mornay:

Melt the butter, add the flour, and cook, stirring, for 1–2 minutes without browning.

Pour in the milk, whisk until smooth, and season to taste with the salt, pepper, and nutmeg. Cook for about 20 minutes, stirring constantly.

Whisk the egg yolk and cream together. Add to the sauce and bring to a boil while stirring.

Pass the sauce through a fine strainer to remove any lumps that may have formed. Heat through again.

Add the cheese and stir until melted. Only then fold in the whipped cream.

POACHED EGGS

well-chilled eggs
4½ cups water, ¼ cup white wine vinegar
lightly salted cold water

Add *only* vinegar to the poaching water; salt is used later to halt the cooking process. Bring the vinegar water to a boil, reduce to a simmer, and poach the eggs one at a time until the white is firm and the yolk still gives to light finger-pressure.

Poaching: cooking eggs
without a shell

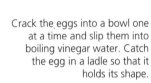

Crack the eggs into a bowl one at a time and slip them into boiling vinegar water. Catch the egg in a ladle so that it holds its shape.

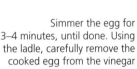

Simmer the egg for 3–4 minutes, until done. Using the ladle, carefully remove the cooked egg from the vinegar water.

Place the poached egg in lukewarm salt water. This stops it from becoming hard.

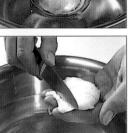

Cut off the trailing bits of the egg white. Keep the eggs in warm water until ready to serve, then drain them on paper towels.

CHEESE OMELET

As well as Parmesan, other types of cheese, such as those from the Gruyère family, piquant sheep's cheeses, Fontina, and butterfat-rich blue cheeses, can be used in this recipe.

Serves 1

For the omelet:

3 eggs, 3 tablespoons grated Parmesan, salt and nutmeg
2 teaspoons butter

For the vegetables:

1 tomato, ⅓ cup sliced zucchini, 2 tablespoons olive oil
a pinch of sugar, chives, parsley

Scald, peel, and core the tomato, and cut its flesh into dice. Sauté the zucchini in olive oil; add the tomato and the sugar, and cook briefly. Sprinkle the chopped herbs on top. To make the omelet, whisk the eggs with the Parmesan and season with salt and nutmeg. Continue as follows:

SCRAMBLED EGGS WITH CHEESE. Serves 4. Beat 8 eggs with 8 tablespoons heavy cream, and season to taste with salt and white pepper. Cut 5 oz cheese into cubes and add to the egg mixture. Finely cut or snip 1 bunch of chives. Melt 3 tablespoons of butter in a frying pan over low heat. Pour in half the egg–cheese mixture and stir with a wooden spoon until it sets in delicate curds. (Cooking half the mixture at a time produces better results.) Keep warm while you cook the other half. Serve sprinkled with the chives.

Heat the butter in a frying pan and pour in the egg–cheese mixture.

Stir the mixture with a fork until it begins to set, taking care not to disturb the bottom layer.

Push the omelet to the edge of the pan with the fork, and fold it over by tilting the pan and rapping its outside edge.

Slide the finished omelet into a warmed baking dish.

Spoon the cooked vegetables over the omelet and serve.

In the frying pan and the oven

EGGS EN COCOTTE

2 oz Emmental, 2 oz boiled ham
2 teaspoons butter, ¼ cup heavy cream
salt and pepper, 4 eggs
1 tablespoon finely snipped chives

Preheat the oven to 350°F. Cut the Emmental and the ham into small cubes. Grease 4 ramekins with the butter, and divide the cheese and ham cubes among them. Heat the cream, season with salt and pepper, and spoon into the ramekins. Crack an egg into each ramekin, sprinkle with chives, and cover with foil. Place in a *bain-marie*, with water coming two-thirds of the way up the sides of the ramekins, and bake for 10–12 minutes. Serve at once.

FILLED CREPES

For the batter:

½ cup all-purpose flour, ⅔ cup milk, 2 eggs

a pinch each salt and pepper

4½ teaspoons melted butter, 3 tablespoons Grana
Padano or Parmigiano Reggiano

2 tablespoons clarified butter for frying

For the filling:

½ onion; 4½ teaspoons butter

1 lb mushrooms; salt and pepper

1½ cups heavy cream, 1 teaspoon chopped parsley

For the sauce:

4 oz Ricotta, 2 eggs, 1½ cups heavy cream

3 tablespoons grated Grana Padano
or Parmigiano Reggiano

salt, pepper, nutmeg

butter for greasing the baking dish

Preheat the oven to 425°F. Prepare crepes as shown in
the adjacent picture sequence. To make the filling, finely
dice the onion and sweat it in the butter. Slice the
mushrooms, add to the onions, season, and cook until the
juices have evaporated. Bring the cream to a boil, strain,
add to the vegetables, and reduce. Divide the filling
among the crepes, roll these up and place in a buttered
casserole. To make the sauce, press the Ricotta through a
strainer, and stir with the eggs and cream until smooth.
Season the sauce, pour it over the crepes, and sprinkle
the Grana Padano on top. Cook on the middle rack of
the oven for 10–12 minutes.

Crepe batter with cheese:

Place the flour in a mixing
bowl, add the milk, and whisk
until smooth.

Crack the eggs into the bowl
and whisk in.

Add the lukewarm melted
butter in a thin stream, stirring
constantly.

Pass this mixture through a fine
strainer. Add the cheese and
leave to stand for about
1 hour.

Melt some of the clarified
butter in a frying pan. Pour in
enough batter to coat the
bottom of the pan thinly.

Cook the crepes until golden
brown on both sides, and leave
to cool thoroughly on a plate.

QUICK FRIED EGGS
WITH SALAMI AND
CHEESE. Melt some
butter in a frying
pan, add
2 slices of salami,
and crack 2 eggs on
top. Over this place 2
slices of Emmental,
season with salt and
herbs, cover, and
cook until done.

CHEESE SOUFFLÉ

A soufflé is the lightest, airiest way to enjoy cheese, and it is not difficult to prepare. It is just a matter of folding the highly sensitive beaten egg whites into the cheese sauce so that it loses as little volume as possible. It is important to prepare the cheese sauce first, and to let it cool. Then, as soon as the egg whites are stiff and supple, fold them into the sauce.

¼ cup butter, ¼ cup all-purpose flour, 1 cup milk
½ teaspoon salt, freshly ground pepper
grated nutmeg
¼ cup cream, 5 egg yolks
1¼ cups grated aged Gouda or Gruyère
5 egg whites, whipped to stiff peaks
butter for greasing the soufflé dish

Preheat the oven to 350°F and grease a 1-quart soufflé dish. Then prepare the cheese soufflé as described in the picture sequence. Place the soufflé dish on a low rack in the oven for 20 minutes, then increase the temperature to 400°F and continue baking for a further 20–25 minutes. The soufflé is ready when it is really well risen and well browned. Serve at once.

Preparing a soufflé:

Melt the butter in a saucepan, and then add the flour all at once.

Whisk vigorously over low heat for about 2–3 minutes, cooking the flour without allowing it to brown.

Stir in the milk a little at a time until it is all incorporated. Season, bring to a boil and simmer gently for 15 minutes, stirring frequently.

Stir through with a whisk, scraping along the base of the pan to prevent the mixture from sticking. Pour in the cream.

Off the heat, stir in the egg yolks one at a time. Add the next yolk only after the preceding one has been fully incorporated.

Finally, add the grated cheese and mix until smooth. Pour the mixture into a bowl and leave to cool while you whisk the egg whites.

Using a spatula, fold the stiffly beaten egg whites into the lukewarm cheese sauce.

Pour the finished batter into the greased soufflé dish, and place in the oven at once.

CHEESE SOUFFLÉS WITH PORT-WINE SAUCE

Like the recipe below, soufflés can be prepared as individual servings in ½-cup ramekins. They are easier to serve, and also require less time in the oven.

For the soufflé:
4 oz Ricotta, 3 egg yolks
⅓ cup rolled oats
⅔ cup grated Provolone Piccante
salt, black pepper, nutmeg
4 egg whites
For greasing the dishes:
2 teaspoons butter, ⅓ cup chopped rolled oats
For the Port wine sauce:
2 teaspoons butter, 1 finely chopped shallot
7 tablespoons each white port, beef broth, and heavy cream
½ teaspoon beurre manié (see right)
salt and pepper
8 red grapes, halved and seeded
1 tablespoon chopped walnuts

Preheat the oven to 425°F. Press the Ricotta through a strainer, add the egg yolks, and stir until smooth. Mix in the rolled oats and the Provolone, and season generously with the salt, pepper, and nutmeg. Butter the ramekins and dust with the chopped oats. Beat the egg whites with a pinch of salt until stiff and fold into the cheese mixture. Place in a *bain-marie*, with water coming ⅔ up the sides of the ramekins, for 12–15 minutes, and bake until done. To make the sauce, sauté the shallot in the butter until golden brown, adding a dash of port from time to time. Pour in the broth and reduce by half. Add the cream, let the liquid reduce slightly, then thicken with the beurre manié. Season to taste with salt and pepper. Turn the soufflés out onto plates and serve with the sauce, the grapes, and the chopped nuts.

BLUE-CHEESE SOUFFLÉ

A good soufflé can be made with very different types of cheese. Here, mild Gorgonzola Dolce is combined with sharp Roquefort, producing a typical blue-cheese taste without pungency. These individual soufflés are made in 1-cup ramekins.

2 tablespoons butter
2 heaping tablespoons flour
½ cup each milk and white wine
1 egg, 2 egg yolks
3½ oz each Gorgonzola Dolce and Roquefort
3 egg whites
salt, pepper, and nutmeg, 1 bunch chives
butter for greasing

Preheat the oven to 425°F. Melt the butter and whisk in the flour, taking care not to let it brown. Add the milk and the white wine, stir until smooth, and bring to a boil. Add the whole egg and the egg yolks one at a time, whisking vigorously to incorporate them. Press the Gorgonzola Dolce and the Roquefort through a strainer and stir into the mixture. Whip the egg whites with a bit of salt until stiff and fold into the soufflé mixture. Season to taste with salt, pepper, and nutmeg; finely slice the chives and fold in. Divide the mixture among the buttered ramekins. Place in a *bain-marie*, with water coming ⅔ up the sides of the ramekins, and bake for 25–30 minutes, until done.

BEURRE MANIÉ is a tried-and-true method of thickening liquids, from soups to sauces. Knead 7 tablespoons of softened butter together with 1 cup of flour to form a paste, and use as needed.

Pasta, polenta, and risotto

Italian cooking in general has a soft spot for cheese, and can draw on a wide variety of native cheeses, from the easy-melting Fontina to the crumbly, relatively low-fat extra-hard cheeses of the Parmesan family. Cheese is extraordinarily compatible with pasta, cornmeal, and rice, but that does not mean we should sprinkle grated cheese over every Italian-sounding dish. While most pasta and risotto dishes harmonize with cheese, there are also quite a few — for example, those that feature fish, mussels, or other shellfish, or those in which a relatively delicate flavor, such as that of mild herbs, is meant to dominate — in which the taste of cheese would jar. Fortunately, these are the exceptions. Cheese not only adds its flavor to pasta and rice, its melting quality also lends a certain creaminess to a dish and helps to bind it together, just as to gratiné it gives it a crust. Not every combination of pasta and cheese is, however, Italian. There are spaetzle from Germany, knöpfli from Switzerland, and the many varied ways of preparing dumplings, known in the Alpine countries as knödeln or nocken, and as gnocchi in Italy.

All recipes serve 4 unless otherwise indicated.

MAKING NOODLES WITH A PASTA MACHINE. The prepared pasta dough, gathered into a ball, is cut into slices and rolled out thin using the pasta maker. The flat band of pasta is then cut into noodles of the desired thickness by the appropriate cutter.

BASIC RECIPE FOR PASTA

There is no more an ideal recipe for pasta dough than there is an ideal pasta, since everyone has his or her own ideas on the subject. The following recipe has won the approval of many critical gourmets.

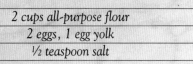

2 cups all-purpose flour
2 eggs, 1 egg yolk
½ teaspoon salt

Prepare the pasta dough as described in the picture sequence below.

Sift the flour onto the work surface and make a well in the center. Crack in the eggs, and add the egg yolk and salt.

Working from the center outwards, mix the eggs and flour together by hand until all the flour is incorporated.

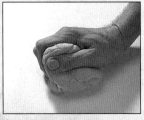

Knead the dough until smooth and elastic. If necessary, add more flour or water, depending on consistency. Wrap in plastic wrap and leave to rest for 1 hour.

Dust the work surface sparingly with flour and roll out the rested dough into as thin a rectangle as possible.

To make flat ribbon noodles (fettuccine or tagliatelle), let the dough dry very briefly, so that it does not stick. Fold the rectangle of dough in towards the center twice.

Use a sharp knife to cut strips ¼ or ⅜ inch wide. To dry, unroll and spread out on a floured cloth.

Homemade pasta in all colors

It is hardly worth debating whether pasta should be bought or made at home. These days, you can buy fresh and dried pasta of the highest quality; it may taste different from the homemade article, but it is almost as good. What you decide, therefore, may depend more on the time you have than on taste. You can buy different colored pastas or make them at home. Pasta dough can be tinted easily with saffron or with tomato paste. A green color requires only a little more effort, since the dye must first be extracted from the spinach. You can use cuttlefish, the ink from cuttlefish, to make black noodles.

GREEN PASTA

For the spinach dye:
7 oz (5 cups) spinach, 2–3 tablespoons water
For the pasta:
1⅓ cups all-purpose flour, 5–6 egg yolks
1 tablespoon olive oil
½ teaspoon salt, 3 tablespoons butter
nutmeg, salt

The spinach dye, being largely neutral in taste, is also suitable for coloring sauces, stuffings, and sweet dishes. The picture sequence below illustrates how to obtain the dye. A food mixer with a dough hook can be a big help in preparing the dough. Place all the ingredients in the mixing bowl and work the dough with the dough hook at the lowest setting, or process in a food processor, until it comes together in a ball. Then knead it again thoroughly by hand on a floured work surface, until nice and smooth.

Salsa di pomodoro. Prepared from fresh, ripe tomatoes and seasoned with a little garlic, it goes with all types of pasta. With freshly grated Parmesan, it's a delicacy in itself!

Spinach coloring:

Finely purée a few spinach leaves with 2–3 tablespoons water in a small blender or processor. Add the remaining spinach gradually and reduce to a purée.

Place the puréed spinach in a cheesecloth. Over a bowl, squeeze out the juice by twisting the cloth from both ends. This is easier with a helper!

The proper way to cook pasta:

It is important to have plenty of salted water at a rolling boil. You need about 5 cups for every 4 oz of pasta, so that the water does not stop boiling after the pasta is added.

Heat the spinach juice in a saucepan to about 150°F, taking care not to boil. Use a tea strainer to skim off and drain the chlorophyll, which will mass together.

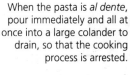

When the pasta is *al dente*, pour immediately and all at once into a large colander to drain, so that the cooking process is arrested.

Tinting the dough:

Add the spinach coloring to the dough ingredients and knead everything to a smooth, supple dough. If necessary, add more flour or water.

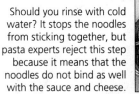

Should you rinse with cold water? It stops the noodles from sticking together, but pasta experts reject this step because it means that the noodles do not bind as well with the sauce and cheese.

Cooking pasta properly requires plenty of boiling water and careful observation. The cooking process must not be interrupted, and the noodles must be drained and served or dealt with further as soon as they are done. Only really freshly cooked hot pasta binds well with the other ingredients, especially with the cheese.

Roll the dough into a ball and wrap with plastic wrap to protect from drying out. Leave to rest for at least 1 hour.

Fettucine, butter and Parmesan

This is the simplest way of combining noodles with cheese, and it is the simplest recipes that require the best ingredients. Even the smallest compromise in quality can jeopardize success. It is equally important to prepare the dish properly. Follow the instructions for cooking pasta on page 169. Remember, the pasta should always be served as soon as it is cooked, especially when it is combined with cheese.

1 cup + 2 teaspoons each all-purpose flour and durum semolina
3 eggs, 1 egg yolk, ½ teaspoon salt
lightly salted water for cooking the pasta
7 tablespoons butter
1 cup freshly grated Parmesan

Prepare a pasta dough as described on page 168, and make it into fettucine. Cook until *al dente*, drain, and pour onto a warmed plate or bowl. Under no circumstances rinse under cold water, since this could prevent the noodles from binding properly with the cheese. It is a good idea to reserve a little of the cooking water in order to moisten the noodles if they become too dry. Mix the butter and Parmesan into the noodles as quickly as possible. Serve at once.

The choice of grating cheeses is not limited to Parmesan. Grana Padano and Grana Trentino, an especially fine extra-hard cheese made from raw milk, also belong to the family of extra-hard cheeses. Cheeses with a higher fat content, too, such as Sbrinz and Provolone Piccante, also taste good with pasta, and sheep's-milk cheeses from the Pecorino and Manchego families lend a distinctive note.

Add the eggs to the whole-wheat and soy flours. Season with salt, add the oil and water, and knead to a smooth, supple dough.

RED TAGLIATELLE WITH FONDUTA AND CAVIAR

Freshly cooked tagliatelle with a freshly prepared fonduta is a delicacy in itself: adding a potent spoonful of caviar turns it into an unforgettable experience.

For the pasta dough:
2¼ cups all-purpose flour
3–4 egg yolks
4 tablespoons melted clarified butter, salt
2 tablespoons tomato paste
about ¼ cup water
For the fonduta:
10 oz Fontina or Emmental
1⅛ cups milk
4 tablespoons butter
3 egg yolks
Sevruga caviar
fresh basil leaves to garnish

Prepare a pasta dough and make into tagliatelle as described on page 168. Cut the cheese into wafer-thin slices, place in a bowl, cover with the milk, and leave to soften at room temperature for at least 2 hours. Melt the butter in a frying pan, add the softened cheese with half of the milk, and stir constantly over low heat until a creamy mass is formed. Add the egg yolks to the sauce one at a time and stir in at once. Cook the tagliatelle in boiling salted water until *al dente*, then drain. Mix the sauce into the fresh, hot noodles and serve on warmed plates, or serve the noodles with the sauce poured on top, so that everyone can mix their own. As a final touch, garnish with caviar and basil.

WHOLE-WHEAT SPAGHETTI WITH GORGONZOLA

This variety of pasta tastes strong and aromatic, and harmonizes ideally with cheese.

For the pasta dough:
3½ cups whole-wheat flour, 1 tablespoon soy flour
2 eggs, 1 teaspoons salt, ground white pepper, 3 tablespoons sunflower oil
5 tablespoons warm water
For the Gorgonzola sauce:
1 clove garlic
1 small onion
1 stalk celery
2 tomatoes
¼ cup black olives
6 anchovy fillets
2 tablespoons butter
pepper and salt
3½ oz Gorgonzola Piccante, cut into cubes
3 tablespoons grated Parmesan

Make pasta dough as described on page 168, roll out thinly, and put through the spaghetti cutter of the pasta machine. Preheat the oven to 425°F. Finely chop the garlic and onions. Cut the celery into narrow strips. Peel, core, and dice the tomatoes. Pit the olives and chop coarsely. Finely chop the anchovy fillets. Sauté the onion, garlic, and celery in the butter until tender. Add the cubed tomato and chopped anchovy fillets, cook briefly, and season with pepper, and with salt if necessary. Cook the spaghetti until *al dente* and drain in a colander. Add the olives and the spaghetti to the sauce, mix well, and put on plates. Scatter the Gorgonzola cubes and the Parmesan on top and cook in the oven until the cheese melts.

FETTUCINE ALFREDO

This dish, named after a Roman pasta chef, is a true paragon of simplicity.

(not illustrated)
10 oz fettucine; salted water; ¼ cup butter
1¼ cups freshly grated Parmesan, 1 cup heavy cream
salt, freshly ground white pepper
a pinch freshly grated nutmeg

Cook the fettucine in plenty of fast-boiling salted water until *al dente*. In a small saucepan bring the cream just to a boil. Melt the butter in a large saucepan, add the well-drained noodles, and toss briefly. Add the Parmesan and mix with 2 forks. Add the warm cream and continue to toss the noodles to mix in well. Season to taste with the salt, pepper, and nutmeg, and serve at once.

PENNE AL MASCARPONE

14 oz penne rigate; salted water
12 cherry tomatoes, ¼ cup butter
⅔ cup grated Parmesan, ½ cup Mascarpone
3 oz ham, cut into cubes
salt, freshly ground pepper, some nutmeg

Cook the penne in boiling salted water until *al dente*. Meanwhile, wash the cherry tomatoes, remove their stems, and cut them in half. Heat 2 teaspoons of the butter in a frying pan, sauté the tomatoes briefly over high heat, and keep warm. Drain the pasta and transfer to a warm bowl. Melt the remaining butter and mix into the pasta with the Parmesan and the Mascarpone until the cheese is melted. Season, and scatter the cubes of ham on top. Serve on warmed plates, garnished with the tomatoes.

PERCIATELLE WITH ZUCCHINI IN A CREAM SAUCE

1 zucchini, 1 yellow pepper
1 onion, diced; 1 garlic clove, crushed
¼ cup butter, 1 cup heavy cream
salt and pepper
14 oz perciatelle or long macaroni
3 tablespoons grated Parmesan, 1 cup grated Fontina

With cheese and cream

A multitude of pasta dishes are traditionally prepared with these ingredients. A creative cook will invent new ones by experimenting with whatever is to hand, such as vegetables, ham, mushrooms, or aromatic fresh herbs. Such pasta dishes are, by virtue of the ingredients they contain, quite filling, and portions do not need to be large. They also make superb hors d'oeuvre, in which case serve only one-third to one-half of the amount intended for a main-course portion.

Slice the zucchini in rounds and dice the pepper. Melt half of the butter in a frying pan, and sweat the onion and garlic until lightly colored. Add the other vegetables and cook for about 5 minutes. Pour in the cream, season, and heat to just below boiling point. In the meantime, cook the pasta in boiling salted water until *al dente*, drain, and mix immediately with the remaining butter, the vegetables, and the cheese. Serve at once.

BLACK NOODLES
ON A BED OF YELLOW PEPPERS

A particularly attractive dish, this would taste no less delicate made with plain yellow noodles. Cuttlefish ink, or cuttlefish, is a neutral-tasting dye, so it tints the dough wonderfully black without affecting the taste. Nor do the black noodles lose any of their color when boiled — and the water remains completely clear (see tip on page 180).

For the noodles:
2½ cups all-purpose flour, 2 eggs, 2 teaspoons olive oil
½ teaspoon salt, 4 teaspoons cuttlefish ink
For the peppers:
2 yellow peppers, 1 garlic clove
2 shallots, 2 tablespoons olive oil, salt and pepper
1 cup heavy cream, 6 oz Fontal or Fontina
3 tablespoons butter
chervil leaves to garnish

Preheat the oven to 485°F. Prepare the pasta dough according to the method on page 168. Halve, stem, and core the peppers, and cut their flesh into fine dice. Finely dice the garlic clove and the shallots. Heat the oil in a frying pan and sweat the shallots and garlic until lightly colored. Add the diced peppers, season to taste with salt and pepper, and sauté until softened; keep warm. Bring the cream to a boil and reduce by about half. Cook the noodles in boiling salted water until *al dente* and drain in a colander. Divide the cooked peppers among 4 plates and arrange the noodles on top. Sprinkle with the cheese, cut into strips, and pour the hot cream on top. Drizzle with the melted butter and in the oven in the oven until the cheese is melted. Garnish with chervil leaves.

GREEN LASAGNE BOLOGNESE

Serves 8 as an appetizer, or 4 as a main course.
For the dough:
3 cups all-purpose flour, 10–12 egg yolks
2 tablespoons olive oil,
1 teaspoon salt, 6 tablespoons butter, nutmeg, salt
2 recipes spinach coloring (see page 169)
For the filling:
3 tablespoons clarified butter
1 lb lean ground meat (half beef, half pork)
½ cup each diced celery, carrots, and onions
salt, black pepper
3 tablespoons tomato paste, 2¼ cups meat broth
1 tablespoon chopped parsley
For the béchamel sauce:
2 tablespoons butter, ¼ cup all-purpose flour
2¼ cups milk
salt, white pepper, grated nutmeg
¾ cup grated Parmesan
butter for greasing

Prepare the pasta dough according to the method on page 168, roll out thinly, and cut into sheets the width of the casserole. Cook the pasta in boiling salted water until *al dente*, rinse in cold water, and drain. Heat the clarified butter in a frying pan, and fry the ground meat over high heat. Add the vegetables and tomato paste. Season with salt and pepper, add the broth and parsley, and cook over moderate heat for 30 minutes. To make the béchamel sauce, melt the butter and whisk in the flour, taking care not to brown it. Pour in the milk, whisk until smooth, and bring to a boil. Season the sauce and cook for about 20 minutes over a low heat, stirring constantly, then pass through a strainer. Preheat the oven to 425°F and grease a large casserole. Cover the bottom of the casserole with sheets of pasta, and spoon on a layer of meat sauce. Place more pasta on top, and pour on some béchamel sauce. Repeat this sequence, using up all the ingredients, finishing with a layer of béchamel sauce. Sprinkle the Parmesan on top. Bake in the center of the oven for about 20 minutes, until golden brown.

Cut the finished lasagne into rectangles, so that you can easily take one serving at a time from the dish.

GREEN RAVIOLI FILLED WITH GOAT CHEESE. Mix 5 oz goat cheese with 1 egg, ⅔ cup grated Parmesan, 4½ teaspoons butter, and some chopped fresh basil. Prepare the ravioli as described in the adjacent recipe and fill with the goat cheese. Serve with tomato quarters that have been sautéed in butter and seasoned with garlic.

MEAT RAVIOLI

For the pasta dough:
2½ cups all-purpose flour, 1 egg, 1 egg yolk
2 tablespoons olive oil, ⅓ cup water, 1 teaspoon salt
For the filling:
4 oz pork, diced, 3 oz calves' liver, diced
1½ tablespoons clarified butter
1 tablespoon finely chopped onion, 4 tablespoons butter
3 tablespoons chopped mixed herbs, nutmeg
1 egg, 1 egg yolk, 1¼ cups grated Parmesan
salt and white pepper

To make the dough, sift the flour onto a work surface and make a well in the center. Add the other ingredients, mix thoroughly, and knead. Form the dough into a ball, wrap in plastic wrap, and leave to rest. Salt and pepper the pork and the calves' liver, and brown in the clarified butter for 2–3 minutes. Allow to cool in a colander. Sweat the onions in the butter until golden, add the herbs, and allow to cool. Mix the pork, liver, and onions, add nutmeg, and put through the finest disk of a meat grinder. Work the egg, egg yolk, half the cheese, and the seasonings into the ground meat. Roll out the dough into two thin sheets of equal size. Mark out squares on one sheet and place a bit of filling in the center of each. Brush the spaces in between the filling with water or egg yolk. Cover with the second sheet of dough and press on well. Cut out squares with a pastry wheel. Cook the ravioli in boiling water until done, drain, and place on plates. Melt the remaining butter, drizzle it over the ravioli, and sprinkle with Parmesan.

RICOTTA AND EGG-YOLK TORTELLI

Tortelli are round ravioli in a single-portion size, just right for serving as an appetizer.

For the pasta dough:
1⅓ cups all-purpose flour, 5 egg yolks
salt, 1 tablespoon olive oil
For the filling:
1½ cups spinach, blanched
¼ cup Ricotta
¾ cup grated Parmesan
salt, pepper, nutmeg
4 eggs, 3 tablespoons butter, 1 small white truffle

Prepare the pasta dough according to the method on page 168, and leave to rest. To make the filling, squeeze the spinach dry and chop finely. Press the Ricotta through a strainer and mix with the spinach and 5 tablespoons of the Parmesan cheese. Season with salt, pepper, and nutmeg. Roll the pasta dough out thinly and cut out 4 circles 4 inches in diameter and 4 circles 4½ inches diameter. Place the filling on the smaller circles and make a well in the center. Separate the eggs and place an egg yolk in each well. Brush the edges of the smaller circles with egg white, cover with the larger circles and press down firmly. Slide the tortelli into boiling salted water and cook for 3–4 minutes. Meanwhile, melt the butter. Drain the tortelli and place on warmed plates, drizzle with melted butter and sprinkle with the remaining Parmesan. As a finishing touch, thinly shave a few truffle slices over the top.

SPINACH RAVIOLI

For the pasta dough:
1¼ cups each rye flour and wheat flour
1 egg, 2 egg yolks, salt, 1 tablespoon oil
For the filling:
1¼ lb spinach leaves, 3 tablespoons chopped parsley
2 teaspoons flour, 6 tablespoons butter
1 cup milk, 1 onion
salt, white pepper, grated nutmeg
¾ cup grated Parmesan, snipped chives

Prepare the pasta dough according to the method on page 168, and leave to rest. To make the filling, trim, wash and blanch the spinach, rinse with cold water, squeeze out well, and purée with the parsley. Melt 2 teaspoons of butter, whisk in the flour, and cook without letting it color. Add the milk, whisk until smooth, and simmer for about 20 minutes. Finely dice the onion and sweat in 4 teaspoons of butter. Add the spinach purée and cook for 2–3 minutes. Strain the sauce onto the purée, mix, and bring to a boil. Season to taste with salt, pepper, and nutmeg, stir in 2 tablespoons of Parmesan, and let cool. Roll out the dough thinly, cut into ovals, and place a bit of filling in the center of each. Brush the edges with water or egg, fold over, and press the edges together firmly. Work quickly to prevent the surface from drying out and the bottom from softening. Cook in boiling salted water for 3–5 minutes. Lift out, drain, and place on plates. Lightly brown the remaining butter and drizzle it over the pasta. Sprinkle with the remaining Parmesan and garnish with chives.

VEGETABLE CANNELLONI

8 cannelloni shells
For the béchamel sauce:
4½ teaspoons butter, ¼ cup all-purpose flour
2¼ cups milk
salt and nutmeg, 2 egg yolks, ½ cup heavy cream
⅔ cup grated Grana Padano or Parmigiano Reggiano
For the vegetable filling:
2 tablespoons butter, ½ cup finely chopped scallions
1 cup chopped leek, ¾ cup chopped carrots
1 cup chopped celery, ½ cup chopped red peppers,
1¾ cups vegetable broth
2¼ cups broccoli flowerets, 1 heaping cup chopped zucchini,
⅓ cup grated Grana Padano or Parmigiano Reggiano
parsley for garnishing

Preheat the oven to 485°F and grease a casserole dish. Prepare a béchamel sauce as described in steps 1–6 of the picture sequence on page 164. Cook the cannelloni shells in plenty of boiling salted water until *al dente*, lift out, and drain. Melt the butter in a saucepan and sauté the scallions, leek, carrots, celery, and peppers. Add the broth and bring to a boil. Cook for 4 minutes, then add the broccoli and zucchini, and cook for a further 4 minutes. Lift out the vegetables, drain thoroughly, and heat in a dry pot for 2–3 minutes, until they are dry. Mix with two-thirds of the sauce. Fill the cannelloni with the mixture, ideally using a pastry bag. Place the cannelloni in the casserole, pour on the remaining sauce, and sprinkle with the grated cheese. Bake on the middle rack of the oven for 20 minutes. Garnish with parsley.

Young, fresh spinach is one of the traditional fillings for pasta dishes and should be replaced with frozen spinach only if absolutely necessary.

Polenta

Polenta is a simple dish that for many generations now has been improved with the addition of cheese. The recipe looks quite easy on paper: 4½ cups water, 1 teaspoon salt, and 1¼ cups cornmeal, plus butter to taste and, of course, cheese. The latter can be an extra-hard Parmesan or Pecorino, or other cheese from the Alpine regions. There, people have always been experts at the proper preparation of polenta, using a copper kettle, a direct wood fire, and lots of time. The copper kettle and the wood fire can, of course, be replaced by a modern high-grade steel pot on a gas or electric stove, but even nowadays a polenta cannot be rushed if it is to be of top quality. Polenta is frequently served as a side dish, like mashed potatoes, or it can be made as in the recipe opposite. The slices of polenta can also be pan-fried in plenty of butter until crisp on both sides, and served with meat or game dishes. Accompanied by a fresh salad, polenta makes a simple but fine main course. Connoisseurs like to nibble the crust that remains on the sides of the pan.

Traditionalists claim that prerequisite for good polenta is stirring in one direction only — for nearly 1 hour.

Traditionally made in a copper kettle:

When the polenta starts to thicken, stirring becomes hard work.

The polenta is done when it pulls away from the kettle. A solid crust remains on the sides of the kettle.

After butter and cheese are worked in, the polenta is turned out onto a board.

POLENTA WITH CHEESE AND HERBS

2½ cups water, 1 teaspoon salt
1¼ cups medium-fine cornmeal
freshly ground pepper, grated nutmeg
¾ cup butter, 1¼ cups grated Parmesan
2 garlic cloves, crushed
2 tablespoons chopped herbs (basil, parsley, sage)

Preheat the oven to 425°F. Bring the salted water to a boil in a large pot, and pour in the cornmeal in a fine stream, stirring constantly. Do not let the water temperature fall below boiling point, as this could cause lumps to form. Season and continue to stir constantly, as shown in the adjacent picture sequence. When the polenta is done, stir in half of the butter and cheese, and adjust the seasoning if necessary. Spread out on a buttered baking sheet to about ¾-inch thickness and let cool thoroughly. Lightly butter a casserole, melt the remaining butter in a saucepan, and sauté the garlic and herbs. Cut the polenta into rectangles of equal size and overlap them in the casserole. Pour the herb butter on top and sprinkle with the remaining cheese. Bake until crusty and brown.

Gnocchi

Traditional Italian recipes bear witness to how well gnocchi combine with cheese. Gnocchi are just as popular as a main course as an accompaniment for meat and vegetable dishes.

POTATO GNOCCHI WITH CHEESE

1 ¾ lb russet or other mealy potatoes, salt
3 egg yolks
1 cup all-purpose flour
1⅔ cups grated Parmesan
grated nutmeg, salt
1 tablespoon chopped herbs (thyme, parsley and chives)
¼ cup butter

Preheat the oven to 450°F. Peel the potatoes, halve if desired, and cook in boiling salted water until done; drain and steam dry in the oven. Pass through a potato ricer or food mill, and work the egg yolks in quickly. Mix in the flour, then 1 cup of cheese, and season to taste with the nutmeg and salt. Form the mixture into ¾-inch long, oval shapes and make a dent in the center of each with the back of a knife. Add the gnocchi to boiling salted water, bring back to a boil, and cook for about 3 minutes, until done. Lift out of the water, drain, and arrange on plates. Sprinkle with the remaining cheese and the herbs. Heat the butter in a saucepan until nut-brown and pour over the gnocchi. An excellent variation is gnocchi au gratin. Proceed as above, then pour reduced cream on top and bake until light brown.

GNOCCHI ALLA ROMANA

2¼ cups milk
¼ cup butter
½ teaspoon salt, white pepper
grated nutmeg
¾ cup durum semolina
2 egg yolks, 1 whole egg
⅔ cup grated Parmesan

Preheat the oven to 425°F and oil a baking sheet. Prepare the semolina according to the instructions opposite and allow to swell. Pour onto the baking sheet, and spread out smoothly to about ¾ inch thick. Sprinkle the grated Parmesan on top and allow to cool. Melt the remaining butter and use some to grease a casserole. Stamp or cut out half-moon shapes from the semolina, place in the casserole, and drizzle with the remaining butter. Bake the gnocchi until golden brown.

Preparing the semolina:

Bring the milk and 2 tablespoons of the butter to a boil. Season with salt, freshly ground pepper, and nutmeg.

As soon as the milk begins to boil, pour in the semolina, stirring constantly.

Stir the egg and the yolks one at a time into the semolina, which will have swelled up. Bring to a rolling boil.

Cheese spaetzle will taste just as good whether produced by a spaetzle mill (top) or cut into ribbons by hand (above).

CHEESE SPAETZLE

As with many regional specialties, there are a number of recipes for cheese spaetzle. A very piquant version worth recommending is made by replacing half of the Emmental with ripe Romadur or Limburger.

3 cups flour
6 eggs
3 tablespoons water
salt
1⅓ cups grated Emmental
2 onions
¼ cup butter

Make a batter by sifting the flour into a bowl and adding the eggs, water, and salt. Beat until bubbly, then leave to stand for several minutes. Using a spaetzle mill, drop the batter into plenty of boiling water. (You can also make spaetzle by hand, but it requires practice and is more time-consuming.) When the spaetzle are cooked, they will rise to the surface: lift them out with a skimmer and drain in a colander. Layer the spaetzle in a serving bowl with the cheese and keep warm in a low oven. Slice the onions, into rings and fry in the butter until golden brown. Pour the onions and butter over the spaetzle, and serve.

CHEESE DUMPLINGS

These light dumplings can be prepared in various ways. Traditionally, they were made in the Tyrol with Graukäse. This recipe with Emmental is equally delicious.

1 cup milk, 9–10 slices stale bread
1 onion, 6 tablespoons butter
9 oz Emmental
1 tablespoon all-purpose flour, 2 eggs, 1 egg yolk
2 tablespoons chopped herbs (parsley and chives)
salt, pepper, nutmeg
½ cup grated Parmesan

Warm the milk and pour over the bread, and allow to soften. Finely dice the onions and sauté in 2 teaspoons of butter until golden brown. Cut the cheese into small cubes, add to the bread with the onion, flour, eggs, and egg yolk, and combine well. Stir the herbs into the mixture and season to taste with the salt, pepper, and nutmeg. Moisten your hands. Then, using a tablespoon, mold dumplings the size of eggs in your wet hand. Cook in boiling salted water for 12–15 minutes until done. Meanwhile, lightly brown the remaining butter. Drain the cooked dumplings on paper towels and arrange on plates. Sprinkle with Parmesan, drizzle with the browned butter, and serve.

Open-pan method:

Heat 4 teaspoons butter in a pot and sweat the onion without letting it color.

Pour in the rice all at once, and begin stirring immediately over a high heat.

Keep stirring the rice until the grains look translucent. Neither the onions nor the rice should brown.

Pour in the wine and continue stirring as it is absorbed.

Keep adding more meat broth as it is absorbed, stirring constantly so that the rice does not stick.

Salt the risotto and cook for another 12–15 minutes until done. Add additional broth as required.

Add the grated cheese and the remaining butter, cover the pot, and remove from the heat.

Risotto

Rice is a mainstay of the Italian kitchen. Risotto dishes show it off to greatest advantage, and in most of these cheese plays its part. The traditional Italian varieties of rice — arborio, carnaroli, and vialone — are particularly suitable for risotto; most of the recipes that follow call for arborio rice, but either of the others can be substituted. The highest quality of rice, called *fino* or *superfino*, absorbs the maximum amount of liquid without losing shape, producing the ideal consistency. Whether beef, veal, or chicken broth is used depends on what the ingredients harmonize with, and on personal taste. The salt content of the broth will determine how much salt you need to add to the risotto.

The picture sequence opposite illustrates the open-pan method. The pot is not covered, and the rice is stirred occasionally until it has absorbed all the liquid it can; it should be *al dente*. Leaving the pot uncovered enables you to adjust the moistness of the risotto by adding broth during the cooking. The other option is to add all the broth at once, cover the pot, and allow the liquid to be absorbed. The consistency then lies somewhere in between the classic moist risotto and a dry pilaf. The following basic recipe may be varied by adding vegetables, meat, herbs, and seasonings.

BASIC RISOTTO RECIPE
2¼ cups arborio rice, ¼ cup butter
1 onion, finely chopped
⅔ cup white wine, 5–5½ cups meat broth, salt

Opinions differ widely on just how wet risotto should be. For this reason, and because of the evaporation during open-pan cooking, the exact quantity of liquid needed cannot be given.

BROWN-RICE RISOTTO

1 onion, finely chopped
6 tablespoons butter
2 cups brown rice
5–5½ cups meat broth
nutmeg and salt
2 small carrots, ½ leek
2 stalks celery
½ cup grated Ragusano or Provolone Piccante
2 tablespoons chopped herbs (chervil, parsley, basil)

Sauté the onions in half of the butter, add the rice, and cook until translucent. Season with nutmeg and salt, cook for 35 minutes, adding the broth in stages and stirring frequently. Dice the carrots and leek, and finely chop the celery. Sweat these vegetables briefly in the remaining butter and remove from the heat. Add to the rice and cook together for 10–15 minutes. Stir the cheese into the risotto and sprinkle the herbs on top. Serve immediately.

RISOTTO NERO

1 onion, chopped; 6 tablespoons butter
2¼ cups arborio rice
⅔ cup dry red wine, preferably Barolo
4 teaspoons cuttlefish ink, 5–5½ cups meat broth
salt, ⅓ cup grated Parmesan
1 boiled lobster tail and chervil to garnish

Sweat the onion in ¼ cup of the butter without letting it color, add the rice, and cook until translucent. Add the Barolo and allow to reduce. Thin the cuttlefish ink with a little broth and stir into the rice. Add the broth in stages and season with salt, stirring constantly, until the rice is cooked, about 12–15 minutes. Stir in the remaining butter and the Parmesan. Garnish each portion with slices of boiled lobster tail and chervil.

To collect the ink from a cuttlefish, pull the head with the insides away from the body. Remove the ink sac at the bottom, cut it open, and squeeze out the black substance. Stir with a little cold water and pass through a fine strainer. You now have a neutral-tasting dye. Cuttlefish ink is also available commercially.

RISOTTO WITH PEAS AND PANCETTA

(not illustrated)
3 oz pancetta (unsmoked Italian-style bacon)
½ cup chopped onion, ½ cup chopped celery
1½ cups round-grain rice, salt and pepper
4½ cups chicken broth
2 cups peas (fresh or frozen)
3 tablespoons butter, ⅔ cup grated Asiago

Dice the pancetta and sweat in a saucepan until the fat runs. Add the onions and celery, and sauté briefly. Add the rice, season, and cook until translucent. Pour in the broth and cook for about 5 minutes with the lid off. Add the peas and cook until done. Add the butter and cheese, replace the lid, and allow the flavors to meld for 3–4 minutes. Stir before serving.

RISOTTO
WITH PORCINI.
Prepare a risotto as on
page 179. Clean and slice 1 lb
porcini mushrooms, fry them quickly
in butter, and mix into the risotto.

SAFFRON RISOTTO

This is the classic Risotto alla Milanese, in which the combined flavors of beef marrow, saffron, and white wine dominate. A young Pinot Bianco is the ideal wine to drink with this. Use only fresh saffron threads, as the quality of saffron powder is unreliable. Experiment to determine the exact amount needed: add the threads in small doses, since with this expensive spice you can very quickly have too much of a good thing in terms of both color and flavor.

1–2 tablespoons beef marrow, 5 tablespoons butter
1 onion, finely chopped
½ clove garlic, crushed
2¼ cups arborio rice
⅔ cup white wine
5–5½ cups meat broth
salt, about ¼ teaspoon saffron threads
¾ cup grated Parmesan

Soak the beef marrow in cold water for 15–30 minutes, then dice, and, over very low heat, render down in 2 tablespoons of the butter. Raise the heat to medium, add the onion and garlic, and sauté. Add the rice and cook until translucent. Moisten with the white wine and let it cook down slightly. Add the saffron to ¼ cup of the broth and stir well. Add the mixture to the rice. Continue to add hot broth as it is absorbed. Add the salt and cook until done, stirring frequently. Lastly, stir in the cheese and the remaining butter. Garnish with butter curls if wished.

You can replace some of the butter or beef marrow with pancetta. This underscores the typical risotto taste that Italians love.

TOMATO RISOTTO

1 onion, chopped finely; 6 tablespoons butter
2¼ cups vialone rice
5–5½ cups meat broth
3 tablespoons tomato paste, 1 cup tomato juice
salt, a pinch of sugar, pepper
2 tomatoes, peeled and seeded
½ cup grated Pecorino
chives to garnish

Sweat the onions in half of the butter without letting them color, then add the rice and cook until translucent. Add some hot broth, followed by the tomato paste and tomato juice, and stir well. Season and continue to add more broth as it is absorbed, stirring frequently. The rice will be done in 15–18 minutes. Cube the tomatoes and add to the risotto. Gently stir the remaining butter and the cheese into the risotto.

Fish, meat, and poultry

International cuisine yields a number of popular dishes in which meat and fish are combined with cheese. Veal Cordon Bleu is a fine example: ham and cheese encased in a breaded veal cutlet. The same method can be used successfully with different meats, especially with turkey breast, and with the wide choice of semi-hard and blue-veined cheeses available. In some cases a filling of cheese alone might be too rich, so it can be combined with mushrooms, vegetables, or fruit. Similarly, there are various ways of coating fish or meat with a mixture containing cheese, whether it be a panada with bread crumbs and grated cheese, or, as in the case of the famous Piccata alla Milanese, a crust of egg and cheese. Meat and fish dishes can also be topped with cheese sauces, or just plain cheese, and baked. Recognizing when and how to use cheese — whether it should be a dominant ingredient or a subordinate seasoning, or whether it should be used at all — is very important. The fish dish illustrated opposite is a good example: a herbed red mullet seasoned inside with salt and pepper, stuffed with fresh herbs, pan-fried, and served with plenty of fresh butter is a delight. However, it can be turned into a real delicacy by sprinkling the stuffed fish with a mixture of two-thirds bread crumbs and one-third grated Parmesan, drizzling generously with butter, baking until the topping is crisp and brown, and serving with broiled cherry tomatoes and a yellow pepper sauce. The creative cook will enjoy experimenting with cheese as a seasoning and a main ingredient, even in combination with foods that are not considered to be very cheese-friendly.

All recipes serve 4 unless otherwise indicated.

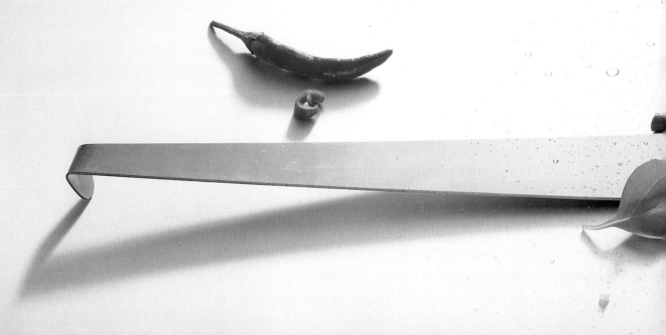

CHICKEN WITH A CHEESE STUFFING

2 small chickens (about 1½ lb each)

salt and pepper

For the stuffing:

1½ stale rolls, 2 tablespoons butter

¼ cup diced onion, 1 garlic clove, crushed

1½ oz smoked bacon, diced (about ¼ cup)

⅓ cup finely chopped chicken livers

½ cup lukewarm milk, 1 egg

3 tablespoons chopped herbs (parsley, basil, and thyme)

salt and pepper

4 oz Gruyère, diced

melted butter for frying and basting

Lightly salt and pepper the chickens inside and out. Cut the half roll into small cubes and fry in half of the butter. Heat the remaining butter and sweat the onions, garlic, and chopped bacon until lightly colored. Add the chicken livers and fry for about 1 minute. Continue as explained on the right. Preheat the oven to 400°F. Brush the chickens with melted butter and roast on a rack for 40–45 minutes. After 30 minutes cooking time, sprinkle with the remaining herbs and again brush generously with butter.

Stuffing the chicken:

Remove the crust from 1 roll. Slice the roll, cover with the milk, and allow to soften.

Add the egg, half of the herbs, and the bacon–chicken liver mixture. Season with salt and pepper.

Add the browned bread cubes and the Gruyère, and mix well together.

Spoon equal amounts of cheese stuffing into each chicken. Do not overstuff.

Use toothpicks or a needle and cotton thread to seal the body cavity. Tie the legs in place.

Cover the freshly roasted chickens with foil and leave to rest for 8–10 minutes. In this way they stay beautifully juicy, and can be cut in half more easily.

VEAL CORDON BLEU

This dish, which has earned its place among the classics of international cuisine, originated in western Switzerland. The original recipe calls for pork cutlet, filled with hearty Gruyère, and is a variation well worth recommending. In the following recipe, the size of the ham and cheese should match that of the veal scaloppine.

4 veal scaloppine
salt, pepper, paprika
4 slices of cooked ham
4 slices of Emmental
flour, 1 egg, beaten
fresh white bread crumbs
butter for frying

Make a pocket for the stuffing in each scaloppine. Season inside and out, fill each with a slice of ham and cheese, and press firmly together. Dredge in flour, dip in beaten egg, and coat with bread crumbs. Melt the butter in a frying pan and fry the scaloppine for 3–4 minutes on each side, until appetizingly brown and crisp. Drain briefly on paper towels and serve with side dishes of your choice.

PORGY STUFFED WITH CHEESE

Stuffed with blue cheese and baked au gratin with Parmesan — two methods that work together to produce a taste treat.

Serves 2
1 porgy, weighing 1–1¼ lb
salt and pepper
1½ oz Bleu des Causses or other blue cheese, ¼ cup butter
1 garlic clove, crushed
1 small zucchini, sliced
2 tomatoes, halved
1 tablespoon each fresh white bread crumbs, grated Parmesan, and chopped parsley

Preheat the oven to 400°F. Scale the gutted fish and cut off all fins. Wash under running water and pat dry with paper towels. Season the cavity with salt and pepper, fill with the blue cheese, and close with toothpicks. Melt half of the butter in a casserole that will comfortably hold the fish, briefly fry the garlic, the zucchini and the tomatoes, and season with salt. Place the stuffed fish on top. Mix the bread crumbs, Parmesan, and parsley, scatter over the fish, and pour on the remaining melted butter. Bake for 10–12 minutes, until the topping is crisp and brown.

VEAL ROLLS WITH GOUDA IN A RICH TOMATO SAUCE

Gouda and prosciutto harmonize superbly with veal, but interesting fillings can also be created from a wide variety of semi-hard and semi-soft cheeses in combination with other types of ham. Turkey cutlets stuffed with cooked ham and Roquefort are a good example.

For the veal rolls:
8 veal scaloppine (2½ oz each)
3 tablespoons olive oil
7 oz medium-aged Gouda
8 small slices prosciutto
8 small sage leaves
salt and white pepper
For the sauce:
2 onions, finely diced
½ cup tomato paste
2 pinches of sugar
2¼ cups meat broth
2 skinned, finely chopped tomatoes
For the bouquet garni:
1 garlic clove
1 piece of green part of leek, 1 sprig of thyme
6 sprigs of parsley

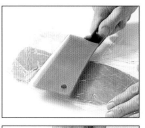

Filet mignon stuffed with Stilton — a splendid-tasting combination. The stuffed filet is wrapped with pork belly held in place with kitchen string, to stop the cheese running out while the meat is cooking.

Cheese — coating and filling

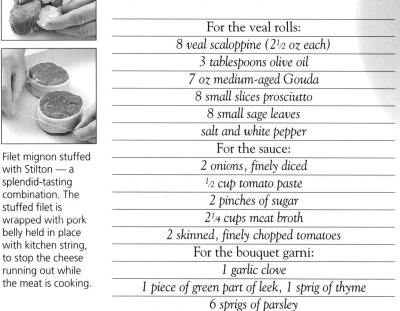

Stuffing and preparing the veal rolls:

Place the veal scaloppine between two pieces of oiled plastic wrap and beat them flat. Cut the Gouda into 8 pieces of equal size, 1–1½ inches narrower than the scaloppine. Wrap each piece of cheese, together with a sage leaf, in a slice of prosciutto.

Salt and pepper the veal and place a prosciutto roll on top of each slice. Fold in the sides of the veal and roll up so that the stuffing is completely enclosed. Tie up the veal rolls with kitchen string.

Heat the oil in a saucepan, fry the veal rolls, turning, until golden brown all over, and place on a rack to drain. Add the onions to the oil in the pan and sauté, then add the tomato paste and sugar, and simmer. Add half the broth, reduce, and return the veal rolls to the pan.

Add the tomatoes. Pour in the remaining broth, bring to a boil, and skim. Tie together the bouquet garni, add to the rolls, and cook for 50–55 minutes until done. Serve the veal rolls with the sauce. Decoratively cut zucchini with diced tomatoes and gnocchi can be served on the side.

PICCATA ALLA MILANESE

This dish consists of little veal scaloppine in an egg-and-cheese crust. Poultry and fish can also be prepared in this way.

8 small veal scaloppine (1½–2 oz each)
3 eggs, 2 tablespoons olive oil
⅔ cup grated Parmesan
flour, salt, and white pepper
¼ cup butter for frying

Flatten the scaloppine as on page 186, then proceed as follows:

Beat the eggs in a bowl, add the oil, and whisk together.

Whisk in the cheese, and let stand for 10–15 minutes.

Pour the flour onto a plate. Salt and pepper the scaloppine and dredge in flour.

Piccata of monkfish.
This fish, which has very few bones, is easy to cut into slices, which should be about ½ inch thick for the piccata. The recipe is the same as for Piccata alla Milanese, right. Salt the slices of fish very sparingly, dredge them in flour, and then, as in the photo sequence below, dip them in the egg–cheese mixture, and fry. Zucchini with peppers and a tomato sauce go well with this.

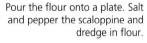

Dip the scaloppine in the egg-cheese mixture, stripping off the excess liquid with your fingers.

Heat the butter in a saucepan. Fry the scaloppine until golden, turning frequently.

BREADING WITH CHEESE

Here is a very appetizing way of breading if you want a strong-tasting crust to contrast with a mild interior. It differs from the usual breading only in that the fresh white bread crumbs are mixed with an equal amount of grated cheese, although the proportion of cheese can be reduced. You can prepare veal, poultry, or even fish in this manner. Cheeses from the Parmesan family are particularly suitable here.

Serve the Piccata with, for example, steamed broccoli, black tagliatelle, and tomato sauce.

Use a fork to dip the seasoned, floured meat in the beaten egg, scraping off the excess liquid against the edge of the container.

Place the meat in the bread crumb and Parmesan mixture and press the coating on firmly. Repeat the process for a thick crust.

Au gratin dishes

SCALLOPS AND CHAMPAGNE SAUCE AU GRATIN

For the sauce:
1 shallot, finely chopped; 2 teaspoons butter
1 cup champagne
1⅓ cups rich white veal stock, 1 cup heavy cream
1 teaspoon beurre manié (see page 165), 1 egg yolk
salt and white pepper
⅓ cup grated Provolone
For the vegetables:
2 tablespoons butter, 9 oz spinach leaves
salt, white pepper, grated nutmeg
You will also need:
4 large sea scallops, with shells if possible
salt and white pepper
2 teaspoons butter, ½ cup champagne

Preheat the oven to 400°F. To make the sauce, sweat the shallots in the butter without letting them color. Add the champagne gradually and then the stock. Reduce by about half. Meanwhile, reserve 2 tablespoons of the cream, reduce the remainder to two-thirds, and strain into the stock. Lightly bind the sauce with the beurre manié. Whisk the egg with the 2 tablespoons of cream and blend into the sauce. Bring just to a boil, season with salt and pepper, and strain. In a frying pan, melt the butter, add the leaf spinach, wilt, and season. Halve the scallop flesh vertically and season with salt and pepper. Grease a saucepan with butter, put in the scallops, and cover with champagne. Carefully simmer the scallops until done, lift out, and drain. Boil down the poaching stock hard and add to the sauce. Drain the spinach and divide among the cleaned, warmed scallop shells or ovenproof gratin dishes. Place two scallop halves on top of each shell, cover with the sauce, and sprinkle with the cheese. Cook on the top rack of the oven until golden brown.

OYSTERS IN SHERRY–CREAM SAUCE AU GRATIN

Prepared with the quantities given here, this dish makes a fine appetizer.

(not illustrated)
For the sauce:
1 shallot, finely diced; 2 teaspoons butter
½ cup medium-dry sherry
½ cup white veal stock
1 cup heavy cream
You will also need:
12 oysters
2 teaspoons butter
¼ cup medium-dry sherry
salt, pepper, cayenne pepper
2 tablespoons grated young Provolone

Preheat the oven to 485°F. Sweat the shallot in the butter without letting it color. Add the sherry and the veal stock, and reduce by half. Reduce the cream separately to two-thirds, strain into the sauce, and cook until creamy. Remove the oysters from their shells, reserving the juices. Wash and dry the deep halves of the shells, and reserve. Grease a saucepan with butter, place the oysters in the pan, add the sherry and the reserved juices, and simmer over a low heat until done. Lift out the oysters, boil down the stock hard, and add to the sherry sauce. Season the sauce to taste and strain. Place the oysters in the cleaned, warmed shells, cover with the sherry-cream sauce, and sprinkle with the cheese. Cook in the oven until golden brown.

Cheese and meat kebabs. Wrap the cheese in thin slices of smoked bacon, so that it doesn't run when roasted. Thread onto the skewer, alternating with cubes of pork, onion, and bell pepper. The kebabs may also be breaded.

VENISON MEDALLIONS WITH FIGS AND BLEU D'AUVERGNE

For the sauce:
1 shallot, finely chopped; 2 teaspoons butter
1½ teaspoons tomato paste
½ cup red port wine, 1¾ cups game roasting-juices or rich brown veal stock, salt and white pepper
To garnish:
4 medium figs, peeled and halved
salt, white pepper, 2 teaspoons butter, ¼ cup red port wine
You will also need:
8 medallions from a saddle of venison
salt and white pepper, 2 tablespoons clarified butter
5½ oz Bleu d'Auvergne, cut into 8 slices

Preheat the oven to 485°F. Sweat the shallot in the butter, add the tomato paste, and continue to cook. Moisten a few times with the port and add the game juices. Bring to a boil, skim, and simmer. Season the figs and fry in the butter. Place in a saucepan with the ¼ cup port. Simmer, turning often, for 3–4 minutes, then lift out. Boil down the stock hard, add to the sauce, season to taste, and strain. Flatten the medallions, season, and fry in clarified butter for 4–5 minutes, turning frequently, until pink inside. Transfer to a casserole, top each with a fig half, cover with the cheese, and bake until it melts. Serve with the sauce.

LAMB CHOPS AU GRATIN

For the cheese mixture:
1 egg, 1 cup grated Gruyère
1½ oz boiled ham
2 tablespoons snipped chives
2 tablespoons whipped cream
salt and pepper
You will also need:
8 lamb rib chops (about 3 oz each)
salt and pepper
1½ tablespoons clarified butter
1¾ cups lamb roasting-juices or rich lamb stock

Preheat the broiler. To make the cheese mixture, mix the egg with the Gruyère. Cut the ham into cubes and fold into the cheese-egg mixture with the chives and cream. Flatten the chops with the flat side of a cleaver, and season with salt and pepper. Heat the clarified butter in a frying pan and fry the lamb chops on both sides until pink inside, remove, and place on a rack. Pour the fat out of the pan, add the lamb roasting-juices, and reduce by half. Place the chops in a casserole, top evenly with the cheese mixture, and place under the broiler for about 3 minutes until golden brown. Serve the lamb chops with the sauce poured around them.

The recipe for Lobster Mornay, opposite, may also be used for langoustines (saltwater crayfish). Separate the tails from the heads, place them in small buttered gratin dishes, cover with the sauce, sprinkle with cheese and brown in a hot oven.

Cheese sauces

Sauces containing cheese can be delightful with fish, shellfish, meat, or poultry, but their flavors must be compatible with the food in question. The more or less pungent taste of cheese means that this is not so easily achieved. Therefore, when experimenting with cheese as a seasoning for sauces, begin with small amounts and avoid cheeses that are very acidic. This applies equally whether the basis of the sauce is a roux, as in the case of a Sauce Mornay, or reduced stock and cream.

LOBSTER MORNAY

For the Sauce Mornay:
2 tablespoons butter, 4½ teaspoons flour, 2¼ cups milk
salt, pepper, nutmeg, 1 bay leaf
2–3 tablespoons heavy cream, 2 egg yolks
½ cup grated Gruyère
You will also need:
2 lobsters weighing about 1½ lb each, poached in a court-bouillon
butter for greasing the gratin dish
⅓ cup grated Gruyère

Preheat the oven to 425°F. Prepare a Sauce Mornay as described on page 161. Halve the cooked lobsters lengthwise and remove the intestines. Remove the flesh from the tails and slice. Crack the claws with a heavy knife so that the claw meat is easier to remove when eating the lobster. Pour some sauce into the empty shells, layer the lobster slices inside, overlapping, and cover with the remaining sauce. Sprinkle the cheese over the lobster halves and bake in the oven for about 10 minutes, until the surface is golden brown. This tastes best accompanied by toasted white bread and a fresh green salad.

BREAST OF DUCK WITH CHIANTI-POACHED PEARS AND ROQUEFORT SAUCE

For the Chianti-poached pears:
2 pears, ½ teaspoon sugar, 1 cup Chianti
1½ inches cinnamon stick, 2 whole cloves
2 crushed peppercorns, a pinch of ground cardamom
For the sauce:
½ onion, finely diced; 2 teaspoons butter
2 tablespoons red wine vinegar, ¼ cup red wine
1 cup duck roasting-juices or rich brown chicken or duck stock, ½ cup heavy cream, 2 oz Roquefort
salt and white pepper
You will also need:
2 duck breasts, skinned and boned (about 10 oz each)
salt and white pepper
2 tablespoons clarified butter
mint for garnishing

Peel, quarter, and core the pears. Lightly caramelize the sugar in a saucepan and pour in the Chianti. Add the spices and bring to a boil. Place the pears in the liquid and poach gently for about 10 minutes, remove the spices, and reserve the pears. To make the sauce, sweat the onion in the butter until golden brown and moisten with the vinegar and wine. Add the roasting juices and boil down hard, then pour in the cream and cook the sauce until creamy. Strain the sauce and work in the Roquefort with a hand-held blender or whisk. Season to taste with salt and pepper if necessary. Salt and pepper the duck breasts. Melt the clarified butter, add the duck breasts, and fry for about 8–10 minutes, turning them often, until pink inside. Leave to rest on a rack. Cut the pears part-way through at ¼-inch intervals and fan out. Boil down the pear stock to about ¼ cup and add it to the sauce, to taste. Slice the duck breasts on the diagonal, and serve with the fanned pears, duchesse potatoes, and the sauce, garnishing with a sprig of fresh mint.

Vegetables and potatoes

Nowadays we have an amazingly wide range of vegetables to choose from, the majority of them available regardless of the season. Cheese, too, apart from a very few types, is available throughout the year. Vegetable and potato dishes are not only accompaniments for meat and fish dishes, but can also be main courses, especially in combination with cheese. They are a delight for creative cooks, especially since, with the large variety of both available, it is not difficult to find the right cheese for each vegetable. There is a wide range of cheeses suitable for potato dishes, the choice being determined by how dominant the taste of the cheese is meant to be.

All recipes serve 4 unless otherwise indicated.

GRATIN OF POTATOES WITH CHEDDAR

Preheat the oven to 400°F. Wash and peel 2¼ lb potatoes, and slice thinly with a mandolin or knife. Grate 10 oz Cheddar. Layer the potato slices in a buttered casserole, sprinkling the cheese in between (see photo). Season with salt and pepper, and pour on 2¼ cups heavy cream to almost cover the potatoes. Place the casserole in the oven and bake for 60–70 minutes, until crispy and brown.

GRATIN OF BOILED POTATOES

Preheat the oven to 425°F. Slice 2¼ lb cold boiled and peeled potatoes, and layer with a chopped onion in a buttered casserole. Top with 8 oz cheese (such as Tomme de Savoie) cut into cubes, season with salt and pepper, and cover with 1¾ cups heavy cream. Place the casserole in the oven and bake for 30–40 minutes.

GRATIN OF POTATOES WITH REBLOCHON

This cheese lends a special touch to the gratin, mild but flavorful. A more piquant variation can be made with Saint-Nectaire, whose rind must be completely removed before use.

2¼ lb potatoes
½ cup each beef broth and cream
1 lb Reblochon
salt, pepper, nutmeg
2 tablespoons butter
1 garlic clove, crushed
1 tablespoon finely chopped onion

Preheat the oven to 425°F. Wash and peel the potatoes and cut into ½-inch cubes. Cook in boiling salted water for 4–5 minutes, drain, and rinse hard under cold running water. Drain thoroughly. Heat the broth with the cream. Thinly pare the rind from the cheese, or scrape off just the outer layer. Slice the cheese thinly, and slowly melt it in the cream mixture over very low heat. Season with salt, pepper, and nutmeg. Melt the butter in a casserole and sweat the garlic and onion until they color slightly. Top with the cubed potatoes, pour on the cheese sauce, and bake for about 20 minutes, then reduce the temperature to 350°F and bake for a further 40–50 minutes, until the potatoes are soft.

GRATIN OF POTATOES AND ZUCCHINI

The combination of potatoes and zucchini in a gratin yields a surprisingly good result. It is ideal as an accompaniment for lamb and rabbit dishes.

14 oz zucchini, 1¼ lb small potatoes
1 garlic clove, crushed, 6 tablespoons butter
½ cup finely chopped shallots, 1 cup meat broth
1 teaspoon thyme leaves
2 teaspoons chopped basil
salt and freshly ground pepper
⅔ cup grated Parmesan
⅔ cup fresh white bread crumbs
butter for greasing the casserole

Preheat the oven to 400°F. Scrub the zucchini under running water and trim the ends, then slice into rounds about ¾ inch thick. Wash and peel the potatoes (which should be of about the same diameter as the zucchini) and cut into slices of uniform thickness. Peel and crush the garlic. Melt half the butter in a frying pan and sweat the shallots and the garlic until lightly colored. Add the broth and cook for 3–4 minutes. Butter a large casserole. Alternate layers of zucchini and potato slices so that they are standing at an angle. Sprinkle with the herbs and seasonings, pour on the broth, and dot the top with the remaining butter. Mix the cheese with the bread crumbs and sprinkle on top. Bake in the center of the oven for 40–45 minutes.

BAKED POTATOES WITH CHEESE AND HERBS.
Fill freshly baked potatoes with a mixture of two-thirds low-fat curd cheese and one-third grated Bergkäse. If necessary, thin with a little cream. Season with salt, pepper, and plenty of fresh chopped herbs.

Potatoes and cheese

Potatoes and cheese are essential staples, and are superbly compatible in taste. Recipes combining them can be found in every household, as well as in the repertoire of top restaurants. A plain baked potato with cheese or potatoes au gratin can be a delicacy in itself, and requires no further embellishment, but by shaving a truffle over these dishes or topping them with a spoonful of caviar, they become the pièce de résistance of a menu. These potato dishes can be main courses, served, for example, with a fresh green salad, or they can be accompaniments for meat, fish, or poultry.

The recipes in this section are intended to serve 4 as a main course, or 8 as a side dish.

CHEESY POTATOES WITH CARAWAY

Cheesy potatoes taste especially good with caraway on its own, but you can also add other seasonings, such as pepper, marjoram, oregano, or paprika.

8 medium potatoes
1¼ cups shredded Gruyère or Allgäuer Bergkäse
caraway seeds

Preheat the oven to 425°F. Wash the potatoes, scrub well, and cook in boiling salted water until just done but still firm. Halve the potatoes lengthwise, sprinkle generously with the grated cheese, and place on a greased baking sheet. Bake for about 10 minutes, until the cheese is melted, then sprinkle with caraway seeds and serve.

CHEESY POTATO ROLLS

For this recipe choose potatoes as near the same size as possible, so that they are done at the same time.

2¼ lb baking potatoes
2 tablespoons butter
2 tablespoons high-quality vegetable oil, salt
1 cup grated Parmesan

Preheat the oven to 425°F and grease a large casserole. Wash and peel the potatoes, and cut down into them about two-thirds of the way through at intervals of no more than ¼ inch. Heat the butter with the oil. Brush the potatoes with some of this mixture, then sprinkle with salt. Place the potatoes in the casserole, and bake. Brush them once more with the oil–butter mixture while they are baking. After 30–40 minutes, depending on the size of the potatoes, sprinkle them with the cheese and cook for a further 10–15 minutes until done.

A splendid variation: Pour ½ cup each of meat broth and heavy cream in a casserole, add the potatoes and sprinkle them with a mixture of ½ cup grated Parmesan and 1 cup finely grated Emmental, then proceed as described above.

POTATO PANCAKES
WITH CHEESE AND PEPPERS

Makes 16
3 eggs, ¼ cup heavy cream, 6 tablespoons flour
2¼ lb baking potatoes
½ cup each chopped red, green, and yellow peppers
2 onions, finely chopped
1 clove garlic, finely chopped
2 oz belly of pork or other fatty pork, finely diced
5 oz Bergkäse or Emmental, finely cubed
Butter and oil for shallow-frying

Mix the eggs, cream and flour in a large bowl.
Wash, peel, and finely shred the potatoes, then
rinse them briefly in cold water, remove and
squeeze dry in a kitchen towel. Add the shredded
potato, chopped peppers, onion, garlic, belly of
pork, and cheese cubes to the batter and mix well.
Heat equal amounts of oil and butter
in a small frying pan, spoon a
heaping tablespoonful of batter
into the pan, spread smooth,
and fry on both sides until
done. Repeat until all the batter
is used.

CORN FRITTERS WITH CHEESE

Makes 8
½ cup milk
2 eggs
4 tablespoons flour
½ teaspoon salt
freshly ground pepper
3 oz belly of pork or other fatty pork
4 oz Tilsit
4 ears very fresh corn
butter and oil for frying

Mix the milk, eggs, and flour to make a batter, and
season with salt and pepper. Finely dice the pork
and cut the cheese into ¼-inch cubes. Using a
knife, remove the corn kernels from the cob by
slicing down from the stalk to the tip of the cob.
Mix the corn, pork, and cheese into the batter.
Heat equal amounts of butter and oil in a frying
pan, add a heaping tablespoonful of batter to the
pan, spread smooth and fry on both sides until
golden brown. Repeat until all the batter is used.

RÖSTI. A good Swiss
rösti can hardly be
improved on, except
by the addition of
cheese. After you flip
over these super
hash-brown
potatoes, sprinkle
grated cheese on the
cooked side, and
allow it to melt. All
sorts of cheese, from
Emmental to
Appenzell, go well
with this dish — the
choice is yours.

LITTLE ZUCCHINI TARTS

Makes eight 4½-inch tarts

For the pastry:

2¼ cups all-purpose flour, ½ cup + 2 teaspoons butter

1 egg yolk

pinch of salt, 1–2 tablespoons water

For the filling:

14 oz zucchini, 6 peeled tomatoes

For the custard:

1 cup heavy cream, 2 eggs

salt, a little pepper

½ teaspoon hot paprika

1 cup each grated Montasio and Parmesan

butter for greasing the flan dishes

parsley for garnishing

Preheat the oven to 400°F and butter 8 small fluted tart molds. Prepare a shortcrust pastry as described on page 213. Use it to line the molds, and bake blind. Slice the zucchini into thin rounds. Core and cube the tomatoes. Whisk together the cream, eggs, seasonings, and cheese. Pour some of the custard mixture into the baked pastry shells, arrange the zucchini slices on top, overlapping in a circle, place the tomato cubes between the slices, and pour on the remaining custard. Bake for 20 minutes until golden brown, sprinkle with parsley, and serve.

LITTLE MUSHROOM PIES

Makes four 4-inch pies

10 oz mushrooms

2 shallots, finely chopped

2 tablespoons butter

salt and black pepper

pinch of nutmeg

7 oz puff pastry

2 eggs, ½ cup shredded Comté

1 bunch chives, finely snipped

butter for greasing the casserole

Preheat the oven to 425°F, and grease four 4-inch tart molds. Wash and trim the mushrooms and cut into wafer-thin slices. Sauté the shallots in hot butter, add the mushrooms and sauté until the liquid has evaporated. Season to taste with the salt, pepper, and nutmeg, and leave to cool. Roll out the puff pastry to a thickness of ¼ inch and cut out circles to line the tart molds. Mix the eggs with the cheese, and season to taste with salt and pepper. Divide the mushrooms among the molds, sprinkle with the chives, and pour in the egg-cheese mixture (top photo). Bake on the lowest rack of the oven for 10 minutes, then lower the temperature to 400°F and bake the pies on the middle rack for a further 10 minutes. Serve warm.

Choosing cheeses for gratin dishes. When vegetables are served au gratin, the same types of cheese are usually used. First and foremost is Parmesan, and with good reason; not only do cheeses from this family of extra-hard cheeses have an agreeably piquant taste, but they form a crispy crust because of their low fat content. In principle, of course, other cheeses can also be used for gratins, including those from the Gruyère and Emmental families, although they have a tendency to become stringy. A lovely crust can also be achieved with these if the grated cheese is mixed with bread crumbs.

Au gratin

The choice of vegetable dishes that can be prepared au gratin is considerable. Almost all types of vegetables are suited to this treatment — just remember to steam them first.

SWISS CHARD STALKS AU GRATIN

1¾ lb broad-stemmed Swiss chard
2 oz smoked bacon
3 tablespoons butter
1 teaspoon flour
1½ cups milk
salt, pepper, and nutmeg
1 cup grated aged Provolone

Preheat the oven to 425°F. Wash the chard and cut the leaves from the stalks. Do not cut off the leafy-green bits from the tender inner stalks. Cut the chard into pieces about 2 inches long and cook in boiling salted water for 5 minutes; lift out and drain well. Finely chop the bacon and fry in a large pot; pour off the fat and add 2 tablespoons of the butter. Sauté the chard in the melted butter for about 5 minutes. Combine the flour with the milk and seasonings, pour over the chard, and simmer over low heat for 8–10 minutes, stirring occasionally. Melt the remaining butter in a baking dish, add the vegetables, and sprinkle with the grated cheese. Bake in the oven until golden brown.

FENNEL
WITH CREAM AND PARMESAN

1¾ lb small fennel bulbs
salted water
¼ cup butter
½ cup heavy cream
freshly ground pepper
1 cup grated Parmesan

Preheat the oven to 400°F. Trim the fennel bulbs, wash, and if necessary remove the hard outer ribs. Cut off the green stalks. Halve the bulbs, or quarter them if very large. Cook in lightly salted boiling water for about 10 minutes, lift out, and drain well. Melt the butter in a baking dish, put in the fennel, and fry briefly on the stove. Add the cream, season with salt and pepper, and sprinkle with the Parmesan. Bake for 20 minutes, until the cheese is crusty and light brown.

MELANZANE CON MOZZARELLA

This vegetable casserole is based on eggplant, which is especially popular in southern Italy.

2¼ lb eggplant
1 heaping tablespoon salt
1¾ lb tomatoes
6 tablespoons extra virgin olive oil
1 onion
1 garlic clove, crushed
salt and pepper
½ cup dry white wine
flour
10 oz fresh Mozzarella, sliced
½ cup grated Parmesan

Preheat the oven to 425°F. Slice the eggplant widthwise, salt each slice, and layer in a colander over a bowl. Weight the eggplant slices, and allow to sweat for 1 hour. Peel and seed the tomatoes. Heat half the olive oil, add the onions, and sauté until they color slightly. Add the chopped tomato flesh, and season with the garlic, salt, and pepper. Pour in the white wine and cook the sauce over low heat for about 40 minutes. Drain off the bitter juices the salt has drawn out of the eggplant, dry the eggplant slices and dredge in flour. Heat the remaining olive oil in a frying pan and fry the eggplant lightly on both sides. Pour the oil remaining in the pan into a casserole, add a layer of eggplant slices, top with Mozzarella slices, and cover with a layer of tomato sauce. Repeat this process until the ingredients are used up, finishing with a layer of tomato sauce. Sprinkle with Parmesan and bake for about 30 minutes.

BELGIAN ENDIVE AU GRATIN

3 heads of Belgian endive (weighing about 7 oz each)
salted water or meat broth
6 slices of boiled ham
6 slices of medium-aged Gouda
1 cup meat broth, ½ cup heavy cream
⅔ cup grated Parmesan
salt and nutmeg
1 tablespoon chopped herbs (parsley and thyme)
2 tablespoons fresh white bread crumbs
3 tablespoons butter

Preheat the oven to 400°F. Wash the endive and cut out and discard the bitter stalk. Poach gently in the salted water or broth for 10 minutes. Lift out, drain, and halve lengthwise. Cover each slice of ham with a slice of cheese, place half a head of endive on top, and roll up. Transfer to a large baking dish. Mix the broth with the cream and the cheese, season with salt, nutmeg, and the herbs, and pour over the endive. Sprinkle with the bread crumbs and dot with butter. Bake for about 20 minutes, until the topping is golden brown.

STUFFED TOMATOES. Preheat the oven to 400°F. Cut lids off 8 ripe tomatoes. Hollow out the tomatoes with a spoon, and season with salt and pepper. Stuff them with a goat cheese and spinach filling (in the recipe for stuffed mushrooms on page 201). Sprinkle with ½ cup grated Provolone, and top each tomato with a dab of butter. Bake for 30 minutes.

MUSHROOMS STUFFED WITH GOAT CHEESE AND SPINACH

18 large mushrooms, trimmed and wiped clean
1 tablespoon lemon juice
For the stuffing:
9 oz spinach leaves
¼ cup dry white wine, 2 tablespoons butter
2 shallots, finely chopped
2 garlic cloves, finely chopped
1 teaspoon chopped thyme
salt and pepper
4 oz Valençay
½ cup fresh white bread crumbs
2 tablespoons grated Ragusano Bianco or Provolone Piccante
butter for greasing the baking dish

Preheat the oven to 350°F and grease a baking dish. Trim the spinach and remove the stalks, then wash, spin dry, and chop coarsely. Twist off the mushroom stalks and chop them finely, then drizzle the cups with lemon juice. Bring the wine and half the butter to a boil in a pot, then sauté the shallots, garlic, thyme, and chopped mushroom stalks for 3–4 minutes. Add the spinach and allow to wilt. Season to taste with salt and pepper. Crumble the goat cheese and fold in, using two forks. Divide the stuffing among the mushrooms and place the mushrooms in the baking dish. Mix the Ragusano or Provolone with the bread crumbs, sprinkle over the stuffed mushrooms, and top each with a dab of the remaining butter. Bake for 20 minutes.

STUFFED ZUCCHINI

4 zucchini (weighing 7 oz each)
For the stuffing:
1 tablespoon olive oil, 1 cup finely chopped onions
½ clove garlic, finely chopped
5 oz aged Asiago
1 lb mixed ground meat (beef, veal, and pork)
2 eggs
1 tablespoon chopped basil
½ teaspoon dried thyme
1 teaspoon each salt and sweet paprika; pepper
1 cup fresh white bread crumbs
½ cup grated Parmesan
¼ cup butter, in pieces
butter for greasing the baking dish

Preheat the oven to 425°F and grease a baking dish. Halve the zucchini lengthwise, hollow out, and cut the flesh into small cubes. Heat the oil in a frying pan and sweat the onions and garlic. Cut the Asiago into small cubes. Place the ground meat in a bowl with the cheese, onions, garlic, cubed zucchini, eggs, herbs, and seasonings. Mix everything together thoroughly and divide among the zucchini halves. Mix the bread crumbs with the grated Parmesan and sprinkle over the stuffed zucchini. Dot the top with butter and bake for 20–25 minutes.

GREEN PEPPERS WITH A SHEEP'S-MILK CHEESE STUFFING

4 green peppers
For the stuffing:
5 oz Bulgarian sheep's-milk cheese or sheep's-milk feta
1 egg, 2 tablespoons sour cream
½ teaspoon salt
¼ cup oil
oil for greasing the baking dish

Preheat the oven to 400°F and grease a baking dish. Place the peppers on a baking sheet and roast until their skins blister, then cool in a covered pot for 10 minutes. Turn the oven down to 350°F. Pull the skin off the peppers, slit them open lengthwise up to the stalk on one side, and open up. Remove the core and the white ribs. Mash the cheese with a fork and mix with the egg and sour cream. Stuff the peppers with the cheese mixture, close them, and place them in the baking dish. Sprinkle with salt and drizzle with oil. Bake for about 40 minutes, until done.

Cheese sauces for vegetables

Whether it is the classic sauce mornay or a type of fonduta, which is popular in Italy, cheese sauce is an ideal way to enhance steamed vegetables. Cheese sauces are particularly popular with members of the cabbage family, such as cauliflower, broccoli, and even Brussels sprouts. Of course, these vegetables can also be sprinkled with grated cheese and cooked au gratin.

CAULIFLOWER WITH SAUCE MORNAY

1 small cauliflower or green cauliflower (about 1¾ lb)
salted water for cooking
For the sauce:
2 tablespoons butter, ¼ cup flour, 2¼ cups milk
salt, pepper, nutmeg
1 egg yolk, ½ cup heavy cream
⅓ cup grated Parmesan
1–2 tablespoons whipped cream

Wash the cauliflower and cut off the stalk. Cook in boiling salted water for about 20 minutes, until done, but by no means too soft. Drain well and place on a platter. Prepare a cheese sauce from the ingredients given, as described on page 161. It is essential that the basic sauce (the béchamel) is cooked through, with no trace of raw flour taste. Pour the sauce over the hot cauliflower and serve at once.

Decorative green cauliflower, or romanesco, is very mild tasting and therefore benefits particularly from being served au gratin with grated Parmesan or Pecorino.

GREEN ASPARAGUS BAKED IN SAUCE MORNAY

This recipe can, of course, also be made with white asparagus, but the stronger-tasting green variety is particularly well suited to this treatment.

2¼ lb green asparagus
2 tablespoons butter
For the sauce:
4 teaspoons butter, 1 tablespoon flour, 1½ cups milk
salt and pepper
2 egg yolks, ½ cup heavy cream, 2 oz Fontina
⅓ cup grated Parmesan for sprinkling
3 tablespoons melted butter

Preheat the oven to 400°F. Wash the asparagus and thinly pare the bottom of the stalks. Tie together in 4 bundles and place in lightly salted boiling water just to cover. Simmer gently over medium heat for 15–20 minutes, depending on the thickness of the stalks. Do not allow the asparagus to overcook. Lift out and drain well. Melt the butter in a large casserole, split the asparagus stalks in the middle, and layer in the dish. Prepare a béchamel sauce from the ingredients given, as described on page 161, and cook for at least 20 minutes. Cut the cheese into cubes and mix well. Pour the sauce over the asparagus and sprinkle with Parmesan. Bake in the oven for about 20 minutes. Drizzle with melted butter and serve at once.

GRATIN OF CELERY

The cheese mixture used in this recipe, consisting of grated Parmesan and Pecorino, harmonizes especially well with celery.

2¼ lb celery
¼ cup butter, 1 tablespoon chopped shallots
2¼ cups meat broth
salt and pepper
2 oz prosciutto, diced
For the sauce:
1 cup heavy cream
⅔ cup grated Pecorino Romano
¾ cup grated Parmesan

Preheat the oven to 425°F. Wash the celery and cut into pieces that fit the size of your baking dish, cutting off the bottom end of the stalks and halving them lengthwise if very thick. Heat the butter in a large saucepan, sweat the shallots until lightly colored, and add the celery stalks. Add the broth and season with salt and pepper. Cook for approximately 20 minutes, until about ½ cup of broth remains. Layer the celery in a baking dish and scatter the diced prosciutto on top. Mix the reduced broth with the cream and cheese, then spoon over the celery. Bake until the top is browned and crisp. Serve garnished with a bit of chopped green from the delicate inner leaves of the celery.

A CHEESE GRATER MADE FROM HIGH-GRADE STEEL. Extra-hard cheese can be grated freshly as required with just such a decorative and practical grater. The grated cheese is caught in the drawer under the grating surface.

Fondue and raclette

The Swiss, who are famous for knowing a thing or two about cheese, claim (although the French and Italians may dispute this) to have invented fondue and raclette, two ways of cooking at the table with cheese as the main ingredient. Raclette is the name of both a meal and its primary ingredient, a cheese that is eaten melted over various vegetables.

Fondue, a truly democratic communal meal that is rustic and delicate at the same time, originated in French-speaking Switzerland. This dish, as nourishing as it is convivial, became an international culinary craze in the 1950s.

Nowadays, cheese fondue has a permanent place in the repertoire of the cook who wishes to make a professional job of entertaining and achieve the maximum impact with the minimum expenditure of effort.

The quality of a fondue is only as good as that of the cheese and wine used to make it. It should be prepared from the best ripe cheese, which is neither too young nor too old, and the wine must have enough acidity, since this binds the cheese; in case of doubt, a little lemon juice helps. Some fondue recipes also call for a small glass of kirsch, which is stirred in with the cornstarch. Drinking a drop of kirsch during the meal also aids digestion. Fondues are eaten by dipping cubes of bread — ideally from a crusty rustic loaf, half white, half rye, or from a baguette — in the hot cheese.

All recipes serve 4 unless otherwise indicated.

BASIC FONDUE RECIPE

1¼ lb cheese, 1 garlic clove

1¼ cups dry white wine, 2 teaspoons cornstarch

freshly ground pepper, grated nutmeg

In making the fondue, it is important to heat the wine and cheese slowly while stirring. When eating the fondue, stir it often: with a bread cube speared on your fork, stir right at the base of the pot, so that the fondue does not burn while on the heat. If the cheese and wine separate, whisk the mixture over high heat until smooth. Prepare the fondue as follows:

Cut the cheese into tiny cubes, which allows it to melt evenly as well as slowly.

Halve the garlic clove and rub over the inside of an earthenware fondue pot. Pour in the wine.

Add half of the cheese (the harder cheese always goes in first) and heat slowly while stirring.

When the cheese is almost melted, add the remaining cheese (the softer type). Keep the fondue at a gentle simmer.

Dissolve the cornstarch in a little wine, add to the fondue, and stir until creamy smooth.

Lastly, add the pepper and nutmeg, place the fondue on a spirit burner, and bring to the table, simmering gently.

White truffles are the exclusive seasoning of Italian fonduta. Their strong flavor contrasts most agreeably with the mild Fontina cheese.

NEUENBURG FONDUE

This is reputed to be the original fondue, at least by the inhabitants of Neuenburg. Hearty Gruyère and mild, nutty Emmental complement each other perfectly.

10 oz each Gruyère and Emmental

1 garlic clove, 1¼ cups white wine

2 teaspoons cornstarch, 2 tablespoons kirsch

pepper and nutmeg

Prepare as in the basic recipe, dissolving the cornstarch in the kirsch and using this mixture to bind the fondue.

WAADTLAND FONDUE

A variation using Raclette cheese, whose flavor is intensified by ripe Gruyère.

14 oz Gruyère, 7 oz Raclette cheese

1 garlic clove

1¼ cups white wine

3 teaspoons cornstarch, ¼ cup kirsch

freshly ground pepper

Prepare as in the basic recipe. To turn this into a meal for a special occasion, shave a large, fresh black truffle over the fondue.

FONDUE MOITIÉ-MOITIÉ

The "half-and-half" fondue from Fribourg, the home of Vacherin, shows off this mild, slightly acidulated cheese to advantage.

10 oz each Gruyère and Vacherin

1 garlic clove

1¼ cups white wine, ¼ cup kirsch

pepper and nutmeg

Prepare as in the basic recipe.

FONDUTA, THE ITALIAN FONDUE

10 oz Fontina, 1 cup milk

3 egg yolks, ¼ cup butter, melted

1 white truffle

4 slices white bread

Cut the cheese into small cubes, pour the milk over it, and leave at room temperature to soften for a few hours. Place the cheese and milk in a double boiler and melt over a low heat. Beat the egg yolks with a little milk and stir slowly into the cheese mixture. Mix in the melted butter. Divide among 4 soup plates, shave wafer-thin slices of the white truffle over the top, and serve with toasted white bread.

Raclette, a tradition from the Valais

This is indisputably one of the simplest cheese dishes, and probably was originally a meal for the farmers and dairymen of the Valais in western Switzerland. It is based on the mountain cheeses of the Valais, which bear the names of the valleys from which they come, such as Bagnes, Illiez, Simplon, Gomser, Binn, and Osières. The ideal cheese for a raclette is aged for three to five months. Its creamy interior melts easily, but does not run. For this reason alone, beware of substitute or alternative cheeses that are often recommended, such as Fontina, which, although it does melt well, runs excessively.

Raclette is just the right meal for an outdoor party, where the glow of a wood fire provides the necessary source of heat. Half a cheese wheel, is placed on a stone, with its cut surface close to the fire. As soon as it turns dark yellow and begins to shine, the first layer can be scraped off onto a plate with a knife. The procedure then begins anew. It is advisable to use a cold stone as a base, otherwise the rind of the cheese softens. Traditionally, the accompaniments are also simple: boiled potatoes, cornichons (tiny pickled gherkins), and pickled onions — but the list can be expanded according to personal taste. For example, marinated artichoke hearts and other pickled vegetables are excellent with raclette. A raclette oven is an electrically heated device used for making this convivial meal possible at home and indoors.

Charcoal is easier to handle than a wood fire. Before the cheese is placed close to the embers, let the ashes burn down, otherwise the smallest gust of wind will swirl them against the surface of the cheese.

With a knife, scrape the melted layer of cheese onto a plate. Watch the cheese carefully, so that it does not become too soft. In any case, a good raclette cheese from the Valais does not run very quickly.

This sort of open-air raclette really does not require any fancy equipment or ingredients, and can be a delightful alternative to a barbecue. Be careful with the drinks you serve, though, as hot melted cheese does not go well with cold drinks, with the exception of schnapps.

Melted in the pan

This raclette bears absolutely no resemblance to its namesake from the Valais. The only point the two dishes have in common is that the cheese is melted. But this little pan and the device it comes with allow you to make a superb job of sizzling the cheese at the table and combining it with meat, vegetables, fish, or fruit. The choice of cheeses is almost unlimited, since even varieties that tend to be very runny can be used, as they are held in one piece in the little pan. In the basic recipe, shown in the picture sequence below, cheese slices are just melted and the traditional accompaniments to raclette handed round. For the more sophisticated combinations shown on the opposite page, the preparations at the table are much more extensive; some of these can be carried out in the kitchen beforehand, for example sweating the onions or steaming the vegetables. Most raclette sets have the broiler and a burner on top, which can be used to preheat the little pan and to fry ingredients. The quantities given in the recipes opposite are sufficient for 4 little pans, which is 1 serving.

Cut the raclette cheese into slices about ⅛ inch thick. Trim the slice to fit the raclette pan and place in the pan.

Preheat the raclette broiler until the coils glow red, then slide the little pan containing the cheese into the machine.

The time it takes for the cheese to melt depends on the type of cheese used and the individual device. However, the cheese should not be allowed to brown too much, as this could give it a bitter taste.

Pour the melted cheese onto the plate or right over a cooked potato or other accompaniment. If necessary, ease it out of the mold with a wooden spatula.

Cheeses that melt nicely are also ideal for gratins. It goes without saying that Raclette cheese (extreme top of photo) takes pride of place here. Piquant Gruyère (second from top), mildly acidulated and easy melting Vacherin from Fribourg (third from top), and the very similar Fontina (bottom of photo) are also ideal. Most other types can also be used, including blue cheeses or, if a really piquant taste is required, ripe washed-rind cheeses.

With tomatoes. Heat 4½ teaspoons butter and ¼ cup chopped smoked bacon in a frying pan, add 1 medium onion, sliced, and sweat. Divide this mixture among the little pans, cover with tomato slices, and sprinkle with salt and freshly ground pepper. Add basil leaves, top with a slice of Fontina, and broil.

With pineapple and prosciutto. Melt 4½ teaspoons butter in a frying pan and gently fry 1 cup fresh pineapple chunks. Season with salt and freshly ground pepper. Divide among the little pans. Cover the contents of each pan with a slice of prosciutto. Dice 5 oz of raclette cheese, divide among the pans, and broil.

With onions and bacon. Sweat ⅓ cup chopped smoked bacon in a frying pan until the fat runs; pour off the fat. Add 1 onion sliced into rings to the pan and sauté until translucent. Divide among the little pans, and season with salt, pepper, and paprika, if wished. Cover with slices of Gruyère, and broil.

With spicy shrimp. Melt 4½ teaspoons butter in a frying pan, and sauté ½ crushed garlic clove, 1 small chile pepper cut into rounds, and ⅓ cup diced shallots until the shallots are translucent. Divide among the little pans with 8 shrimp, season with salt, and sauté briefly. Cover with 1-oz slices of Vacherin, and broil.

Freshly baked potatoes in a basket. This traditional and simple accompaniment for raclette can also be served with the modern variations of this dish.

With steak and Roquefort. Melt 4½ teaspoons butter in a frying pan and sauté ¼ cup diced shallots until transparent. Add 4 slices of tender boneless beef (about 2 oz each) and brown on one side. Divide the shallots among the little pans, place a steak in each, and salt. Top each with a slice of Roquefort and a slice of raclette cheese, and broil.

With vegetables. Melt 4½ teaspoons butter in a frying pan, and sweat ¼ cup diced onion. Add ¾ cup sliced zucchini, and ⅓ cup each of finely diced leek, carrot, and bell pepper, and cook for 3 minutes. Divide among the little pans, add salt and pepper, top with slices of raclette cheese, and broil. Sprinkle with chopped parsley.

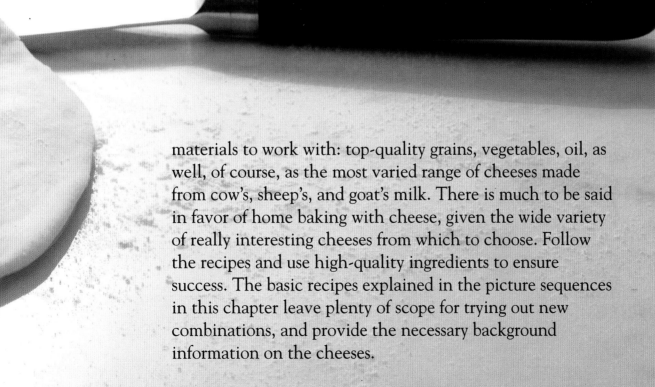

Baking with cheese

Cheese has earned a permanent place in bakeries the world over. Every country has developed its own varieties of sweet and savory dishes depending on the cheeses it produces. It is not surprising that the most successful specialties come from the areas around the Mediterranean, since these climatically blessed regions have such abundant and high-quality raw

materials to work with: top-quality grains, vegetables, oil, as well, of course, as the most varied range of cheeses made from cow's, sheep's, and goat's milk. There is much to be said in favor of home baking with cheese, given the wide variety of really interesting cheeses from which to choose. Follow the recipes and use high-quality ingredients to ensure success. The basic recipes explained in the picture sequences in this chapter leave plenty of scope for trying out new combinations, and provide the necessary background information on the cheeses.

All recipes serve 4 unless otherwise indicated.

Short and crisp

Shortcrust pastry with cheese:

Place the butter, cheese, and seasonings in a mixing bowl. Pour in the cream and mix to a smooth dough with a wooden spoon. There should be no pieces of butter remaining.

Sift the flour with the baking powder onto the work surface and work by hand into the butter mixture. Rub all the ingredients together until the mixture is the consistency of bread crumbs.

Knead to a smooth dough. Work as quickly as possible, since excessive kneading makes the pastry brittle. Gather together into a ball, wrap in plastic wrap, and refrigerate for about 2 hours. Roll out the pastry on a lightly floured work surface to a thickness of ¼ inch.

Preheat the oven to 400°F. Cut out a variety of shapes and place them on an ungreased baking sheet (the pastry contains sufficient fat to prevent it from sticking). Brush the cookies with egg yolk and sprinkle with poppy seeds, pistachios, sesame seeds, coarse salt, caraway, or almonds. Bake for 10–15 minutes.

SHORTCRUST CHEESE COOKIES

These are best fresh from the oven, or briefly rewarmed in a preheated oven until crisp.

¾ cup butter, softened; ⅔ cup grated Sbrinz
1¼ cup grated Greyerzer or Gruyère
½ teaspoon salt, 1 teaspoon sweet paprika
½ cup heavy cream
2¼ cups all-purpose flour, ½ teaspoon baking powder
2 egg yolks

For decorating:
Poppy seeds, sesame seeds, chopped pistachios, caraway seeds, coarse salt, skinned and halved almonds.

Preheat the oven to 400°F. Prepare the pastry as follows:

Savory shortcrust pastry:

Sift the flour onto the work surface. Make a well in the center and add the butter, egg yolk, and salt. Mix well with a pastry blender or metal spatula, and chop to the consistency of crumbs.

Add the water. Knead by hand to a smooth dough and form into a ball, working quickly so that the butter does not become too soft.

Wrap the ball of pastry in plastic wrap and chill for about 30 minutes. Grease 10 boat-shaped molds and place them close together. Roll out the pastry thinly and position over the molds.

Press the pastry down slightly into the molds and go over the top with a rolling pin, so that the pastry is cut to size.

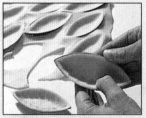

Using your thumbs, carefully press the pastry into the molds, making sure that there are no air bubbles between them and the pastry.

Cut off the excess pastry with a knife. Pierce the pastry on the base of the molds several times with a fork, to prevent air bubbles from forming during baking.

Baking blind:

Preheat the oven to 350°F. Fill the molds with dried lentils or "baking beans," so that the sides of the pastry do not collapse during baking.

Bake until light brown, about 10 minutes. Remove the lentils from the pastry shells with a spoon, then carefully turn the pastry out of the molds.

PASTRY BOATS

Savory shortcrust pastry is ideal for making shells that can be filled, for example, with fresh-cheese creams or cheese salad. Preheat the oven to 350°F and bake the pastry blind (with a pastry weight or dry beans), as shown. The shells freeze well and can easily be rewarmed until crisp in a 425°F oven.

2¼ cups all-purpose flour
½ cup butter, coarsely diced
1 egg yolk
a pinch of salt
1–2 tablespoons water

Make the pastry boats as described in the picture sequence opposite.

TO MAKE THE CHEESE SALAD: Slice 4 oz young Gouda into thin strips. Mix with ½ cup finely diced red, green, and yellow peppers. Mix 2 tablespoons finely chopped onions with 1 tablespoon vinegar, 2 tablespoons oil, 1 tablespoon chopped chives, and salt and pepper. Toss the salad in this dressing and divide among the pastry boats.

Hearty quiches and pies

Cheese quiches and pies can be made in all shapes and sizes. The most varied types of cheese can be used, but the basis is always a custard made from cheese, eggs, and milk or cream. Savory pies and quiches should always be eaten fresh from the oven, so that the flavors can be appreciated fully. They can, however, be made in advance, and easily reheated until crisp without any loss of quality. The base for savory pies and quiches can be shortcrust, yeast or puff pastry. Shortcrust pastry offers the most advantages: it bakes crisp throughout, reheats well, and is easy to cut. Yeast pastry should be rolled out thinly and left to rise before being filled. The sides of a pie made with puff pastry become crisp and flaky, but the more or less liquid filling means that the base does not rise and remains doughy.

BACON AND ONION QUICHE

Makes one 10-inch pie
For the pastry:
1¾ cups all-purpose flour, ½ cup butter
1 egg yolk, ½ teaspoon salt, 1 tablespoon water
For the filling:
2 tablespoons butter, 1 onion
½ cup finely chopped smoked bacon
2 heaping cups shredded Gruyère
For the custard:
½ cup each milk and heavy cream, 4½ teaspoons flour
2 eggs, separated
½ teaspoon salt, freshly ground pepper

Preheat the oven to 400°F. Prepare a shortcrust pastry from the above ingredients, as described on page 213. Wrap in plastic wrap and refrigerate for 1 hour. Roll out into a circle on a floured work surface and use to line an ungreased fluted tart pan with a removable bottom. Crimp the edges and trim off the excess pastry with a knife. Refrigerate until needed. For the filling, slice the onion into thin rings and fry in the butter until translucent. Add the bacon and sweat for 5 minutes. Leave to cool, then spread over the pastry base. Sprinkle the Gruyère on top. To make the custard, combine the milk and cream with the flour, egg yolks, salt, and pepper. Beat the egg whites until stiff and fold in with a whisk. Pour the custard evenly over the base and bake the quiche for 35–40 minutes, until golden brown.

BACON AND HERB QUICHE

Makes one 9-inch pie
For the pastry:
1¾ cups Graham flour, ½ cup butter, cubed
¼ teaspoons salt, ¼ cup water
For the filling:
1¼ cups chopped smoked bacon
1¼ cups shredded Emmental
4 eggs, ¼ teaspoons salt and freshly ground pepper
2–3 tablespoons fresh chopped herbs (parsley, basil, and thyme)
1 cup heavy cream

Preheat the oven to 400°F. Prepare a shortcrust pastry as described in steps 1 and 2 of the picture sequence on page 213. Wrap the balls of pastry in plastic wrap and chill for 30 minutes, then proceed as shown in the picture sequence opposite. Bake the quiche in the center of the oven for 35 minutes.

Preparing and filling the bacon and herb quiche:

Roll out the pastry to an even thickness, roll around a rolling pin, and unroll over an ungreased fluted quiche pan.

Crimp the edges, using your fingers or a ball of dough. Trim off the excess pastry with a knife.

Place the cooked smoked bacon in a mixing bowl and add the cheese.

Add the eggs, one at a time.

Add the salt, pepper, and chopped herbs, followed by the cream.

Using a whisk, combine all the ingredients briefly, but do not beat, as this would tint the mixture green.

Pour into the lined pie dish and smooth the top with a spatula.

SWISS TARTLETS

Makes fifteen 3-inch tartlets
For the pastry:
2¼ cups all-purpose flour, ½ cup + 2 teaspoons butter
1 egg
¼ teaspoon salt, 1–2 tablespoons water
For the filling:
2 teaspoons each heavy cream and milk, 3 eggs
2 cups grated Greyerzer or Gruyère
1 cup grated Emmental
salt, pepper, nutmeg

Preheat the oven to 425°F. Sift the flour onto the work surface and make a well in the center. Cut the butter into pieces. Place the butter, egg, salt, and water in the well and work quickly into a smooth dough. Wrap in plastic wrap and refrigerate for 1–2 hours. To make the filling, whisk the cream, milk, and eggs together until smooth. Mix in the cheese and season to taste with salt, pepper, and nutmeg. Dust the work surface with flour, roll out the pastry thinly, and use to line the tartlet molds. Fill to just below the edge of the pastry (top photo). Bake for about 25 minutes.

For a hearty version of the little cheese pies shown above, slice 4 oz coppa (coarse Italian pork salami) or smoked bacon into thin strips and add to the filling with 1 tablespoon chopped parsley.

MINI SESAME–CHEESE PIES

Makes eight 4-inch pies
For the pastry:
1¾ cups Graham flour, ½ cup butter
¼ teaspoon salt, ¼ cup water
For the filling:
3 egg yolks, ⅔ cup heavy cream
1 cup grated Manchego
1½ cups grated Bergkäse or Emmental
salt, pepper, and cayenne pepper
3 stiffly beaten egg whites
white and black sesame seeds

Preheat the oven to 400°F. Prepare a shortcrust pastry from the first set of ingredients as described on page 213, and refrigerate for at least 30 minutes. To make the filling, mix the egg yolks and cream, and add the grated cheese. Season generously to taste with salt, pepper, and cayenne. Roll out the pastry and use to line the molds. Carefully fold the egg whites into the cheese custard. Divide the filling among the pastry-lined molds and sprinkle with sesame seeds (top photo). Bake for 20–25 minutes.

OBWALD CHEESE PIE

This classic cheese pie from Switzerland is made simply from cheese, eggs, milk, and cream, without further embellishment. Salt and pepper are sufficient as seasoning.

Makes one 11-inch pie
For the pastry:
1¾ cups all-purpose flour, ½ cup softened butter
½ cup grated Sbrinz
⅓ cup water, ½ teaspoon salt
For the filling:
1½ cups each grated Sbrinz and Emmental
⅞ cup each milk and heavy cream
2 eggs, separated
salt and freshly ground pepper

Preheat the oven to 400°F. Prepare a shortcrust pastry from the first set of ingredients, as described on page 213. Wrap in plastic wrap and refrigerate for 1 hour. Next, roll out the pastry on a floured work surface and use to line an ungreased pie dish. Prick the pastry base in several places with a fork and sprinkle with the combined Emmental and Sbrinz. To make the filling, thoroughly mix the milk with the cream and the egg yolks. Beat the egg whites until stiff, carefully fold into the custard, and season. Pour the custard into the pastry shell, evening out with a spatula if necessary. Place the dish on a baking sheet and bake for 30–35 minutes, until the custard is set and the top is golden brown.

To make the Obwald cheese pie, first sprinkle the mixed, grated cheeses over the pastry base, then pour the custard evenly on top.

CHEESE WAFFLES

These taste best hot off the waffle iron, but you could also sandwich two cooled waffles together with a spicy cream cheese and cut into strips.

Makes 10 square waffles
1 cup butter, ½ teaspoon salt, 4 eggs
1¾ cups all-purpose flour, ½ teaspoon baking powder
¾ cup grated Colby or Monterey Jack
1 teaspoon hot paprika
6–8 tablespoons lukewarm milk
oil for greasing the waffle iron

Prepare the waffles as described in the picture sequence below: To make the batter even lighter, separate the eggs. Beat the egg yolks with the butter until creamy and whip the egg whites until they form stiff peaks. Carefully fold the beaten egg whites with the flour into the butter mixture.

VATRUSHKY

Makes 12
For the pastry:
2½ cups all-purpose flour, ½ teaspoon baking powder,
½ teaspoon salt, 6 tablespoons butter, softened
1 egg, ½ cup sour cream
For the filling:
2½ cups low-fat Quark or Ricotta
1 tablespoon sour cream, 2 eggs
½ teaspoon salt, freshly ground pepper, 1 teaspoon sugar
1 egg yolk, beaten, for glazing

Beat the butter and salt together with a hand mixer. Mix in the eggs one at a time, adding 1 tablespoon flour after each to prevent the mixture from curdling.

Stir in the remaining flour, the baking powder, the cheese, and the paprika with a wooden spoon. Add the milk and work the mixture into a smooth batter.

Heat the waffle iron to 400°F and oil it. Spoon some batter onto the waffle iron and cook for 2 minutes. Lift out with a two-pronged fork.

Preheat the oven to 400°F. Sift the flour and baking powder into a bowl, make a well in the center, add the salt and butter, and mix with a little flour. Add the egg and sour cream and, using a wooden spoon, work into a smooth dough. Form into a ball, wrap in parchment paper, and chill for at least 45 minutes. Drain the Quark well, push through a strainer, and combine with the sour cream, eggs, salt, pepper, and sugar. Chill for at least 45 minutes also. Roll out the pastry to ⅛ inch thick and cut out 12 rounds each of 3½ and 4½ inches. Spoon filling into the center of the larger rounds, and cover with the smaller rounds. Brush the edges with beaten egg yolk. Draw up the lower edges and crimp together at intervals. Glaze, prick with a fork, and bake for about 20 minutes.

PUFF PASTRY WITH QUARK

This is not really an authentic puff pastry, since the butter is added to the pastry at the beginning and is not supposed to be blended in completely. The little lumps of butter and the acidity of the Quark give the dough extra lift, the result being a very light, airy pastry. This pastry can be worked and cut into shapes just like classic puff pastry. Round shapes are not very economical, since the leftover bits must be kneaded together again, which stops them from rising as well.

Makes 32 pastry puffs
For the pastry:
4¼ cups all-purpose flour, 2 cups butter
2½ cups Quark, 1 teaspoon salt
1 egg yolk, beaten
For the ham and cheese filling:
½ cup finely chopped onions
1¼ cups finely cubed ham, ¾ cup grated Manchego
salt and pepper
1 stiffly beaten egg white
For the mushroom and cheese filling:
¾ cup finely chopped onions
2¾ cups finely chopped mushrooms
1 tablespoon finely chopped parsley
1 tablespoon butter
4 oz Bergkäse or Emmental, cut into small cubes
salt and pepper
1 beaten egg

The picture sequence shows how to make square pastry puffs. Preheat the oven to 425°F. To make the ham filling, mix the onions, ham, cheese, and seasonings in a bowl, beat the egg white until stiff, and fold in. To make the mushroom filling, sauté the onions, mushrooms, and parsley in the butter for 3–4 minutes. Cool the mixture, then stir in the cheese, salt, pepper, and egg. Fill half the pastry puffs with each filling, bake for about 20 minutes, and serve immediately.

Have all the ingredients ready. Sift the flour onto the work surface and make a wide well in the center. Add the butter, cut up small, the Quark, and the salt.

Working always from the outside inwards, chop the ingredients with a metal spatula until the flour is completely incorporated. Using your hands, quickly work into a dough. Wrap in plastic wrap and refrigerate for about 30 minutes.

Roll out the pastry to a 8 x 13-inch rectangle about ½ inch thick. Fold the shorter sides in towards the center, overlapping slightly. Refrigerate for about 30 minutes, then repeat the entire process twice.

Roll out half the dough to 12 x 12 inches. Cut into eight 3 x 6-inch pieces, and divide the ham filling between them. Brush the edges with egg yolk, fold over, and seal tightly with a fork. Brush the top with egg yolk. Repeat with the remaining dough and mushroom filling.

SHORTCRUST CHEESE STRAWS

The strong cheese flavor of these shortcrust-pastry straws comes from a combination of two really piquant cheeses: aged Gouda as a filling, because it melts well and thus combines easily with the pastry, and Parmesan sprinkled on top.

2¼ cups all-purpose flour, ½ cup butter, 1 egg
a little salt, 1 tablespoon water
1 egg white
5 oz aged Gouda
1 cup grated Parmesan

Make a shortcrust pastry from the flour, butter, egg, salt, and water, as described in steps 1–3 of the picture sequence on page 213. Wrap in plastic wrap, refrigerate for at least 1 hour, then preheat the oven to 400°F and proceed as described below:

Roll out the pastry to a 6 x 24-inch rectangle of even thickness, brush one half generously with egg white, and sprinkle with the Bergkäse. Now brush the other half with egg white.

Fold the plain half over the cheese-strewn half, brush the top with egg white, and sprinkle with the Parmesan. Using a pastry wheel, cut clean edges all around and halve the sheet of pastry lengthwise.

Using the pastry wheel and a ruler, cut cheese straws measuring ½ x 3 inches. Place the straws on a baking sheet and bake for 10–12 minutes, until golden brown.

CHEESE *SABLÉS*

These crunchy cheese pastries can be made milder or more piquant by varying the type of cheese used. In this recipe Laguiole, a French cheese related to Cantal, is used, giving the *sablés* a highly aromatic flavor. For a mild version, replace the Laguiole with 4 oz medium-aged Gouda and ¾ cup ground almonds.

Makes 150
¾ cups + 2 tablespoons softened butter, ¼ cup milk
1¾ cups grated Laguiole
1 egg, 1 teaspoon salt
3 cups all-purpose flour, a pinch of baking powder

Place the softened butter, milk, cheese, egg, and salt in a bowl and mix well. Mix the flour with the baking powder and work into the mixture. Knead the pastry briefly on the work surface and form into cylinders 1 inch in diameter. Refrigerate them for 30 minutes, then preheat the oven to 400°F and proceed as explained in the picture sequence below:

Using a sharp knife, cut the cylinders into ¼-inch-thick rounds. Slicing through two cylinders at once is twice as fast.

Space the pastry "chips" on a baking sheet and bake for 8–10 minutes.

CROISSANTS WITH A HAM-AND-CHEESE FILLING

Makes 10
For the pastry:
10 oz frozen puff pastry
For the filling:
⅓ cup diced uncooked ham
½ cup grated Cantal or Cheddar
⅛ cup fresh cheese, 1 egg yolk
salt, pepper, nutmeg
1 egg yolk for glazing

Preheat the oven to 425°F. Mix the ham, cheeses, and egg yolk together and season to taste. Roll out the puff pastry to 12 x 18 inches, halve this lengthwise, and cut into triangles with a 3½-inch baseline. Make a 1-inch cut in the center of this baseline. Divide the filling evenly among the triangles and proceed as follows:

Paint the apex of the triangles with egg yolk, avoiding the cut edges. Pull open the cut base a little, place over the filling, and fold over once.

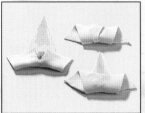

Fold the point over the cut edge and press tightly against the underside. Brush the surface with egg yolk, sprinkle with sesame seeds, and bake for 12–15 minutes.

CHEESE BOWTIES

The Sbrinz can be replaced by another cheese from the Parmesan family.

Makes 16
10 oz frozen puff pastry
1 egg yolk, 2 tablespoons finely grated Sbrinz
salt and pepper

Roll out the puff pastry to 8 x 12 inches. Cut crosswise into 3 equal pieces (8 x 4 inches each). Brush two pieces thickly with egg yolk to help the cheese stick better. Sprinkle on the cheese and season with salt and pepper. Place one sheet of pastry on top of the other so that the cheese is on top, then proceed as shown in the picture sequence below:

Brush the third sheet of pastry thickly with egg yolk, and place egg-side down on top of the other two sheets. Using a rolling pin, roll out to 4½ x 8½ inches, pressing down firmly so that the sheets stick together. Cut the edges straight. Cut into ½-inch wide strips.

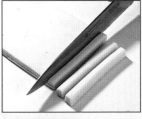

Use a very sharp knife to cut the pastry all the way through.

Hold the strips carefully in the center with both hands (do not press) and twist 180° in opposite directions.

Place on an ungreased baking sheet with one of the cut edges underneath, spacing the twists out sufficiently, and bake for 10–12 minutes, until golden brown.

CHEESE STRAWS
Makes 24

10 oz frozen puff pastry
1 cup grated Asiago, coarsely crushed pepper
2 egg yolks beaten with water; caraway seeds

Preheat the oven to 425 °F, and prepare the cheese straws as described in the picture sequence below.

CHEESE-AND-MEAT TURNOVERS
Makes 9
For the filling:

1 small onion, 1 garlic clove, both finely chopped
3 oz Bergkäse or Gruyère, cut into small cubes
1 cup chopped bell peppers (red, green, and yellow)
1¼ cups ground meat (beef or pork, or both)
1 teaspoon mustard, 1 tablespoon chopped parsley
½ teaspoon chopped green peppercorns, salt to taste

You will also need:

10 oz frozen puff pastry, 1 egg yolk, beaten

Preheat the oven to 450°F. Mix all the ingredients together. Roll out the pastry to a 12-inch square and cut into nine 4-inch squares. Divide the filling evenly among the squares, brush the edges with egg yolk, and fold over into triangles. Seal the edges firmly with a fork. Place the turnovers on a baking sheet moistened with water. Bake for 12–15 minutes.

It is easy to vary the taste of these cheese straws by making them, for example, with Pecorino or Parmesan, and sprinkling them with coarse salt, poppy seeds, or sesame seeds.

Making cheese straws:

Roll out the puff pastry to 12 x 12 inches and brush with egg yolk. Sprinkle cheese over one half of the pastry and season with pepper. Fold over the pastry to cover the cheese.

Roll over the pastry several times with the rolling pin in order to combine the cheese with the pastry. Using a pastry wheel and a ruler, cut into ½-inch-wide strips.

Holding the strips at either end, carefully corkscrew them by twisting each end in the opposite direction. Place on a baking sheet that has been moistened with water.

Glaze the cheese straws with the remaining egg yolk and sprinkle with caraway seeds. Bake for about 10 minutes, until golden brown.

A well-seasoned filling

Puff pastry, containing salt but no sugar, is naturally suited to spicy fillings, as the following recipe shows. Lighter fillings can be used too: for example, whipped cream mixed with grated cheese and appropriate seasonings, or combinations of fresh cheese, stirred until fluffy, grated cheese, and plenty of whipped cream.

FRESH-CHEESE TORTE

10 oz puff pastry
For the filling:
3¼ cups fresh cream cheese, scant ½ cup heavy cream
1 teaspoon salt, white pepper, 2 teaspoons lemon juice
⅔ cup finely diced red pepper
1 tablespoon finely chopped onions
1 tablespoon sweet paprika
5 green olives, 2 teaspoons capers, ½ clove garlic, all chopped
⅓ cup finely diced green pepper
1 tablespoon chopped mixed fresh herbs
For garnishing:
½ cup flaked, toasted almonds
a few stuffed olives, 1 cooked carrot
parsley
little pickled chile peppers

Preheat the oven to 425°F. Cut the puff pastry into rough pieces and knead together briefly so that it does not rise too high when baked. Divide into three equal pieces, form into balls, and roll out into 10-inch rounds. Line a baking sheet with parchment paper and place the pastry circles on top; prick with a fork, let rest for 15 minutes, and bake for 12–15 minutes. Remove from the oven when golden. Meanwhile, beat the fresh cheese with a hand mixer or whisk until fluffy. Whip the cream until it forms soft peaks and fold in. The cheese cream should have the consistency of very stiffly whipped cream. Season with salt, pepper, and lemon juice. Divide the cheese cream equally among three bowls. Stir the red pepper, onion, and paprika into one of the creams, spread evenly over one of the puff pastry circles and cover with a second pastry circle. Mix the green olives, capers, garlic, green pepper, and herbs into the second cream. Spread this mixture over the second pastry circle, top with the third circle, and spread this last one thinly with some of the remaining fresh-cheese cream. Mark the top of the torte into 16 slices. Fill a pastry bag with a star tip with the remaining fresh-cheese cream and decorate the torte. Decorate the sides and center of the torte with the toasted flaked almonds. Garnish each wedge with carrot and olive slices, parsley, and a pickled chile pepper.

This spicy torte should be prepared just before serving, since the moist filling will eventually soften the crunchy puff-pastry base. Alternatively, you can bake the base in advance and reheat it in a preheated oven until crisp, shortly before filling it.

Choux pastry

Choux pastry is the ideal base for many savory creations, since it is made without sugar. It is therefore well suited to combining with cheese. The cheese can be stirred into the pastry before baking, or a plain baked choux pastry can be filled with a cheese cream or a cheese salad. Piquant hard and semi-hard cheeses are the ones best suited for adding to the pastry itself — for example, an aged, properly stored Emmental or Gruyère, or an extra-hard cheese such as Parmesan or Pecorino. In these cases, however, halve the amount of salt in the pastry — especially if the pastry is also to be strewn with coarse salt — since the cheese itself adds saltiness.

BASIC RECIPE

½ cup each milk and water
½ cup butter, ½ teaspoon salt
2 cups all-purpose flour, 5–6 eggs
coarse salt and caraway seeds
For the choux pastry with cheese:
1½ cups grated Gruyère

Making choux pastry:

Bring the milk, water, butter, and salt to a boil in a saucepan.

Add the flour to the boiling liquid all at once, and immediately stir the mixture with a wooden spoon until smooth.

Stir the pastry until it forms a large ball and a white film covers the base of the pot.

Transfer the pastry to a mixing bowl and allow to cool a little. Add the eggs to the pastry one at a time.

Add the next egg only after the previous one has been fully incorporated.

For the cheese choux pastry, add the grated cheese and mix in thoroughly.

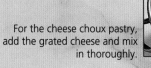

CHEESE CRUNCHIES. Preheat the oven to 400°F. Using a pastry bag with a round tip, pipe cheese choux pastry onto a baking sheet, spacing out well, and sprinkle with salt and caraway. Bake for 12 minutes. Serve fresh or freeze and rewarm in the oven until crisp, as needed.

These choux rings are sprinkled with coarse salt and caraway seeds before they are baked. After baking, halve horizontally and fill with the fresh-cheese cream on page 128.

Gougère ring with a savory cheese and cream filling. This choux ring is a variation of the original gougère balls. Preheat the oven to 450°F. Pipe the balls onto a baking sheet to form a ring, and steam-bake for 20–22 minutes. Halve the baked gougère lengthwise with a suitable knife (top photo), and spoon the cheese and cream filling onto its base (center photo). Place the top half of the choux ring on top of the filling.

GOUGÈRE:
LITTLE CHOUX PASTRY BALLS

1½ cups water
½ heaping cup butter, a pinch of salt
2¼ cups all-purpose flour
5 large eggs
8 oz Gruyère, cut into small pieces
salt and freshly ground pepper
1 egg for glazing

Preheat the oven to 450°F. Prepare a choux pastry from the above ingredients, as described in the picture sequence on the opposite page. Pipe little balls of pastry onto a buttered baking sheet. Beat the egg thoroughly and use to glaze the pastry. Steam-bake the gougère for 15 minutes: place it in the oven, pour a cup of water into a shallow pan on the floor of the oven, and close the door immediately. The steam thus produced helps the pastry to rise higher.

CHEESE AND CREAM FILLING FOR
THE GOUGÈRE RING

5 oz fresh goat cheese
5 oz fresh cream cheese
⅔ cup grated Gruyère
chopped parsley
salt and pepper
1 cup whipped cream

Whisk together all the ingredients except the cream. Then fold the cream into the mixture gradually.

Gougère, a choux pastry with cheese, is a specialty of Burgundy. Eaten cold or lukewarm, it goes superbly with the wines of the region. Plain or filled, these make delicate canapés.

Preparing pizza dough:

Make a well in the flour, crumble in the yeast and pour the water over the yeast.

Using a wooden spoon or your fingers, break up the yeast until dissolved. Cover this with a layer of flour and leave to rise.

When the mixture has obvious cracks on its surface, add the oil.

Work the ingredients into a dough with a wooden spoon or your hands.

Turn the ball of dough out onto a floured work surface and knead until smooth. The dough should be firm but elastic. Let rise again until doubled in size.

The dough, divided into portion-size balls, can be wrapped in plastic wrap and frozen for use later.

Divide the dough into pieces and roll by hand into balls. With the aid of a rolling pin, roll out into circles.

With a floured hand, stretch the dough from the center outwards, so that the edge is a bit thicker. Prick several times with a fork.

Top the pizza bases with the ingredients in the proper order, leaving the slightly raised, thicker edge free.

Pizza

Pizza would be almost unthinkable without cheese or its main partner, tomatoes. It is a theme with countless variations, since vegetables, ham, sausage, and even fish and shellfish can quite happily be combined on the crusty yeast-dough base.

BASIC RECIPE FOR PIZZA DOUGH

Makes four 8-inch pizzas
2½ cups all-purpose flour, 1 cake (⅗ oz) fresh yeast or
1½ teaspoons dry yeast, ½ cup tepid water
½ teaspoon salt, 2 tablespoons olive oil

The absence of eggs, butter, and milk in this simple recipe is what makes the dough so beautifully crusty, when prepared as shown in the picture sequence opposite. It can also be made by combining all the ingredients at once, but then must be left to rise a bit longer. The finished dough should be firm but elastic, so that it can be stretched out easily. The edge of the pizza should always be a bit thicker than the rest of it, to prevent the liquid from the tomatoes and the topping from running off while the pizza is baking.

CHEESE PIZZA

Makes two 11-inch pizzas
1 recipe basic pizza dough
14 oz tomatoes, 2 garlic cloves
salt and pepper, 2 tablespoons olive oil
3 oz Gorgonzola Piccante, 3 oz Fontal or Fontina

Preheat the oven to 425°F. Divide the dough in half and stretch into two pizza bases about 11 inches in diameter. Dip the tomatoes briefly in boiling water, peel, core, and slice them, and distribute over the bases. Slice the garlic wafer-thin, scatter over the top, season, and drizzle with the oil. Top with slices of Gorgonzola. Cut the Fontal into cubes and scatter on top. Bake for about 20 minutes, until crusty and brown.

Sfincione, the pizza of Sicily

It would be inexcusable to call this Sicilian specialty a pizza, for although it is indisputably related to that Neapolitan dish, sfincione is a typically Sicilian food, made from the harvest of the land. Sicilians also maintain that sfincione existed long before the rest of Italy even dreamt of pizza. This is a "poor man's meal," eaten by farmers and laborers: even so, there is a great variety of toppings, and above all seasonings; but the basic ingredients always remain the same. Sfincioni are usually baked in small rounds, but are also sometimes made into larger pies.

Sfincione, a rustic specialty from Sicily, is still baked there in the traditional manner, in old stone ovens. Originally, sfincione toppings were dictated by the harvest of one's own garden.

The pizza dough can be prepared by combining all the ingredients at once. The yeast dough should be soft enough to knead. Most importantly, it must stretch easily into small, round flat cakes about 8 inches in diameter.

For the topping, peel and chop tomatoes, and marinate in olive oil with onion rings, salt, and chopped garlic. Spread this mixture over the dough bases. Scatter pitted, halved black olives, a bit of oregano, and crumbled sheep's cheese on top.

The crusty result from the stone oven cannot be duplicated in a gas or electric oven, but will still be very good. Preheat the oven to at least 425°F and bake the sfincioni for about 15–20 minutes. Drizzle them with good olive oil immediately.

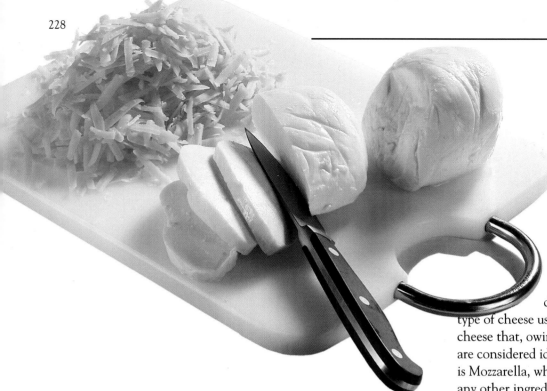

Cheese for pizza: shredded or sliced

Whether a pizza is topped with sliced, shredded, or grated cheese depends to a large extent on the type of cheese used. There are certain kinds of cheese that, owing to their good melting qualities, are considered ideal for pizza. Probably best known is Mozzarella, which adapts superbly to the flavor of any other ingredients. Since it is soft, it is naturally sliced. Mild Gouda and Steppe cheese, on the other hand, are suited to shredding, and the extra-hard cheeses, such as Parmesan and its relatives, are grated. Because of their strong taste, however, the latter are used more as a seasoning than as a main ingredient, sometimes in addition to a mild pizza cheese.

PIZZA MARGHERITA

Green basil, white Mozzarella, red tomatoes: the famous pizza in the colors of the Italian flag was, so the story goes, created by a Neapolitan pizza-maker in honor of Queen Margherita of Savoy. This recipe is intended for a pizza made on a 13 x 17-inch baking sheet. Alternatively, the dough can be divided to make two round pizzas, as in the photo.

For the dough:
2½ cups all-purpose flour, 1 cake (⅗ oz) fresh yeast or 1½ teaspoons dry yeast
½ cup lukewarm water
½ teaspoon salt, 2 tablespoons olive oil
For the topping:
3½ cups peeled tomatoes
10 oz fresh Mozzarella
salt, black pepper
20 basil leaves, ½ cup olive oil

Preheat the oven to 425°F. Work the first set of ingredients into a light yeast dough as described on page 226. Dust the work surface with flour, roll out the dough to an even thickness, place on the lightly oiled baking sheet, and prick several times with a fork. Top the pizza as illustrated in the picture sequence opposite. Allow it to rise again for 10–15 minutes, then drizzle with the olive oil, and bake in the center of the oven for 18–22 minutes.

The cheese on the baked pizza should be nicely melted, and yellow to light brown (never dark brown), according to type. However, the baking times for the pizza shell and topping are not always the same. If the cheese is meant to stay light in color, it is best to put it on the pizza a third or even half of the way through the total cooking time.

Topping the pizza Margherita :

Drain the tomatoes in a strainer, chop coarsely, and place on the pizza base.

Distribute the Mozzarella slices evenly over the base, and season with salt and pepper.

Place the fresh basil leaves on top. Their taste is more evenly distributed if they are chopped, but the whole leaves are more decorative.

Using a spoon or oil can, drizzle the olive oil over the pizza.

The Pizza Margherita should emerge from the oven with a crusty base and a juicy, soft topping.

VEGETABLE AND SALAMI PIZZA

For the dough:

2½ cups all-purpose flour, 1 cake (⅗ oz) fresh yeast
or 1½ teaspoons dry yeast
½ cup lukewarm water
½ teaspoon salt, 2 tablespoons olive oil

For the topping:

1 onion, 1 lb tomatoes, 10 oz zucchini
2 yellow peppers
10 oz Mozzarella, 4 oz Italian salami
1 teaspoon salt, black pepper
1 tablespoon each basil and oregano
¼ cup olive oil, 10 black olives

Preheat the oven to 425°F. Work the first set of ingredients into a light yeast dough as described on page 226. Dust the work surface with flour, roll out the dough to an even thickness, place on a lightly oiled baking sheet, and prick several times with a fork. To make the topping, cut the onions into rings, the tomatoes and zucchini into rounds, and the peppers into strips. Arrange the vegetables on the dough base, alternating with slices of Mozzarella and salami, and sprinkle with the salt, pepper, and herbs. Let the pizza rise again for about 10 minutes, then drizzle with the oil, and top with the olives. Bake in the center of the oven for 20–25 minutes.

Mini pizzas: smaller size, greater variety

Little individual pizzas are just the right size if you feel like a snack. If you are seriously hungry, two should hit the spot, but with different toppings, of course. To make them, prepare a yeast dough according to the basic recipe on page 226. Divide the dough into 5. Form each piece into a circle about 6 inches in diameter, and top with the other ingredients. Just how varied and plentiful these ingredients should be depends to a large extent on personal taste, which is why quantities have not been specified in the following suggestions. Bake the pizzas in a preheated oven at 400°F for about 15 minutes, or until crisp. With pizzas, as with all dough or pastry bases, make a sight check for the ideal degree of doneness during the last third of the baking time.

WITH MUSSELS

Steam fresh mussels in a little seasoned water until they open. Remove them from their shells and scatter them over the pizza base with plenty of onion rings and crushed garlic. Top with peeled, chopped tomatoes and sprinkle with cubed Provolone. Season with salt and pepper, sprinkle with chopped basil, and drizzle with olive oil (top pizza pictured).

SPICY, WITH CHILE PEPPERS

Place peeled, chopped tomatoes on the pizza base, scatter diced onion over them, and top with peeled yellow peppers. Salt lightly, and place some halved, seeded chile peppers on top. Sprinkle with shredded Asiago. Bake until done, garnishing with olives halfway through the baking time (second pizza).

WITH TOMATOES AND ITALIAN SAUSAGE

Scatter a little diced onion and some crushed garlic over the pizza base, then top with halved, peeled tomatoes. Place slices of Italian sausage and Fontina in between. Lightly salt the pizza, season with pepper, and sprinkle with grated Parmesan (third pizza).

WITH EGGPLANT

Cut an eggplant into cubes and fry in a little oil for 3–4 minutes. Spread over the pizza base, and top with onion rings and peeled, diced tomatoes. Season with salt, pepper, and thyme. Top with shredded Provolone and sprinkle with a bit of grated aged Pecorino (bottom pizza).

SAVORY ROLLS AND SPIRALS

Makes 20

4½ cups Graham flour

2 cakes fresh yeast or 1 package dry yeast

½ cup each lukewarm water and milk

1 egg, 1 teaspoon salt

Filling for the spirals or rolls:

4 oz smoked bacon, ½ cup diced onions

5 oz Gruyère, finely cubed

freshly ground pepper

2 tablespoons chopped herbs (parsley, chives)

6 tablespoons butter

egg yolk for glazing

coarse salt, poppyseeds, sunflower seeds, and sesame seeds

Place the flour in a bowl, make a well in the center, and crumble in the yeast. Pour the mixture of milk and water over the yeast, and break it up until dissolved. Sprinkle a layer of flour over this. Cover with a cloth and leave in a warm place to rise until the layer of flour has obvious cracks in it (15–20 minutes). Add the egg and salt, and work into a smooth dough. Knead firmly on the work surface, return to the bowl, and allow to rise again for about 30 minutes, until the dough has doubled in size.

Meanwhile, make the filling. Finely chop the bacon and fry with the diced onion for 2–3 minutes until the onions are translucent. Cool, then mix with the cheese, pepper, and herbs. Roll out the dough to about 12 x 24 inches and spread with the cheese mixture, leaving a long edge free. Brush this edge with water and roll up the dough from the opposite side. Cut the dough roll into 1-inch slices.

Preheat the oven to 425°F. Melt the butter in a baking dish, roll the sides of the spirals in the butter, then place in the dish, cut surface up. Cover the spirals and leave to rise again for 30 minutes, then bake for about 25 minutes, until crusty and brown.

To make the rolls, roll the dough into a cylinder and divide into 20 pieces of equal size. Cupping your hand, roll each piece on the work surface into a ball, then press into round flat cakes about 4 inches in diameter. Place a spoonful of filling on each, pinch the edges of the dough together, and roll until they are round. Place the rolls, well spaced out, on a baking sheet. Cover and leave to rise in a warm, draft-free spot, until they have almost doubled in size. Preheat the oven to 425°F. Brush the top of the rolls with egg yolk and sprinkle with coarse salt, sesame or sunflower seeds, poppyseeds or cheese, and bake.

CRUSTY CHEESE ROLLS

Called *buchteln*, these rolls are an example of typical Austrian baking. Serve them still slightly warm.

Makes 36
For the dough:
4½ cups flour, 1 oz fresh yeast or 2 teaspoons dry yeast, about 1 cup milk
¼ cup butter, ¼ cup sugar, ¼ teaspoon salt
grated peel of ½ lemon, 2 eggs
For the filling:
1 cup milk, ⅓ cup sugar, ½ teaspoon vanilla extract
4 teaspoons cornstarch, 2 egg yolks, 1¾ cups Quark or Ricotta, strained
⅔ cup raisins soaked in 4 teaspoons rum
7 tablespoons butter for greasing the baking dish
confectioner's sugar

Preheat the oven to 400°F. Sift the flour into a bowl, make a well in the center, and crumble in the yeast. Pour in the milk, work the yeast until dissolved, and cover with flour. Cover the bowl with a cloth and leave to rest in a warm spot, until the flour has cracks in it (15–20 minutes). Melt the butter and stir with the sugar, salt, lemon peel, and eggs until creamy. Add to the bowl and work into a smooth, dry dough that leaves the sides of the bowl. If necessary, add a little milk. Cover and leave to rise for 15 minutes. To make the filling, bring the milk and sugar to a boil. Dissolve the cornstarch in a little milk, add to the rest of the milk and cook through, stirring. Remove from the heat and stir in the vanilla extract and the egg yolks one at a time. Add the Quark and fold in the raisins. Continue as described in the pictures opposite.

All dry curd cheeses, including Quark and Ricotta, should be strained when used in baking or to make cheese creams. Press through a strainer with a flexible spatula.

Filling the *buchteln*:

Divide the dough into 9 equal pieces and quarter each of these.

Form the small pieces of dough into balls by rolling them with a circular motion against the work surface, hand cupped.

With a rolling pin, roll out the balls of dough into small, circles of even thickness, 3–4 inches in diameter.

Use a spoon to divide the filling among the circles of dough. Place the filling in the exact center of each, so that the rolls can be sealed more easily.

Holding the dough in your cupped hand, pull the edges upwards. Carefully pinch the dough closed over the filling and then roll again into a ball.

Turn the *buchteln* in the melted butter and place right up against each other. Bake for 15 minutes, then at 425°F for 25 minutes, until golden brown.

QUARK CRUMB CAKE

For a more elaborate treat, arrange halved fresh apricots or plums over the Quark cream, then top with the crumb mixture, and increase the baking time by a few minutes.

Makes 18–21
For the dough:
3¼ cups all-purpose flour, 1 oz fresh yeast or 2 teaspoons dry yeast, ½ cup milk, 6 tablespoons butter
¼ cup sugar, ½ teaspoon salt
grated rind of 1 lemon, pinch of allspice, 2 eggs
For the Quark cream:
1 cup milk, scant 1 cup sugar, 4 teaspoons cornstarch
3 egg yolks, 1¾ cups Quark or Ricotta, drained
juice and grated rind of ½ lemon, 1 tablespoon rum
For the crumb topping:
3 cups all-purpose flour, ¾ cup + 2 tablespoons butter
1 cup sugar, ½ vanilla bean

Preheat the oven to 400°F and grease a 13 x 17-inch baking sheet. Prepare a dough from the first set of ingredients, as described in the recipe for *buchteln* (opposite page). Roll out the dough on a floured work surface to fit the baking sheet, then transfer to it. Prick with a fork at close intervals, to prevent the dough from developing bubbles as it bakes. To make the filling, bring the milk to a boil with the sugar. Blend the cornstarch with a little milk and add to the milk mixture. Stir in the egg yolks, followed by the Quark, lemon juice, grated lemon peel, and rum. Leave to cool, then spread over the dough. If you like, add ⅔ cup raisins to the Quark cream. To make the topping, rub the flour, butter, sugar, and the contents of the vanilla bean together

to form coarse crumbs, and spread evenly over the cake. Bake for 20–25 minutes. When cool, cut the cake into 3 strips lengthwise, and each strip into 6–7 pieces widthwise.

Quark cream:
Bring the milk and sugar to a boil and bind with the dissolved cornstarch. Cook through thoroughly, then remove from the heat.

Stir in the egg yolks one at a time, then add the strained Quark, lemon juice, lemon peel, and rum.

Filling the cheesecake:

Drain the cheese as dry as possible, then push through a fine-mesh strainer.

Separate the eggs. Using a whisk or a hand mixer, blend in the egg yolks and half of the sugar, beating until fluffy.

Heat the butter, clarify, and pour into the mixture in a thin stream, stirring constantly. Sift in the flour and add the salt and the grated lemon peel.

Add the raisins, stirring only briefly so as not to turn the mixture brown.

Try replacing the Quark with Ricotta — sheep's-milk Ricotta in particular makes a highly piquant cheesecake. Prepare as in the recipe opposite.

Beat the egg whites with the remaining sugar to stiff peaks, and carefully fold into the cheese mixture with a wooden or rubber spatula.

Pour the mixture into the prebaked shortcrust pastry shell.

Smooth the top and bake the cheesecake in the preheated oven for about 45 minutes, until golden brown. Turn out upside down onto a cake rack.

When the cake is completely cool, turn it over and sift some confectioner's sugar over the top. Use a red-hot skewer to create a lattice pattern.

CHEESECAKE

Makes one 10-inch cake

For the shortcrust pastry:

2 cups all-purpose flour, ½ cup butter

½ cup confectioner's sugar

1 egg yolk, a pinch of salt

For the cheese mixture:

2½ cups Quark or Ricotta, 4 eggs, ¾ cup sugar

½ cup butter, ½ cup all-purpose flour, a pinch of salt

grated rind of 1 lemon

½ cup raisins soaked in 4 teaspoons kirsch or rum

confectioner's sugar for dusting

Prepare a shortcrust pastry as on page 213, and refrigerate for 1–2 hours. Preheat the oven to 375°F. Roll out to a circle 13 inches in diameter and use to line a fluted tart pan. Crimp the sides and trim off any excess pastry. Pierce the base at intervals with a fork, and bake blind as described on page 213. Prepare the cheese mixture as in the picture sequence opposite. Lower the oven heat to 300°F. Do not bake the cheesecake at a higher temperature, as this would cause it to rise too high and crack, then collapse. Baked at the proper temperature it rises only slightly, and remains light and moist.

These tartlets are prepared according to the recipe opposite but apricots are used instead of sour cherries.

CHEESECAKE WITH SOUR CHERRIES

Makes one 9½-inch pie
For the pastry:
¾ cup butter, ¾ cup confectioner's sugar
grated rind of ½ lemon
1 egg yolk, pinch of salt, 2¼ cups all-purpose flour
For the filling:
1 jar of sour cherries (drained weight: 1 lb)
1¾ cups sugar, pinch of cinnamon, 2 teaspoons cornstarch
3 egg yolks, pinch of salt
⅔ cup milk, 2½ teaspoons gelatin
¾ lb fresh goat cheese
grated rind of ½ lemon
1 tablespoon lemon juice, 2 cups heavy cream
cocoa powder for dusting

Place the butter and confectioner's sugar on a work surface and work until the mixture is smooth. Add the lemon rind and egg yolk, followed by the flour and salt, kneading them in quickly. Form this pastry into a ball, wrap in plastic wrap, and refrigerate for 1 hour. Preheat the oven to 375°F. Roll out the pastry and line a fluted tart pan. Crimp the edges with your thumb and trim off any excess pastry with a knife. Bake blind as described on page 213; after about 15 minutes remove the beans or pie weight and continue baking the shell for another 10–15 minutes, until crisp and brown.

To make the filling, drain the sour cherries, reserve the juice and bring it to the boil with 2 tablespoons of the sugar and the cinnamon. Mix the cornstarch in a little of the juice and use to thicken the mixture. Reserve a few cherries for decoration. Add the rest to the syrup and let cool completely. Mix the egg yolks with the remaining sugar, the salt, and the milk, and heat to just below boiling point, until thick enough to coat the back of a spoon (see page 236). Dissolve the gelatin in this cream mixture. Pass the cheese through a fine-meshed strainer and stir in. Add the lemon peel and lemon juice. Whip the cream until stiff and stir two-thirds of it into the slightly cooled cheese cream. Using a pastry bag and a large plain tip, pipe part of the cheese cream into rings on the pastry base and fill them and gaps between them with the sour cherry syrup. Pour in the remaining cheese cream and smooth the top. Refrigerate until set. Dust the top with cocoa powder, mark out slices with a knife, and use the remaining cream to pipe a rosette onto each piece, decorating with a cherry.

Preparing the cheese filling:

Beat the egg yolks, sugar, lemon rind, and salt with the milk. Heat slowly over medium heat, stirring.

The custard should be heated to just below boiling point, until it is thick enough to coat the back of the spoon.

Soften the gelatin in cold water, squeeze out well, and dissolve in the hot custard, or follow package directions for powdered gelatin.

Strain the cheese into a bowl and pour the slightly cooled custard over it, then mix.

Stir until you have a smooth cream, and let it cool to lukewarm.

Stir the whipped cream into the cheese mixture. A whisk is faster, but a wooden spatula does the job more gently.

Pile the filling on the pastry base encircled by a ring, and smooth the top with a spatula. Chill the torte.

Remove the ring. Using the ring to keep the cut pieces together, slide the second shortcrust base on top.

Fresh berries are a fine addition to a cheese-cream torte. Sweeten the fruit with sugar if necessary, then spread over the shortcrust base and cover with the cheese-cream filling.

TANGY CHEESE TORTE

Be sure the Quark or Ricotta is dry. If necessary, drain it for 1–2 hours before use. This means you may need more cheese than the amount given in the recipe, in order to compensate for the lost liquid.

Makes one 10-inch cake
For the shortcrust pastry:
½ cup butter, ½ cup confectioner's sugar
1 egg yolk, 1¾ cups all-purpose flour
For the cheese filling:
4 egg yolks, 1 cup sugar
grated peel of 1 lemon, pinch of salt, 1 cup milk
4 ⅔ sheets gelatin or 1 tablespoon + ½ teaspoon powdered gelatin
2½ cups dry Quark or Ricotta
2¼ cups heavy cream
confectioner's sugar for dusting

Work the butter, confectioner's sugar, egg yolk and flour into a shortcrust pastry and refrigerate for 1 hour. Preheat the oven to 400°F. Roll out the pastry into two 10-inch bases and bake in springform pans for 8–10 minutes, until golden brown. Cut 1 base into the desired number of pieces while still warm and in its pan. Prepare the filling as in the picture sequence opposite and dust the finished torte with confectioner's sugar.

FLAKY CRANBERRY CHEESECAKE

If possible, prepare this light cream torte no more than 2–3 hours before serving, otherwise the moist filling will soften the crisp pastry.

Makes one 10-inch cake
For the pastry:
1 cup water, ½ cup + 2 teaspoons butter, ½ teaspoon salt
2 cups all-purpose flour, 5–6 eggs
For the cranberry compote:
1 tablespoon honey, ½ cup brown sugar
juice of 1 orange, ½ cup red wine, 2 cups fresh cranberries
For the filling:
3 egg yolks, ½ heaping cup sugar, a pinch of salt
⅔ cup milk
3 sheets gelatin or 2½ teaspoons powdered gelatin
1¾ cups dry or well-drained Quark or Ricotta
3¼ cups stiffly whipped cream
confectioner's sugar for dusting

Preheat the oven to 450°F. Use the first set of ingredients to prepare a choux pastry as described on page 224. Pipe out five 10-inch bases on baking sheets lightly dusted with flour, and bake until crisp and light brown. Choose the three nicest bases for filling, and cut or break the two remaining bases into small pieces for the flakes.

To make the cranberry compote, bring the honey, sugar, orange juice, and wine to a boil. Cook for 5 minutes. Add the cranberries and simmer for 5 minutes. Allow to cool.

To make the filling, prepare a cream mixture as shown in the picture sequence on the opposite page. Stir about half of the whipped cream into the cheese mixture. Spread half of the cheese-cream mixture onto the first base and top with half the cranberry compote, arranged in little mounds. Cover with the second base, press down firmly, and top with the remaining cheese mixture and cranberry compote, reserving a little of each for decoration. Finally, place the third base on top and press down firmly. Spread some of the remaining whipped cream on top and cover generously with the choux pastry flakes. Dust the top with confectioner's sugar, pipe on rosettes with the remaining whipped cream, and decorate with cranberry compote.

Desserts

Fresh white cheeses are particularly well suited to sweet creations. The traditional Quark desserts of southern Germany, Bohemia, and Austria, are also worthy of attention and can be varied almost infinitely with different fillings or sophisticated sauces. Ricotta cheeses are ideally suited for sweet desserts and can be used instead of Quark in the recipes here. The various fresh goat cheeses have a delicate, fresh flavor before they ripen (the typical "goaty" character is almost undetectable at this stage), and make a particularly good dessert combined with fresh fruit.

Many desserts made from fresh white cheeses are based on very simple recipes — a fresh *fromage blanc* with a hint of sugar or honey, combined with fresh berries, mixed into fruit salads, or used to fill fruit produces a lovely end to a meal. Take, for example a fruit salad with cottage cheese (insert, opposite page). Fresh fruit — in this instance strawberries, blackberries, halved physalis (Cape gooseberries), figs and two slices of star fruit — is arranged on a plate. Some stiffly whipped cream is folded into the cottage cheese, which is then piled onto the fruit and topped with raspberry sauce.

All recipes serve 4 unless otherwise indicated.

STRAWBERRIES
WITH QUARK GRATIN
Serves 4–8

1 cup milk, ½ vanilla bean

¾ cup confectioner's sugar, a pinch of salt

2 teaspoons cornstarch

2 egg yolks, 1 cup dry or well-drained Quark

2 egg whites, ½ cup heavy cream

9 oz strawberries

confectioner's sugar for dusting

toasted flaked almonds

Prepare the gratin according to the picture sequence opposite.

QUARK GRATIN
WITH TROPICAL FRUITS
Serves 4–8

1 cup milk, ½ vanilla bean

½ cup sugar, a pinch of salt

3 teaspoons cornstarch, 3 eggs, separated

2 cups dry or well-drained Quark

10 oz fresh tropical fruits (mango, guavas, kiwis, etc.)

confectioner's sugar for dusting

Prepare the gratin according to the picture sequence opposite, leaving out the cream. Cut up the fruit, arrange on plates or in gratin dishes, top with the Quark mixture, and brown under the broiler.

Preparing a Quark gratin:

Bring the milk, vanilla bean, half the sugar, and the salt to a boil in a large saucepan.

Blend the cornstarch with a little milk and add to the boiling milk. Boil hard until cooked through. Remove the vanilla bean.

Remove from the heat and whisk in the egg yolks one at a time.

Press the Quark through a fine-mesh strainer and fold into the custard with the whisk.

Beat the egg whites to stiff peaks with the remaining sugar and stir into the Quark-custard mixture.

Using a whisk or a wooden spatula, carefully fold the stiffly whipped cream into the custard.

Arrange the strawberries on plates and pour the Quark custard over them. Place under the broiler until the top browns.

Dust the gratin with confectioner's sugar and decorate with a few toasted slivered almonds. Serve at once.

LÍVANCE: BOHEMIAN PANCAKES WITH QUARK

The pancakes can be made either in an authentic
lívance pan with a base 3 inches in diameter, or in a
regular frying pan. In the latter case take care not to
make the batter too runny, or you will end up with
crepes.

Makes 16–20 pancakes
2¼ cups all-purpose flour, ½ oz fresh yeast
1 cup lukewarm milk
3 tablespoons butter, 1 egg, ½ teaspoon salt
2 tablespoons sugar
grated rind of ½ lemon
½ cup dry or well-drained Quark
butter for greasing the pan
For the filling:
1 cup dry or well-drained Quark, strained; 1 egg yolk
1 teaspoon lemon juice, ¼ cup sugar
½ recipe cranberry compote (see page 237)
confectioner's sugar for dusting

Sift the flour into a bowl and make a well in the
center. Crumble in the yeast and add the milk to
dissolve it. Sprinkle a layer of flour on top, cover
the bowl with a cloth, and leave to rise in a warm
place until the surface develops obvious cracks,
about 15 minutes. Melt the butter and mix with the
egg, salt, sugar, and lemon rind. Add to the dough
and stir to a smooth, almost liquid yeast batter. Stir
in the Quark, if necessary thinning the batter
further with a little milk, and leave to rise again.
Grease the pan generously with melted butter, pour
in the batter, and cook over moderate heat for
about 2 minutes per side until an appetizing light
brown; keep warm. To make the filling, mix the
Quark with the egg yolk, lemon juice, and sugar.
Sandwich the *lívance* together with the Quark
filling and a spoonful of cranberry compote, and
dust with confectioner's sugar.

QUARK STRUDEL

This authentic strudel recipe is from Austria, of
course, where it would be called *topfen* strudel. It
should always be served slightly warm,
accompanied, for example, by a cold fruit sauce.

For the pastry:
1½ cups all-purpose flour, 1 egg yolk, ¼ teaspoon salt
4 teaspoons oil
butter for greasing the baking sheet
For the filling:
2½ cups drained Quark
⅔ cup sugar, 2 eggs
grated rind and juice of ½ lemon
1 tablespoon cornstarch, ¼ cup raisins, 4 teaspoons rum
½ cup clarified butter for spreading
confectioner's sugar for dusting

Preheat the oven to 400°F. Sift the flour onto the
work surface, make a well in the center, and add the
egg yolk, salt, and oil. First stir briefly with a fork,
and then knead with both hands to a smooth,
supple dough. Form into a ball, wrap in plastic
wrap, and leave to rest for at least 30 minutes.
Next, roll out the dough on a floured work surface.
Lay a large dish towel on the table, dust evenly with
flour, and place the rolled-out dough on top. Using
both hands, stretch the dough out from the center
to the edges, until it is uniformly thin all over. For
the filling, push the drained Quark through a
strainer into a bowl and blend with the sugar, eggs,
lemon juice, lemon rind, and cornstarch. Steep the
raisins briefly in the rum and add them to the other
ingredients. Spread the mixture onto the strudel
dough, leaving a border free around the edges. Roll
up the strudel, lifting the end of the dish towel to
help. Carefully place it on a buttered baking sheet
and bake for about 40 minutes, until nicely golden
brown and crisp. While still hot, spread clarified
butter on top, dust with confectioner's sugar, and
cut into pieces.

Cranberries
harmonize
particularly well with
sweet Quark. Their
strong taste is
beautifully
compatible with the
acidity of fresh white
cheese.

MASCARPONE CREAM

This cream can be served in long-stemmed glasses or bowls, piled on top of ladyfingers dipped in coffee liqueur, or used as a filling for shortcrust-pastry tartlets, cream puffs, or, as here, almond-paste tubes.

Makes 40

For the pastry tubes:

1¾ cups confectioner's sugar, 2 oz almond paste
pinch of cinnamon, 3 eggs
1¼ cups all-purpose flour, ¼ cup heavy cream

For the Mascarpone cream:

3 egg yolks, 1 cup confectioner's sugar
2¼ cups Mascarpone
bitter chocolate for decorating

Preheat the oven to 375°F. Draw 40 4-inch circles on parchment paper, and use to line baking sheets. To make the pastry tubes, combine the confectioner's sugar with the almond paste, cinnamon, and 1 egg till smooth, then add the remaining eggs and the flour. Leave the pastry to rest for 1 hour, then stir in the cream. Spread the mixture onto the circles with a palette knife, and bake till golden brown. Working quickly, pull the baking sheet halfway out of the oven and, leaving the oven door open, remove the pastry circles one at a time, roll at once around a rolling pin or 1-inch dowel, and remove immediately, as the pastry hardens very quickly. To make the filling, beat the egg yolks to a fluffy, creamy mass with the confectioner's sugar, then stir in the Mascarpone. Using a pastry bag with a star tip, pipe this mixture into the prepared pastry tubes. Using a paper cone, pipe melted chocolate over the filled tubes.

Mascarpone cream in long-stemmed glasses. Crumble ladyfingers into the glasses, drizzle with mocha and coffee liqueur, and top with the Mascarpone cream. Sprinkle the top with chocolate curls and dust with confectioner's sugar.

Almond-paste tubes with Mascarpone cream. Fill the tubes immediately before serving if possible, as the Mascarpone cream softens the crisp pastry relatively quickly.

Light and airy creams

RICOTTA-AND-LEMON CREAM

juice and grated rind of 2 lemons

⅔ cup sugar, 1½ cups Ricotta

2 eggs, separated; 1 cup heavy cream

9 oz fresh berries (redcurrants, raspberries, and strawberries, preferably wild)

4 teaspoons maraschino liqueur

1 tablespoon natural honey

Scrub the lemons under hot running water and grate just the zest (outermost yellow part). Place the zest with the lemon juice and half the sugar in a saucepan, and reduce to about one-fourth of its original volume, then leave to cool. Strain the Ricotta and mix with the reduced lemon juice and the egg yolks. Whip the cream until stiff and refrigerate. Beat the egg whites to stiff peaks with the remaining sugar, stir into the Ricotta mixture, and fold in two-thirds of the cream. Divide the berries among long-stemmed glasses, reserving a few redcurrants, drizzle over the maraschino and honey, and top with the Ricotta-cream mixture. Spoon the remaining whipped cream into a pastry bag with a star tip, pipe a rosette on top of the contents of each glass, and decorate with redcurrants.

QUARK-AND-ORANGE CREAM WITH PASSION FRUIT SAUCE

Makes 6

grated rind of 1 orange

½ cup orange juice

⅔ cup sugar, 3 eggs, separated

1 tablespoon powdered gelatin

2 cups drained Quark

½ cup heavy cream

For the sauce:

1 teaspoon butter, ½ cup sugar

juice of 2 oranges

4 passion fruits, fresh fruit for decorating

Scrub the orange well under hot running water and grate the peel thinly. Place the peel and the juice, half the sugar, and the egg yolks in a large saucepan, and heat to just below boiling point, whisking constantly. Soften the gelatin in a little cold water and dissolve in the orange juice mixture. Push the Quark through a strainer and mix in. Whip the cream until stiff and refrigerate, then beat the egg whites to stiff peaks with the remaining sugar and fold into the Quark mixture. Fold in the cream, spoon immediately into ½-cup molds, and chill until set. To turn out the molds, dip them briefly in hot water to help release the contents. While the molds are chilling, make the sauce: melt the butter and sugar in a saucepan, stirring constantly. Pour in the orange juice all at once, add the pulp and seeds of the passion fruit, and boil the sauce until the caramel has dissolved completely. Serve the Quark creams with fresh fruit and the cooled sauce.

These sweet pastry tubes, called cannoli in Italy, are filled with a Ricotta cream studded with candied fruit that has been steeped in Amaretto.

Filling and cooking the apricot dumplings:

Roll the dough into a cylinder on a floured work surface, and cut into 16 equal slices.

With floured hands, pat into little round cakes, placing an apricot filled with a sugar cube on top of each.

Cover the apricots with the dough, pinch the edges together to seal, and roll lightly in your hand into a round dumpling.

Lower the dumplings into lightly salted boiling water and simmer gently for 12–15 minutes, until they rise to the surface.

Drain the dumplings well and roll in the toasted bread crumbs until completely coated.

Try to use only untreated lemons, which still need to be scrubbed under hot running water. Grate only the outermost yellow part of the peel (the zest).

APRICOT DUMPLINGS

The taste and consistency of a Quark dough harmonize really well with fruit such as apricots and plums. Preparation is, admittedly, a bit of an effort, as the dough is relatively soft, making it slightly difficult to roll into nice round fruit-filled dumplings. The dough can be made somewhat firmer by adding bread crumbs, but add only as much as is absolutely necessary.

Serves 4 as a main course, 8 as a dessert
2½ cups drained Quark
3 tablespoons softened butter, 2 tablespoons sugar, ¼ teaspoon salt
grated rind of ½ lemon
2 eggs, 1½ cups fresh white bread crumbs, ¾ cup semolina
16 apricots, 16 small sugar cubes
For the crumb coating:
2 cups fresh white bread crumbs, 2 tablespoons butter
confectioner's sugar for dusting
6 tablespoons browned butter

Press the Quark through a fine strainer. Stir the butter until almost liquid, then add the cheese, sugar, salt, and lemon rind. Stir in the eggs, followed by the bread crumbs and semolina. Let this soft dough swell for at least 30 minutes, then turn out onto a floured work surface and form into a cylinder. Wash, cut open, and pit the apricots. If they are ripe and sweet, do not use the sugar cubes. Melt the butter in a frying pan and toast the bread crumbs till golden brown, stirring constantly. Prepare the dumplings as shown in the picture sequence opposite. Sift a little confectioner's sugar over the dumplings and serve with the browned butter.

Plums instead of apricots is a nice variation. Use only dry, ripe fruit with a low moisture content. If the plums are too tart, use a sugar cube, as with the apricots.

A sauce made from blood oranges goes well with both the soufflé and the Viennese stuffed crepes. The juice of the oranges is reduced with sugar, and seasoned to taste with bitter Campari.

QUARK SOUFFLÉ

This recipe is wonderful plain, and a delightful with fresh fruit — for example, strawberries, raspberries, or apricots — which should be placed on the bottom of the soufflé dish.

Serves 4–6
1 cup milk, ⅔ cup sugar
½ vanilla bean
4 teaspoons each cornstarch and flour
5 eggs, separated
1½ cups drained Quark
½ cup raisins soaked in 4 teaspoons rum
butter and sugar for the soufflé dish

Preheat the oven to 400°F. Butter a 1-qt soufflé dish and dust with sugar. Bring the milk to a boil with half the sugar and the vanilla bean. Dissolve the flour and the cornstarch in a little cold milk and mix in. Allow to boil vigorously till cooked through and thickened, then remove the vanilla bean. Fold in the egg yolks. Push the Quark through a strainer and add to the pot. Mix in the raisins, stirring only briefly. Beat the egg whites to stiff peaks with the remaining sugar, and carefully fold into the Quark mixture. Spoon the mixture into the soufflé dish, smoothing the top flat. Place the dish in a water bath of at least 175°F, with the water coming halfway up the side of the dish. Bake about 45 minutes, until cooked and well risen.

VIENNESE CREPES WITH QUARK

Makes 8–10
1 cup all-purpose flour, ½ cup milk, ¼ cup heavy cream
2 eggs, a pinch of salt, 1 teaspoon sugar, 1 tablespoon oil
butter for frying
For the filling:
⅓ cup raisins, 4 teaspoons dark rum
¼ cup butter, ½ cup sugar, ¼ teaspoon salt
grated rind of 1 lemon
2 eggs, separated; 2 cups drained Quark
For the topping:
1 egg, ¼ cup cream, 1 tablespoon sugar
small pieces of butter, confectioner's sugar

Preheat the oven to 400°F. Place the flour in a bowl, and add the milk, cream, eggs, salt, sugar, and oil, and stir to a smooth, thin batter. Leave to rest for 1 hour. Stir the batter, then melt some butter in a 7-inch frying pan and use the batter to make 8–10 thin crepes. To make the filling, steep the raisins in the rum for 1 hour. Beat the softened butter with half the sugar, the salt, and the lemon rind till foamy, then stir in the egg yolks. Mix in the Quark and the raisins. Beat the egg whites with the remaining sugar until stiff and fold into the Quark mixture. Spread a thick strip of Quark down the center of each crepe and fold in the sides. Butter a casserole and place the crepes in it with the fold underneath. To make the topping, whisk together the egg, cream, and sugar, and pour over the crepes. Dot with butter and bake for 25 minutes. Dust with confectioner's sugar and serve immediately.

Cheese and wine

An age-old theme

Both cheese and wine, with their centuries-old traditions, are natural products that are tended painstakingly, and frequently consumed together. However, we have refrained from recommending particular wines to accompany specific cheeses and cheese dishes. To attempt a serious treatment of this complex problem in limited space would do neither the cheese nor the wine justice. In addition, the relationship between cheese and wine is often portrayed as being more intimate than it actually is. A good cheese does not necessarily require wine to complement its taste and, conversely, a truly great wine can be enjoyed simply on its own. Nonetheless, we will make some very general recommendations.

Try regional combinations

A glass of wine with a piece of cheese and some crusty bread is an image of the simple life, immortalized in still lifes and pastoral scenes painted throughout the ages. What we often see depicted in such paintings are the food and beverages of the artist's locale, and this provides us with a simple principle to follow: try combining cheese and wine from the same region. A young Pecorino from Tuscany is, for example, ideally suited to a fruity Chianti, and a goat cheese from the Loire is a brilliant combination with a fresh Sancerre. These are solid and dependable products from regions where the cheese is tended as carefully as the wine, and where there seems to be a natural harmony between the two. Of course, regional combinations are not without risk, since there may be very wide selections of both cheese and wine available now, so start by selecting traditional types of each.

Basic principles

Although committed gourmets and specialists in both fields have long endeavored to determine the best combinations of cheese and wine by conducting tastings, it is very difficult to translate the results into general recommendations, since they always apply to the tasting in question. Ultimately, we are dealing with living products that undergo constant changes. In spite of this, dedicated consumers can use such results, together with their own experience, to reach usable conclusions, and can create new combinations by experimenting. With the usual reservations, here are a few principles that seem to hold true.

Not all red wines harmonize with cheese. It is the fruity, light red wines, mostly the simple, plain ones, that are best suited to cheese. Merlot and Pinot Noir are recommended.

Red wines high in tannin are compatible with highly aromatic cheeses only in exceptional cases, or when the tannin is round and soft in wines with a relatively high alcohol content.

Cleanly developed, balanced white wines harmonize with many types of cheese. Fresh, fruity wines with sufficient acidity, not too high in alcohol and with a low tannin content, are generally the right ones. White burgundy, Silvaner and Riesling are recommended.

Dry, fresh rosés are suitable for soft cheeses, particularly fresh cheeses, and for fresh goat cheeses.

Tangy, dry champagnes pair well with fresh goat cheeses as well as with soft cheeses with bloomy white rinds.

Not many sweet wines are ideal with cheese. Beerenausleses, Sauternes, or Vin Santo harmonize with blue-veined cheeses, provided they have enough acidity.

Cheese occasions

The different customs and occasions associated with the consumption of cheese show how difficult it is to select the right wine to go with a particular cheese. When an individual type of cheese is eaten in the form of a canapé or other hors d'oeuvre with a glass of wine, the wine can be chosen quite deliberately to complement it. However, when a selection of four or five types of cheese with interesting taste variations is being offered, it might be very difficult to choose a single wine that will harmonize with them all. For this reason, it is usually advisable to restrict the selection of cheese used in hors d'oeuvre or presented on a cheeseboard to about three that complement each other. Then choosing a single suitable wine is possible.

When cheese is served in combination with other foods in cold dishes, it is often a matter of how much cheese there is in the dish, and whether the cheese is mild, and subordinate in terms of flavor, or piquant, and dominant even in terms of its aroma. In such instances, the choice of the wine will always be a compromise. When cheese is one of the main ingredients in a warm dish, it is usually so dominant in terms of taste that the wine should be matched to it.

It goes without saying that wine should be served at the proper temperature. The same also applies to cheese, which, depending on type, should be served at 59–68°F: fresh, young cheeses towards the cooler end of this range, and ripe, semi-hard, and hard cheeses correspondingly warmer. Therefore, take the cheeses out of your pantry or refrigerator in good time and leave them covered so that they can slowly come to room temperature.

Bibliography

AID/Auswertungs-und Informationsdienst für Erndhrung, Landwirtschaft und Forsten e.V., *1090 Kdse* (Niederauer, T., edited by F. Beyer). Bonn, 1989.
ANAOF: *Les fromages d'appellation d'origine*, Paris, 1984.
Androuët, P.: *Le Livre d'Or du Fromage*, Paris 1984.
Androuët, P.: *Les fromages de chèvre*, Tours, 1986.
Arroyo Gonzalez, M. and Fernández de Arroyo, C.: *Los quesos en Cantabria*, Santander, 1981.
Association de l'Industrie de la Fonte de Fromage de la CEE (ASSIFONTE): *Rapport Annuel 1988/89*, Paris, Bonn, 1989.
Cantin, C.: *Les Fromages*, Paris, 1978.
Carr, S.: *Guía de los Quesos*, Barcelona, 1988.
Centre de Publications de l'Université de Caen: *Histoire et Géographie des Fromages*, Caen, 1987.
di Corato, R.: *Formaggio in Tavola e in Cucina*, Milan, 1986.
Davis, J.G.: *Cheese, Vol. III. Manufacturing Methods*, London, 1976.
Deutsche Landwirtschafts-Gesellschaft: *DLG-Prüfbestimmungen für Milch und Milchprodukte einschliesslich Speiseeis*, Frankfurt, 1989, 3rd edn.
Eck, A.: *Le Fromage*, Paris, 1986.
Eck, A.: *Cheesemaking*, Paris, 1987.
Eekhof-Stork, N.: *Der grosse Käseatlas*, Berne, 1979.
Food and Agriculture Organization of the United Nations: *Codex Alimentarius Vol XVI*, Rome, 1984.
Food and Agriculture Organization of the United Nations: *La fromagerie et les variétés de fromages du bassin Méditerraneén*, (Ramet, J.P.). Rome, 1985.
Hartner, H.: *Roquefort, Stilton & Co.*, Düsseldorf, 1989.
International Dairy Federation: *Production and Utilization of Goat's and Ewe's Milk*, Doc. 158, Brussels, 1983.
International Dairy Federation: *World Dairy Situation in 1989*, Bulletin No. 243, Brussels, 1989.
Kammerlehner, J.: *Labkdse-Technologie*, Vols. 1 and II, Gelsenkirchen-Buer 1986 and 1988.
Kielwein, G. and Luh, H.K.: *Internationale Käsekunde*, Stuttgart, 1979.
Klupsch, H.J.: *Saure Milcherzeugnisse - Milchmischgetränke und Desserts*, Gelsenkirchen-Buer, 1984.
Kosikowski, F.V.: *Cheese and Fermented Milk Foods*, Michigan, 1977.
Le Jaouen, J.C.: *La fabrication du fromage de chèvre fermier*, Paris, 1982.
Lolkema, H. and Blaauw, J.: *Kaasbereiding*, Apeldoorn, 1974.
Luquet, F.M.: *Laits et Produits Laitiers*, Vol. 2, Paris, 1985.
Mair-Waldburg, H.: *Handbuch der Käse*, Kempten, 1974.
Marcos, A.: *Spanish and Portuguese Cheese Varieties*, in: *Cheese*, Vol. 2 (ed. P.F. Fox), London, 1987.
Mietton, B.: *Les technologies pâtes molles et dérivés*, in: F.M. Luquet, : *Laits et Produits Laitiers*, Vol. 2, Paris, 1985.
Milchindustrie-Verband: *Milchindustrie 1988/89. Geschäftsbericht und Statistischer Anhang*, Bonn, 1989.
Mills, S.: *The World Guide to Cheese*, New York, 1988.
Ministerio de Agricultura: *Catalogo de Quesos Españoles*, Madrid, 1973.
Ministero dell'Agricoltura e delle Foreste: *Käse aus Italien. Handbuch*, Milan, 1984.
Mit Messer, Draht und Käsespaten, Neuwied, 1982.
National Cheese Institute: *Cheese Varieties and Descriptions*, USDA Agriculture Handbook 54, Washington D.C., 1978.
Peeters, E.-G.: *Le Guide de la Diététique*, Verviers, 1971.
Price, W.V.: *Cheese*, Atascadero, California, 1979.
Renner, E. and Renz-Schauen, A.: *Nährwerttabellen für Milch und Milchprodukte*, Giessen, 1986.
Rossi, G.: *Manuale di Tecnologia Casearia*, Bologna, 1977.
Scott, R.: *Cheesemaking Practice*, London, 1986.
Souci, S., W. Fachmann, W. and Kraut, H.: *Die Zusammensetzung der Lebensmittel Nährwert-Tabellen 1989/1990*, Stuttgart, 1989.
Stobart, T.: *Lexikon der Gewürze, Kräuter und Würzmittel*, Bonn, 1972.
Sunset: *Cheese*, Menlo Park, California, 1986.
Waren- und Verkaufskunde Käse in Bedienung, Bonn-Bad Godesberg, Remagen-Rolandseck, 1988.
Wilster, G.H.: *Practical Cheese Making*, Corvallis, Oregon, 1980.
Zentrale Markt- und Presiberichtstelle für Erzeugnisse der Land-, Forst- und Erndhrungswirtschaft: *ZMP Bilanz '88 Milch*, Bonn, 1989.

Acknowledgements

The authors and publishers wish to thank all those who have contributed to this book with their advice, help, and expertise.
In particular, we wish to thank the following for their contributions:
Dr. R. Arnold, Regierungsdirektor, Referat Ernährung und Ernährungswissenschaft, Bayerisches Staatsministerium für Ernährung, Landwirtschaft und Forsten, Munich, ("Cheese: a healthy food").
Dr. G. Kautz, Käserei Champignon, Bereich Forschung und Produktentwicklung, Heising, Allgäu ("Milk"; "How Cheese is Made").
Dr. W. Sturm, Stellvertretender Direktor, Leiter Technik, Alcan Rorschach AG, Rorschach, Switzerland ("Packaging to Preserve Quality").

Our thanks also to:
L.A. Barrón del Castillo, Chief, Meat and Dairy Service, Animal Production and Health Division, Food and Agriculture Organization of the United Nations, Rome; Dr. L. Bartoli, Direttore, Istituto di Tecnica e Sperimentazione Lattiero-Casearia, Thiene, Italy; Dipl.agr. F. Beyer, Direktor, Milchwirtschaftliche Untersuchungs- und Versuchsanstalt, Kempten, Allgäu; Dr. G.C. Emaldi, Istituto Sperimentale Lattiero Caseario, Lodi (Mi), Italy; D. Emmons, Food Research Centre Agriculture Canada, Ottawa; Food and Drug Administration, Department of Health and Human Services, Washington D.C.; M. Hardy, Fromagerie Hardy, Affineur, Meusnes, Selles-sur-Cher, France; J. Hennart, Hennart Frères, Affineur, Sequedin, France; G. Hölzle, Direktor, Vorsitzender, Süddeutsche Butter- und Käse-Börse, Kempten, Allgäu; J Hueber, Président, Association Nationale des Appellations d'Origine des Fromages (ANAOF), Paris; P. Jachnik, Chef du Service Economique et des Affaires Internationales, Fédération Nationale des Coopératives Laitières, Paris; o. Prof. Dr. H. Klostermeyer, Direktor, Institut für Chemie und Physik, Süddeutsche Versuchs- und Forschungsanstalt für Milchwirtschaft, Freising-Weihenstephan, Inhaber des Lehrstuhls für Milchwissenschaft, Technische Universität, Munich; Dipl. Landwirt H. Mairock, Direktor, Landesvereinigung der Bayerischen Milchwirtschaft, Munich; Dr. A. Nienhaus, Geschäftsführung, Centrale Marketinggesellschaft der Deutschen Agrarwirtschaft (CMA), Bonn; Prof. N.F. Olson, Department of Food Science, University of Wisconsin, Madison; W.J. Roth, Obmann INTERLAB, Switzerland; Prof. Dr. V. Sadini, Università Padova, ehedem Kommission der Europäischen Gemeinschaften, Generaldirektion VI Landwirtschaft, Brussels; Dr. D. Scheer, C.Fr. Scheer, Willstätt-Sand, Präsident, Union Européenne du Commerce des Produits Laitiers et Dérivés, Brussels; P. Staal, past Secretary General, E. Hopkin, Secretary General, International Dairy Federation, Brussels; Prof. Dr. G. Terplan, Inhaber des Lehrstuhls für Hygiene und Technologie der Milch der Ludwig-Maximilians-Universität München, Munich; Ir. J.M. van der Bas, Direktor, Zuivelcontrole Instituut, Netherlands Controlling Authority for Milk and Milk Products, Leusden, Netherlands; Ir. E. Verhenne, Dienstchef, Ost- und Westflandern, Nationale Zuiveldienst, Melle, Belgium; RA G. Werner, Geschäftsführer, Milchindustrie-Verband, Bonn; Wisconsin Department of Agriculture, Trade and Consumer Protection, Madison.
Androuët, Affineur, Paris; Katja Bremer, SOPEXA, Förderungsgemeinschaft für französische Landwirtschaftserzeugnisse, Düsseldorf; Frau Chmielewski, Roquefort-Société (Informationsbüro), Frankfurt; Geschäftsstelle für Appenzeller Käse, St. Gallen; Herr Ginsburg, Frau G. Schärer, Frau L. Stähli, all at the Schweizerische Käseunion, Berne; Caroline Gledhill, Paxton & Whitfield, London; Hugo Hieber, Chalet de fromage, Munich; ICE, Istituto Nazionale Commercio Estero, Düsseldorf; Herr Klopsch, Informationszentrum ungarische Weine, Hamburg; Königlich Dänisches Generalkonsulat, Munich; Königlich Norwegisches Generalkonsulat - Handelsabteilung, Düsseldorf; Herr Lang, Käsereigenossenschaft, Lehern; Milk Marketing Board of England and Wales; Molkerei-Zentrale Bayern, Nuremberg, Kempten; Moorhayes Farm, Wincanton, England; Niederländisches Büro für Milcherzeugnisse, Aachen; Jytte Nielsen, Marktinformationsstelle der Dänischen Molkereiwirtschaft, Düsseldorf; Norske Meierier GmbH, Hamburg; G.S. Overbeek, Benschop, Holland; Kristina Polzin, Schwedischer Aussenwirtschaftsrat, Düsseldorf; John Sanders, "James' Cheesemongers", Beckenham, Kent; Schwedische Botschaft - Handelsabteilung, Bonn; SGWH, Schweizer Gesellschaft für Weich- und Halbhartkäse, Berne; Société Fromagère de la Brie, Saint Siméon; Spanisches Generalkonsulat - Handelsabteilung, Düsseldorf; Herr Steineck, Beck Import GmbH, Munich; Käserei Stich, Ruderatshofen; K. Toft and P. Tuborgh, beide MD Foods Deutschland GmbH, Flensburg; Wisconsin Milk Marketing Board, Madison.

Picture credits

Drawing, p. 10, margin: Helmuth D. Flubacher; 7 photos pp.14 and 15: Fritz Grunder; 3 photos p. 71, top right, bottom right and margin: Marktinformationsstelle der Dänischen Molkereiwirtschaft; 2 photos, p. 70, right: Roquefort Société; 1 photo, p. 71, margin: Dirk Rüther; 2 photos, p. 26, left and top; 3 photos, p. 27, bottom; 3 photos, p. 29 top; 1 photo, p. 30, left; 2 photos, p. 116, top left; 2 photos, p. 118, left; and p. 207, center right: Schweizerische Käseunion.

Subject index

This index contains the names of all the cheeses mentioned in the Cheese Encyclopedia. Boldface numbers refer to illustrations.

Recipe index